MODEST PROPOSAL
ANTHOLOGY

MODEST PROPOSAL ANTHOLOGY

INTERVIEWS WITH TOP COMEDIANS
RIGHT BEFORE COMEDY WENT
VIRAL, AND OTHER STUFF

Edited by Ryan McKee

Original Cover Art by Mike Hollingsworth

NEW DEGREE PRESS

MODEST PROPOSAL ANTHOLOGY
*Interviews with Top Comedians Right before
Comedy Went Viral, and Other Stuff*

ISBN

978-1-64137-976-2 *Paperback*

978-1-64137-861-1 *Kindle Ebook*

978-1-64137-862-8 *Digital Ebook*

In loving memory of Scott Sanders.

*Thank you for giving Modest Proposal, a stage
and second home at The Paper Heart.*

*Thank you for believing in us before anyone else,
and frankly, before anyone should have.*

*Thank you for not getting angry when Ron
accidentally lit the stage on fire.*

*Without you, many of our stories
never would've happened.*

We never thanked you enough.

Editor's Note

Hey, it's Ryan here. You might remember me from the book cover. My name is listed under *Emmy Award Winner*, which I still feel weird about having on the cover. But the publisher told me to just tell people, "The publisher made me do it." So ... "I know, right. The publisher made me put that on there."

This is a collection of things we published in *Modest Proposal Magazine* from 2003 through 2006. It offers a snapshot of comedy right before YouTube, Twitter, Facebook, Snapchat, Myspace, and Reddit changed everything. No one even knew what the hell to do with Friendster yet... including Friendster. Blogs were a punchline. Netflix mailed you DVDs of stuff they didn't even produce.

It's fun to reminisce about comedy back then. But this anthology by no means captures the breadth of comedians during this time. As I've grown over these fifteen years, I've realized how many voices I wasn't listening to back then.

The goal of releasing this anthology is to re-launch the *Modest Proposal* brand with the commitment to celebrate a much wider range of the funniest people in the world. Our website will feature new interviews, writing, videos, and whatever new technology we can figure out. Here's to the next fifteen years.

Please reach out if you need technical support with this book: ryan@modestproposal.co

CONTENTS

ACKNOWLEDGMENTS

As founder of *Modest Proposal* and editor of this book, I'd like to acknowledge the following things in no particular order:

1. I stole the concept of this Acknowledgments page from Dave Eggers's *A Heartbreaking Work of Staggering Genius.* This is appropriate because many of my ideas for *Modest Proposal* were totally swiped from that book.

2. There is an unacceptable lack of ethnic, gender, and sexual diversity in this book. I absolutely should have sought out a greater variety of voices during the time we published *Modest Proposal Magazine.*

3. Writing a book is much harder than I expected.

4. We published several dumb references, bad jokes, and stupid decisions in our original magazines. Many of those are preserved in this book as historic record and as a means to roast ourselves.

5. Many of my account passwords during the first decade of this century contained Dave Eggers's name.

6. Most of the updated content in this anthology was written from March through June of 2020. Due to the COVID-19 pandemic, live comedy shows, as well as TV and film productions are shut down. This fact creeps into a few of the updated interviews and writings.

7. As I write this, large-scale protests are occurring around the world, sparked by the murder of George Floyd. There's an immense amount of sadness and racism and injustice and fear.

8. Eric Koester is a Georgetown professor, Creator Institute founder, husband, father, wide-smiler, and the reason this anthology exists. He pushed me to do it, listened to an unfair number of complaints and excuses, and delivered numerous pep talks. His patience and optimism seem inexhaustible. Trust me, I've done everything in my power over twenty years of friendship to exhaust both.

9. Ron Babcock also helped.

10. While this book is already too long, even more articles, comic strips, jokes, illustrations, and interviews deserved to be included. So many talented people contributed to *Modest Proposal Magazine*. I just couldn't include everything. Also, I forgot some stuff and misplaced other stuff.

11. I need to work on my time management and organizational skills.

12. Content I should've published in this anthology, but didn't, will find its way onto ModestProposal.co. Yes, ModestProposal.co—NOT .com. We've failed at acquiring that .com domain since 2002.

13. I should stretch more. Does anyone else feel tight all the time?

14. Everyone at New Degree Press has been very nice and professional with me. If they called me names like Whinin' Ryan, Cryin' Ryan, or Fuckin' Shitbrain, I never heard it and probably deserved it.

15. If you want to hack my Myspace account, the password is leggomyeggers.

16. Writing a book is really fucking hard.

17. Hopefully you're reading this in a future where pandemics of violence and hate, illness and death feel out of place in a comedy book. Right now, though, they're impossible not to mention.

18. I'm amazed at how generous friends, family, comedians, and strangers have been with their time, support, and money to make this happen. Not just this book, but also our original magazines, videos, and live shows. I'll do my best to thank every one of you but will fall short in letting you know how much it means to me.

19. Ron Babcock helped out more than I previously led you to believe.

20. I can only make one guarantee about this book. Their are no typo.

WHY A MAGAZINE?

———

By Ryan McKee

June 2020

"Spend as much money as you can. She will be worth it," he said. "Your ex-girlfriend has to see you've moved on. You're with some new sexy, mystery lady. She'll get jealous and you'll have her back like that."

Who knew Mensa meetings happened at midnight in bars that smell like piss? Because this guy was a genius.

For months, my friends told me to move on from Emily. But I just wasn't ready. And now, a plan! I had action items. Find a woman on Craigslist. Pay her money. Take her to a comedy show at Upright Citizens Brigade Theatre, where Emily worked. Make Emily jealous. Win Emily back.

A few escorts hung up on me before I realized I shouldn't open with, "I'm not looking for sex. I just want a date for a comedy show."

Eventually, I reached Michelle and explained the situation. As luck would have it, Michelle must've been in Mensa too. She agreed this plan would totally work. She sounded kind of drunk at 3 p.m. Nevertheless, she was ready to haggle. For the special rate of $150 per hour, she promised to show up looking "bomb-ass hot."

In the early days of UCB Theatre LA, no one showed up dressed for bottle service at a Russian after-hours club. I had on a Misfits T-shirt and old Vans. Michelle wore a tight, black mini-skirt, shiny black stilettos, platinum blond hair, and tanning-bed golden skin. Everyone stared as we stood in line.

"Don't worry," Michelle said as she looked down at her cleavage. "These'll make her jealous."

We didn't see Emily at the box office. No sign of her in the showroom either. *Did she call in sick? Did I just overdraw my checking account to spend $300 for no reason?*

Finally, after the show, we walked out and my stomach jumped to my throat. There she stood. Emily. In sneakers and jeans.

Doing my best to act *totally casual*, I introduced her to my *totally normal* date.

"Nice to meet you. Hope you had a great time," Emily said, genuinely friendly.

"That fucking shit was hilarious," Michelle said.

And that was it. We were shuffled out with the rest of the crowd to make room for the next show.

Out on the sidewalk, I said, "She didn't care at all."

"No, she's totally jealous," Michelle said, "I can tell. It's a girl thing. She'll call you."

Emily never called me. When I told her this story five years later, she laughed and said, "I think I kinda remember that." It didn't make her jealous, but she did "kinda remember," she thinks.

I have the stubborn tendency to ignore good advice and work very hard on an overcomplicated plan toward a goal, even when—no, **especially** when—a more direct path is evident and more rational. I could've been upfront with Emily and told her how strong my feelings were for her. If she didn't reciprocate, my friends were right, and I could move on. Most likely, she wouldn't have come back either way. The straightforward approach would've saved me $300 (plus overdraft fees), not to mention time and anxiety.

But where's the fun in that? The complicated way gave me a much better story to tell.

The same character traits motivated me to create *Modest Proposal*. After college, I really wanted to be a novelist. Step one should have been—write a novel. Instead, I wrote half of one and then got really distracted by *Freaks and Geeks, Insomniac with Dave Attell* and Dave Eggers's *A Heartbreaking Work of Staggering Genius*.

In Dave Eggers's book, he describes creating *Might* magazine with his friends. Even though the publication folded for financial reasons, they built a cult following, and critics loved it. That led to Dave getting freelance work for bigger magazines like *Esquire* and then a book deal, which became the best-selling *Heartbreaking Work*. I'm sure that's oversimplified and factually flawed, but that's what I believed at the time.

So, I took Dave's advice—advice that, admittedly, he didn't give me, but I thought he had implied—and devised a totally uncomplicated plan.

1. Create a magazine with my friends.

2. Cover comedy in it because I love talking to comedians.

3. Make it funny and clever and offbeat.

4. Write most of the articles myself.

5. Ensure critics adore the magazine.

6. Never sell out. At least, not until *Playboy* and *Esquire* offer to hire me.

7. Lose enough money on the magazine that eventually, we'll be forced to close down.

8. Let the fans know we kept it real as long as we could. They'll bemoan the loss but understand it's not my fault.

9. Field offers from multiple book publishers. They'll love the magazine too but agree it can't be profitable because it's *too* good for the masses.

10. Publish my novel (once I finish it).

I chose the name *Modest Proposal* after Jonathan Swift's satirical essay about selling Irish babies as food. I thought it made us seem smart and a little dangerous.

Many of my friends liked the idea and wanted to help—only because when I'd pitch it, I didn't reveal the entire plan as listed above. Kristen Hof offered to draw illustrations. Teresa Aguilera designed our logo of the baby holding the knife and fork. Mike Hollingsworth gave us comic strips. Eric Koester devised a business plan that would've been profitable, had I listened to him. Chrystyna Golloher allowed our house to become *Modest Proposal* offices and helped however she could. Mikey Cramer gave us collage art. Jen Wood, Chris Keener, John Espinoza, Lora Bodmer, Nic Wegener, Mat Snapp, Todd Valdini, Emily Stone, and Kevin Polowy all said they'd write articles and followed through. All for no money and all before they even saw Issue #1.

And Ron Babcock had the best response. I emailed him to see if he'd like to help. I meant "help" as in, write something or brainstorm with me. He responded, "Yes! I'll move out to Arizona and join the team." He lived three thousand miles away in Wilkes-Barre, Pennsylvania, at the time. Thank god he was looking for any reason to move out of his parents' house. I never would have followed through with the idea if he hadn't.

I got to #4 on my uncomplicated plan and then jumped to #7. Some may quibble with #3, claiming we never accomplished "funny" or "clever." Ultimately, I forgot to finish the novel and focused instead on performing stand-up, producing live shows, making videos, and chasing Hollywood fame.

While neither of my plans succeeded in winning back my ex-girlfriend or publishing a novel, they did lead to fun stories. Many of those are collected in this book for the first time. Since we made the magazine before comedy went viral, or before "going viral" was even a possibility, we never published our content online. Actually, online publishing was a big part of Eric's business plan for us… I really should've listened to him.

INTERVIEWS
WITH UPDATES

Original articles from 2002 to 2006, along with updates from the subject in 2020. Most of the new responses are directly below the interviewees' original answers, except for a few interviews where footnotes seemed more appropriate.

DAVID CROSS

———

By Ryan McKee

Original Interview: November 2002

Updates: May 2020

For a person sinking his entire life savings into a cutting-edge comedy magazine, I was painfully ignorant on the subject. Despite living right by the legendary stand-up comedy club Tempe Improv all through college, I only paid money to see one show there, Dustin "Screech" Diamond. You could count the number of headliners I'd seen live on one hand: Dave Chappelle, Janeane Garofalo, Lewis Black, Andrew Dice Clay, and Bill Maher. Well, two hands if you count Screech.

Prior to purchasing David Cross's double-CD, *Shut Up, You Fucking Baby!* I'd only bought two comedy albums, *"Weird Al" Yankovic's Greatest Hits* and *The Jerky Boys* (and only one of which aged well). At that point, I only knew three things about David. His "Chicken Pot, Chicken Pot, Chicken Pot Pie" appearance on *Just Shoot Me!* Sub Pop (the label that brought us Nirvana and The Shins) released his album. Cool people and zine publishers liked him.

I hadn't seen *Mr. Show with Bob and David.* Hadn't seen David's 1999 HBO special *The Pride Is Back.* Didn't know about the '90s alternative comedy scene in LA. However, people I spoke with at the two indie music stores by my house (Eastside Records and Zia Records) and at our foppish neighborhood bar (Casey Moore's)—aka cool people—led me to believe I should idolize David Cross.

If I wanted my comedy magazine to be cool, I needed an interview with David Cross. I made it #1 on my *Modest Proposal Magazine* To-Do List.

I had an unpaid internship at *The Hollywood Reporter* the summer between my junior and senior years of college. I only learned two things of value that summer: 1) Lost & Found on National Blvd. makes the best Bloody Marys 2) ANYONE could call the Screen Actors Guild and get contact information for ANY of their members. Denzel Washington, Helen Mirren, Kelly from *Saved by the Bell*... you could call anyone, or at least their assistant, manager, agent, or publicist. One time that summer, while drunk on Lost & Found Bloody Marys, I called Johnny Depp's publicist, just because I could, and asked her to mail me his headshot. I still remember the contempt in her voice, "Johnny Depp doesn't do fucking headshots!"

I called SAG, wrote the phone number for David Cross's manager on a piece of paper, tacked it on my bulletin board, and stared at it for a week, too nervous to call because I expected her to answer with, "David Cross doesn't do fucking interviews with losers!" Finally, one day around 6 p.m., I decided she had probably left the office for the day, so I'd just call and leave a message. She picked up on the third ring.

"Uhhh, hello, uhhh, my name is Ryan McKee and I, uhhhhh, run a magazine, a comedy magazine, called *Modest Proposal*, and I wanna... would like to... request an interview with David Cross... I know, he's..."

"Just email me the info and he can do twenty minutes on Friday," she said.

That was it! She agreed without debate. Item #1 off the to-do list! Modest Proposal's first win!

Two years later in 2004, *Modest Proposal* co-produced a comedy benefit show *Putting the Mock Back in Democracy* to register college-aged voters. It featured Patton Oswalt, Nick Swardson, Brian Posehn, Dave Anthony, Naked Trucker, and David Cross as the headliner. Ron and Ryan (my duo comedy act with Ron Babcock) got a spot on the show as well since we did so much work to help produce it.

Everyone seemed stoked backstage to perform for a packed 2,500-seat theater, except Dave who quietly nursed a Heineken in the corner. I tried reminding him of this interview and telling him how much it inspired us to push forward with the magazine. I didn't expect him to remember, and I was correct. He had no idea what I was talking about. Then he moved to the other side of the green room and avoided me for the rest of the night. It probably didn't help that Ron kept shout-whispering, "I can't believe we're hanging out with David Cross!"

I'm not resentful. First, I wouldn't want to talk to a twenty-five-year-old me either. Second, I'll always be grateful to him for this interview. He gave twenty minutes of his time to an ignorant, nervous kid who claimed to run a publication but didn't have a copy of said publication or even a website to show for it. Numerous people (mostly those aforementioned cool people) later said they only took us seriously when they saw his name on the cover.

Eighteen years later, David Cross's PR team is the first email I sent to request his updated comments on the original interview. True to form, they got right back to me and said David was happy to do it.

Ryan McKee: Why did you play music venues instead of comedy clubs on the *Shut Up, You Fucking Baby!* tour?
David Cross: First of all, I love working with bands. I was at the very end of this tour with this one band, where we did like ten cities. Sub Pop called me up out of the blue—I had never talked to anybody over there—and asked if I'd like to record a comedy album. I explained the situation of what I was doing and said I'll just get another tour together. So, we went home and four or five weeks later we were back on the road recording it.

I don't like comedy clubs that much anyway. It's much more fun to do it with bands opening up and at music clubs. I don't like the structure of a club. I don't like the ticket price and the two-drink minimum. It's not all ages. You can only do an hour. Usually, you don't get to pick the people who open for you. It's just shitty.

2020 UPDATE: Well perhaps, "shitty," isn't the best way to describe it, but for me, the comedy clubs at the time, especially for what my status was, were waaaaaay less fun. Also, the set I was doing that eventually became SUYFB was fueled by alcohol, and I was doing anywhere from two- to three-hour sets each show, so I could not have done that at a club.

How much were your tickets?
I was able to charge $10 to $15 depending on the city. There's no way you're going to find a $10 ticket price at a comedy club for a 10 o'clock Friday show. They charge like $20.

True. Don't forget about the two-drink minimum as well.

Besides Ultrababyfat, what bands opened for you?
In various places, we had Arlo, the Greenhorns, the 45s, and Mooney Suzuki opened the Baltimore show.

Again, rock-solid truths!

Do you think independent music has influenced you as much as comedy?
In a sense, yeah. There's that idea of what is successful. The idea that if you're critically successful, you don't have to reach billions of people. If you're satisfied with your work and people you respect like it, that's success. It's indie credo that you do it for yourself and fuck everybody else.

Hmmmm, not sure what I was going for here. I kind of understand it, but when someone says, "indie credo," it makes me question everything that came before it. Sounds to me like a bit of a justification for not being (or trying to be) "successful"... which it was.

In 1990, Robin Hordon said that stand-up comedy had its height in the '80s and was overdone. He predicted that anti-comedy or alternative comedy was the future. Did his prediction come true?
It's certainly so widely accepted now that people don't even think of it as anti-comedy. They just think of it as a type of comedy now. It doesn't have the baggage it used to. There're more people like Janeane Garofalo and people like that getting accepted and seen here and there. Subconsciously people just think of them as comedians and not anti-comedians.

It's so startling to read this and remember, Yeah, back then what would become known as "alternative comedy" was really new and foreign to people outside of a few places: New York, Los Angeles, Boston, San Francisco, and that was about it. It made people uncomfortable and most people didn't like it at all. It's similar to realizing that a lot of the music the world listens to and enjoys now without second thought (R.E.M., U2, The Cure, The Smiths, I could go on and on) were considered "weird" back then and people would pick on you or beat you up if you listened to it. It seems so crazy to realize some people had a visceral hatred of "alternative" comics.

Bill Hicks CDs from ten years ago are still applicable today. Do you think your CD will be the same way in ten years?
I don't know. I think maybe not to someone who's sixteen or seventeen, but maybe if you just substitute the names for

whoever is in office at the time. It's unfair to Bill Hicks to compare me to Bill Hicks because Bill Hicks was great. While I touch on that stuff and have always touched on that stuff, I think it seems more prominent than it is. Really only thirty-three percent of the album is that; it just stands out because of the unique time we're in. I guess the comparisons are because most people are just pussies about it, and they don't really say anything. The jokes they make don't really have any teeth to them. Some people call themselves political comics, and then they talk about how Barbara Bush looks like the guy on the Quaker Oats jar. And that's not political comedy.

"Jar"? Quaker Oats "jar"? Quaker Oats don't come in a fucking jar! I call bullshit on this!

How long did you wait after September 11th before you made jokes about it?
Two weeks and that's just because I couldn't get up and do a set. I just didn't know what to say. It was actually the 28th to be exact.

Can't dispute that.

Is that where you got in front of the crowd and asked if it's all right to do jokes about George Bush now?
You know, I've said that in interviews, and they've left out the part that's really important, and that's that I saw Marc Maron do that, except he did it as a joke. And I talked to him afterward, and I said, "You gotta keep doing that, that's really smart." But then I suggested to him, "Don't do it as a joke. Just really ask it." And he said he didn't know. Then I was like, "Well, I'm going to ask it. I'm going to use that and ask

them. Just to feel people out." So, I didn't come up with that idea. Although I turned it into something serious whereas he made jokes about it. It became a really good thing. When I was out on the road, every single time I would ask it, people would go fucking nuts.

Glad I was able to give Marc the credit for this. I remember this well. I remember the first gig I had after that; it was at Northwestern University. I split the bill with Lewis Black, and I did a couple of minutes of innocuous stuff and then asked the audience. As I describe above, they responded enthusiastically, "Oh my god, please, yes!"

What's the moment you realized you could make a living in comedy?
About twenty minutes ago. No, really, when I was in Boston. I was able to support myself, albeit in a very low budget way. I had three roommates in this shitty apartment in the projects area— cockroaches and everything. I didn't eat really well, but I was able get by without having a day job and just playing softball all day and fucking around. Then doing comedy at night. That's when it became a real thing.

Adorable. What I considered "a living" was having just enough money for heat, rent, ramen, alcohol, drugs, and gas money. Ah, youth.

Boston has cultivated a lot of comedians. What is it about that city?
I don't know. A lot of the comics who are out of Boston were not from Boston and left because they didn't get a lot of work— people you see constantly now like Janeane Garofalo, Louis

C.K., and Marc Maron, Bobcat, Dana Gould. There's a lot of them. They got work there, but not enough and had to move on. I know Emerson College had some weird part in it. When I was there, [Boston] had a really great scene for the amount of people there. Everyone and their brother was opening up a comedy night at their whatever bar, bowling alley, T.G. Applebee's, whatever. There was comedy everywhere. In every other city in America, there wasn't that much work to go around, so you couldn't have that many comics. I don't why, though.

Well, this isn't necessarily true. Certainly, all those folks I listed above could get work. They left for New York or Los Angeles because you were more visible to people who worked in the entertainment industry there. Pretty simple. Not sure why I answered that way. One thing about Boston (back then) was that it had a co-mingling of two very different types of people in respect to class, education, and political bent in a way that other cities don't quite have. Boston is the most parochial, provincial place in America—the ultimate version of the "slobs vs the snobs" mentality you can imagine. So that lent itself to some interesting comics and shows.

How'd the *Mr. Show* live tour go?
Great. That was really fun. We'll go out at the end of April, beginning of May, and hit the rest of the country.

I believe every word of this.

Do you think you reached people who didn't know *Mr. Show* before?
I suppose we did. Some of them. I don't know why people would go pay, whatever it was, thirty bucks a ticket to go

see something they didn't know. Maybe some people were dragged there by other people.

I'm disregarding contest winners here and I apologize for that.

Did HBO always give you guys full creative control with the show?
All the time. That was just the rule. They never said anything.

And in exchange we made no money!

Did you do *Scary Movie 2* just for money?
Yeah pretty much.

True dat.

Did you enjoy it?
Yes and no. Everybody I was working with was really fun. The movie was kind of a bummer because I was kind of embroiled in my own frustrations with a movie I'd just made, which I thought was smarter and funnier. We were trying to raise $100,000 to make a cut, and these guys were spending $100,000 on like a lighting joke. It was kind of frustrating. But I don't have any regrets about doing that movie. It gave me the money to move to New York, which I wanted to do. For my sanity. Also, when I do something like that, the idea is that maybe it will lead to more work and better work. It didn't, but that's why I'd spend two and a half, three months, working on something that I'm not that crazy about. Also, I don't care if somebody is bummed out that I did *Scary Movie 2*. I just don't give a shit. It doesn't affect me.

I'm clearly referencing Run Ronnie Run! *(which was a bitter disappointment for Bob Odenkirk and me). I don't know why I'm being so coy. All of this still applies, though. And this was before* Alvin and His Chippingmunks!

And you moved from LA?

Yeah, I didn't like it when I moved there, and eight and half years later, I still didn't like it.

And guess what, motherfuckers! I STILL don't like it.

I read that you dug the movie *Battlefield Earth*. Are you into Scientology?

I just find it fascinating. I'm a little obsessed with it. It's just the strangest... I mean all religions are a little silly, but I understand the traditions and the history to them. But Scientology is just garbage. It's so patently false, immediately. I'm kind of obsessed with people who are Scientologists because they're so plain looking, and you can kind of pick them out from a distance.

Ha. Okay then. I think I'm underplaying it by saying I was "a little" obsessed with it. Back then, and even before that, I was a LOT obsessed with Scientology. It was like a hobby. I read so many books about it and read a couple of biographies of L. Ron Hubbard, how he just made shit up to inflate his résumé, and what a fragile narcissist he was. He is basically Trump but smarter and less evil. I applied for a job at the Scientology Center when I was living in Boston just to get inside and see what the fuck the machinations were. I have been locked in various rooms and watched the recruitment films. I have taken the "Standardized Oxford Personality Test" or whatever bullshit name they give to it twice. I've signed up for ASHO and Sea Org, and I've even done that nonsense with the E-meter. It's SO CLEARLY BULLSHIT! I was fascinated to say the least.

Why do you think so many celebrities have latched on to it?
Well, they weren't celebrities when they latched on to it. I think that's the big qualifier. I mean, if you want to be a star, go to Hollywood and be a star. You've already got something wrong with you. Something's fucked up. If you're already self-involved, self-important, have an inflated sense of ego, I think Scientology gives you some convenient answers. Answers for people like that who need an explanation for why things aren't going right. Why people might be keeping them down.

And if Scientology doesn't do it for you, there's always QAnon.

Were you brought up practicing Judaism?
Not strict. But it was important to my mom to go to synagogue on the holidays. We celebrated all the holidays.

Can't argue that. Although my mom and I got in a tiff last Hanukkah when I didn't want to introduce my daughter to the ritual of it, but my mom won out (my daughter loves to light the menorah). I kept adding my dark, atheist addendums to what my mom was saying about it to her, so I feel a compromise was struck.

Was it tough in the South growing up Jewish?
I met some really phenomenally ignorant people. Not necessarily that they were anti-Semitic but really ignorant. I was a curiosity. There were a couple situations of anti-Semitism,

you know, people would throw pennies at me or my sister or spit on us. But that was rare. Certainly, that atmosphere fostered that attitude.

Boy, I seem surprisingly forgiving here. "Oh, you know, just being spit on and having change whipped at our heads. No big deal." I must've been in a very good mood when I said that.

Do you feel like Atlanta is home to you?
Yes and no. It's really the only place that feels like home because I was there for so long. My mom lives in Florida, and my little sister lives in North Carolina. I've got one sister who lives in Atlanta, and that's where we all go. I'm there like three or four times a year. I've got a lot of friends there, and it's very comfortable. Though Atlanta's changed so drastically over the last fifteen years and not for the better. It's kind of lost what little charm it had and just wants to be a big city and seem that way. Which is too bad. It's a big sprawling LA-ified metropolis.

I still have very complicated feelings about Atlanta. I am there a lot more now than I used to be. My mom moved back there, and I still have a bunch of friends there. The comedy scene is pretty good, once I move past my predictable old man whining about how "it's all changed." It used to be great before it got too big for its britches (which is true by the way—Atlanta peaked around 2000). I can see it through my wife and daughter's eyes (they love it), and I can experience the friendliness and the pace and just general quality of life there that can be so great. And there's great food there too! And most of the bars I grew up going to are still there (although the Stein Club is no longer with us).

I've got a friend who's going bald and trying to get into stand-up comedy. Any advice?

Get a wig, man. Bald people do not make it in today's world. Get a wig and fill that wig with Rogaine.

I failed to reveal that I was COO of Rogaine at the time of this interview and was banned by the SEC from doing anything else to promote them after this interview came out. I apologize.

BETH LISICK

———

By Ryan McKee

Original Interview: December 2002

Updates: March 2019

ALLOW ME TO SET THE SCENE ...

It's Valentine's Day and I'm on a date with Beth Lisick. Yes, our mutual friend Stephen T. Brophy is also there. And yes, I'm meeting her in person for the first time. And, full disclosure, she is happily married with a son. And okay, if you want to get technical, the word *date* was never mentioned, but the terms *hang out*, *grab beers*, and *no big deal* were. Still, it is Valentine's Day, and we are at a bar and we're talking and laughing, so in my head, I'm totally on a date with Beth Lisick.

SOME BACK STORY ...

Five years earlier, I had never heard of Beth Lisick. I had a job at a record store called Orbit Music and noticed my manager James, who had one long pinky fingernail and obsessed over the band The Jesus and Mary Chain, had thrown some books into the store's dollar bin. The title *Monkey Girl* caught my eye, and I started reading it when no customers were there… which, in the middle of a South Bend, Indiana, winter, happened fairly often. Lisick's writing made me laugh so hard that James walked out from his office to make sure the bleak weather hadn't made me go *The Shining*-"Here's Johnny!"-level crazy. Laughing out loud in an empty record store is creepy.

I threw a dollar in the cash register, took the book home, and so began my Beth Lisick fandom. I found her second book, *This Too Can Be Yours*, on Amazon and ordered it immediately, at full price. After online stalking her to the best of anyone's capabilities in 2002 before social media, I contacted her and did the following interview over email. While she's not a comedian per se, I had her at the top of my wish list for *Modest Proposal* interviews, right after David Cross.

BACK TO VALENTINE'S DAY …

Beth and I (and Stephen) are laughing like longtime friends. Since Stephen and Beth are longtime friends, this totally makes sense, but they're doing a great job of including me too. This date is going awesome.

It's time to go and I offer her a ride back to where she's staying.

"Are you sure?" she asks. "I'm staying in Westwood."

Crap! That's all the way across LA and in the opposite direction from my place...

"Absolutely!" I say. "Not a problem at all."

During the long car ride, we're still talking and laughing, and I tell her I first discovered her book in the dollar bin. She stops laughing. "Why would I think that's funny?" She seems bummed.

I don't have a good answer. To me, Beth is so successful and awesome, why would it bother her that a book of poetry she'd written a decade prior ended up in the dollar bin of a crappy record store in South Bend? Her third book, the memoir *Everyone into the Pool*, is a *New York Times* bestseller, and she had a deal for her fourth book, which later became the national bestseller *Helping Me Help Myself*.

Beth shakes off my stupid comment, and the car ride ends warmly. Before getting out of the car, she gives me a big hug and kiss on the cheek. Best Valentine's Day date ever.

On the hour-long drive back to my studio apartment, I play Beth's dollar-bin reaction over and over in my head. I realize no matter how awesome you are or how successful others perceive you, it still stings when someone makes a shitty comment about your work.

In the thirteen years since, we've seen countless celebrities lose their shit on social media because of what faceless trolls are saying, so my realization is like "duh." But that Valentine's night with Beth Lisick was the first time I learned it.

Ryan McKee: How do you take your coffee?
Beth Lisick: Cream, no sugar.

2019 Update: Major life update! For the past three years, I have been drinking my coffee black. Getting more bitter with age.

Be honest, have you ever laughed at a bumper sticker?
Are you kidding? I laugh at bumper stickers all the time. Just seeing a bumper sticker, any bumper sticker, on a car makes me laugh. I love picturing the person actually selecting the bumper sticker. Or maybe someone gives it to them as a gift because they think it really sums up that person's philosophy. Then they have to decide which part of the bumper it goes on. They probably clean their bumper and then carefully peel off the backing and try really hard to put it on straight. All for the purpose of expressing themselves to total strangers passing them on the freeway. Of course, I laugh at bumper stickers.

Another major shift over the years. Social media is the new bumper sticker, and I am not laughing anymore.

Let's just say you have a bumper sticker, even if you don't. What does it say?
I have revisited this question after a week's time and have determined it cannot be answered. Try answering it yourself and you'll see what I mean.

I'm mature enough to answer now. My favorite style of bumper stickers are the ones where it's very clear the person should not be operating a vehicle. So, something like "Honk If You're Also Being Raptured" or "I'm Doing My Kegels."

Both *Monkey Girl* and *This Too Can Be Yours* have stories set in office situations. Have you been able to quit your office job?
It's been about two years since I've had a regular job. My last job was working as a writer for an internet animation company. One week we got fancy new ergonomic chairs and bottles of Dom Perignon, and the next week we were clearing out our desks because all the money was gone.

I had a good, long run of not having a regular day job but about eight months ago, I started working part-time as the non-sexual paid companion to a gay millionaire with dementia and I love it.

Many stories in the new collection are interlaced. Was there a conscious attempt to tie the stories together more in this book than *Monkey Girl*?
It was definitely conscious. I wanted to create a little world where the characters were intertwined. Like in life!

"I Got the Beat" in *This Too Can Be Yours*, the character has to play a beat poet. Do people really still believe in beat poets?
The only thing I can say here is that story is one hundred percent true. I got a call from a technology company asking me to read poems at a party. When I got there, it turned out they wanted me to dress up as a beat poet in a black turtleneck and beret and read poems that the CEO had written about his new product. I love that they didn't think of hiring an actor.

Do you harbor any ill-feelings toward the movie *So I Married an Axe Murderer*?

Only because this is where that CEO got the idea for humiliating me like that. Some of my poet friends were supposed to be extras for that movie, but they got too drunk and were replaced at the eleventh hour by more professional extras.

How many shitty jobs would you say you've had in the last ten years?

I've done my fair share of lame crap for money, the lamest definitely being that story. To clarify, I didn't know they wanted me to play a beat poet until after I got there. Mostly for the last five years, I've had writing and editing jobs. I also used to be a baker.

I had a really funny shitty job for a month about five years ago. I worked as a customer service rep for a company that rents out designer gowns by mail. All day long, I had to field phone calls from women across the US who were opening packages, hoping to feel like Cinderella but then disappointed and repulsed when their Karl Lagerfeld gown smelled like BO or weed.

I felt bad when I read "Punchlining" for the first time because I had just written a joke at a mime's expense and found it incredibly witty at the time. But you're right, mime jokes are easy. Why are they such easy targets?

That story was fun to write because there I am talking about how easy it is to laugh at mimes, but I'm basically making jokes at the mime's expense the whole time. Sure, he is a performance artist dressed up as a mime in order to conduct a social experiment, but still. And people do love to laugh at those nutty performance artists as well. The first big mime gag I remember seeing was in *Spinal Tap* when Billy Crystal is the angry caterer mime. Amazing that it was nearly twenty years ago and people can still get an easy laugh by mentioning the word "mime."

Nothing has changed here. Still makes me angry that it's such an easy way to get a laugh. Being a good mime requires years of hard work and dedication, and I think the unrelenting jokes could potentially be causing a mime shortage. And then what are we supposed to do?

Do you consider yourself a poet first or a fiction writer?
I definitely don't consider myself a poet. The stuff in *Monkey Girl* was mostly written to perform out loud, so I consider it more "performance text" or something. I'm not sure I can call myself a fiction writer yet either. Now I'm working on a book of essays. Maybe I'll discover I'm a nonfiction writer. What am I? Help me.

Hey! I just finished my first novel. It's called Edie on the Green Screen *and comes out March 2020. I'm a fiction writer!*

I read a story about a Lollapalooza road poet. In it, she realizes very few people in the audience care about poetry. The audience is there to see the bands and they throw things at the poets. She begins to hate the other poets she's with and ends up hanging out with a group of people who run a burrito stand instead. Did you have similar problems on the Lollapalooza Tour?
First of all, I love burritos and the people who make them. Secondly, opening for musical acts usually sucks because no one is ever there to see you. I have really grown to hate speaking into

a microphone in a crowded club environment because most of the time you have to raise your voice to be heard and then you become Weird Woman Yelling into Microphone. Outdoor events are even worse. A couple of years ago I did something on an outdoor stage, and I vowed never to do it again. I felt like an evangelist or a political activist or something. My voice bouncing off the walls in a public plaza. Gross.

I would like to add that I often attend events where activists are yelling into microphones in public spaces. I just don't want to be the person with the microphone.

With all you do, how do you still have enough time to go out and cover culture for your SFGate.com column?
I am barely hanging in there. I have a nine-month-old son who hates to sleep, so that doesn't help either. I actually went to the bookstore today and bought a book called *The No Cry Sleep Solution.* There I was completely haggard with little Gus suspended in one of those Baby Bjorn carriers, and he's laughing maniacally, eyes blazing with exhaustion. I got back to my car and noticed that my fly was unzipped.

I find it really hard to take seriously that I ever could have been embarrassed or ashamed that my fly was unzipped. Really, past Beth? I wrote a book a few years ago about all my shameful moments (Yokohama Threeway: And Other Small Shames) and there is nary an unzipped fly in the Top Fifty of my life's shames.

Do you find people in the art/independent/underground scene often take themselves too seriously?
A lot of people take themselves too seriously. I mean, some people create incredible works of art that are very serious

in nature, and I love that. I want to go to a movie and be devastated sometimes. I want to sit in the dark and cry like a baby because the world can be so awful. Just because I don't make that kind of thing doesn't mean I don't appreciate it.

One such uptight indie guy the other night told me that comedies are throwaway films. How do you feel about that?
It's ridiculous for someone to say a comedy is a throwaway. Who would say that? Surely not a multi-dimensional human person from Earth. Yes, most commercial comedy films are bullshit, but so are most "serious" films. Down with crap. That's the real enemy.

Could you list some of your favorite comedies?
The world is held together by the wind that blows through Christopher Guest's hair.

How did you become a part of White Noise Radio Theater?
I used to work with Les and Stephen at the aforementioned animation company. I was a big fan of their material and would go see all their shows. They opened for my band once. Finally, they got tired of me hanging around, yelling out their punchlines during performances and trying to get them into bed, so they asked me to join.

Did you do much sketch comedy before?
Never.

How did you become a part of Sketchfest?
It's organized by a San Francisco sketch group called Totally False People. They are also Totally Funny People and Totally Organized People. Totally Nice People as well because they asked us to be part of their festival.

I just took part in the eighteenth-annual Sketchfest a few months ago! I think I've only missed two or three of them ever.

Why did The Beth Lisick Ordeal break up?
"Creative differences." Please leave that in quotes.

Tell us about your new bands.
The Loins and the Gold Dust Twins are both duos with my husband, Eli Crews. The Gold Dust Twins is spoken word and electronic music, and The Loins is a big spazfest where we wear matching jumpsuits and dance around a lot. We even do a mid-set belt change. Someone who saw us recently said it was sort of like watching a weird form of therapy, and that's exactly how we feel about it. Instead of paying a marriage counselor we make a few bucks from the door and get drunk for free.

Eli and I are gearing up for a real horror show: Starting to play music together again as super olds. Also, it's too bad that our son will never join our band because he is more interested in commerce than in art. Maybe good that someone in this family is smart about money.

How did you get involved with Sparklehorse's "Piano Fire" music video?
The director saw me performing with White Noise and thought I could fill out the cop uniform nicely. I was a couple of months pregnant at the time, so I kept having to whip off the utility belt to pee.

What famous person were you most excited to meet?
Parker Posey fawned all over Gus at a boutique in New York. That was pretty exciting!

Did a grip-and-grin with Tommy Wiseau.

Some person named Nish on posthoc.com stated, "I believe that no matter which woman I end up falling in love with, there is always going to be a place in my heart for Beth Lisick, and my girl better understand." Do you get some creepy people falling in love with you?
The things you can find out from a Google search! It doesn't really creep me out, but maybe I'd feel differently if I had stalkers. I've had some funny bar napkin notes passed to me, but nothing to get too weirded out by.

In the intervening years, I found out who this person is. Nish Nadaraja. One of the founding employees of Yelp. My life could have been really different if I just paid attention to more of these guys.

What's up lately?
I acted in a couple of short films over the summer and I have a stand-up comedy duo with my friend Tara Jepsen. We are Carole Murphy and Mitzi Fitzsimmons—Lady Comediennes! We talk about chocolate and men like we were in a *Cathy* cartoon. Everything is about to take an awful turn as Carole finds out that Mitzi has been cutting herself, though.

I made a short film with my friend Jonn Herschend that is opening at the San Francisco International Film Festival. It's called Director's Commentary, *and it's the director's commentary on a film about a married couple hoping to have wild hotel sex before they are cockblocked by the director's commentary because the director has some unfinished business with the actors. I also have some screenwriting projects with Jonn and*

Tara that will hopefully go somewhere. Also, my novel! And my son is almost done with high school and things are really going to open up for me when I no longer have to wake up at 7:30 in the morning.

With everything going on, how does Beth Lisick keep it real?
Herbal tea, calisthenics, and old-fashioned love.

I finally started enjoying weed! So fun to know that I can finally fulfill my lifelong dream of being a stoner at age fifty.

ANTHONY JESELNIK

—

BY RON BABCOCK
Original Interview: 2006

Updates: April 2020

I first saw Anthony Jeselnik perform in the basement of a Ramada Inn. He brought an apple on stage and said, "A lot of people ask me, 'Hey Anthony, why do you bring an apple on stage? It's so unprofessional.' And I say to them, 'So I have something to do during the applause breaks.'" Then he took a bite as the audience lost it.

I fucking hated it. Not because it wasn't funny; I hated it out of pure jealousy, which I know would make Anthony happy.

Anthony had something I and most other young comics didn't have—confidence. And not just confidence. I mean staggering confidence. He's like a vintage leather jacket that grew arms and legs. With his excellent writing and unique stage presence, he could back it up as well. In a world of self-deprecating comics, here was the one comedian who only did the opposite of self-deprecating material.

He's been described as shocking, arrogant, and amoral, but that's just his stage persona. Off-stage, he's friendly and complimentary. Still incredibly, incredibly confident, but not a dick about it.

Shortly after the UCB Theatre opened in LA, Anthony and I were both booked on a show there. I'd been in LA less than a year; nobody knew my face yet. Anthony was a relative newcomer, but everyone already seemed to know he'd be successful. Lucky for me, he swaggered on stage after my set, not before it.

After the show, I introduced myself and he immediately said, "Hey, good set." His positive feedback kept my spirits up through another three weeks of soul-sucking open mics. Later, I reminded him of that show and what he said. He remembered and said, "Honestly, I didn't even watch your set. I was just being nice." *See? He has a good heart.*

We ended up hanging out with Anthony quite a bit and booked him for our Paper Heart show in Phoenix a couple of times. During his sets, I loved watching Arizona audiences go from offended to hysterical very quickly. We slept on our friends' floors and drank Miller High Life. Anthony was always thankful and complimentary.

Since this interview, Anthony's career took off. In fact, he's more successful than even he expected. He used to speculate his stand-up act would have a relatively short shelf life, but it would lead to great writing opportunities.

And he was right. When Jimmy Fallon took over *Late Night* from Conan, they hired Anthony as the first monologue writer. He was wrong about the limitations on his stand-up act though. He's one of the top headlining comedians from our generation. When something terrible happens in the world, you go to his Twitter account to see how he can possibly turn this into a joke. And goddamnit, he rarely disappoints.

Anyway, enough blowing smoke up his ass. Here's an interview from a time when Anthony Jeselnik had barely twenty minutes of stand-up material.

Ron Babcock: Stand-up in LA is so conversational, but your style is the complete opposite. Did you start out that way?

Anthony Jeselnik: When I started out, I was nervous and deadpan. I eventually evolved into the son of a bitch I am today when the jokes started getting a powerful response and I was able to really put my shoulder into the crowd. And I've only been at this for three and a half years, including the year I started out and performed three times with a true story about my girlfriend accidentally burning down my apartment. Can you imagine how big a jerk I'll be in another three years? You can't, of course, but here's a hint. It will be stunning.

2020 Update: It was stunning. Haha. I can't believe I had the balls to be so cocky less than four years into comedy. What an asshole.

When was the last time you hugged someone?
I hug people constantly, but I make sure to start with the handshake and get that forearm between us, so they know I don't love them.

If I answered this question today, I would not have an answer.

Before you started comedy, what else were you confident about?
You name it: running errands, shaving, Jenga...

It is actually just those four things, but I trail off to make it seem like there are more.

If your ego was an actual physical size, what size would it be? And could it defeat a bear?
I get this question a lot. My ego would be about the size of the T-1000 from *Terminator 2*, with all the same abilities. Of course, it could not only defeat a bear but all bears at once.

This holds up. I stand by it.

What do you say to people who think you're arrogant?
You either don't know me well enough or entirely too well.

Today, my answer would be: Yes.

Do you think your ego has ever hurt you?
If egos hurt careers, the world would be a very different place.

As true today as it was when it was written.

Tell us about this year's Aspen Comedy Festival.
Aspen was amazing and all four of my shows were a huge
success. I think it's typical to get your hopes up for a festival
because of all the million-dollar-deal stories, but I was very
lucky to have a lot of comedian friends with festival experience tell me just to have a good time and do the best I could
but not to expect anything at all. I think that's a great way
to approach not just the festival circuit but stand-up comedy
in general.

Aspen was my first festival. I loved them until I got about five
festivals deep.

What do you think of self-deprecating comics?
If not for self-deprecating comics, I wouldn't be so very special.
Thank you, self-deprecating, i.e., ALL, comedians.

Publicly slamming all my peers with a gross generalization.
Classic Jeselnik.

Do you do crowd work?
I've been trying to do more and more. Audiences love
that crap.

I would give this exact same answer today.

What is something you are not good at?
Trying to hide how annoyed I am with doing an entire interview about my ego.

Solid slam.

Have you ever been punched in the face?
I have, but not since high school. The last time I got punched in the face was in the parking lot of an all-night diner after a concert. I was drunk and a group of kids started something. I forget what I said, although I'm sure it was hysterical, but one guy stepped up and unloaded five or six punches right into my face. One punch took a chunk out of my bottom front tooth. And I'll never get it fixed because, hey, who wants to be perfect?

I have since been reminded that the group asked me if I had a problem, and I told them to suck my dick. And I never got the tooth fixed.

Is stand-up a stepping-stone to acting?
I got into stand-up to showcase my writing, but I'm enjoying myself so much that as long as I can keep cranking out these unbelievable jokes, I'll do it forever.

I got a writing job once. Didn't work out. Now I don't get writing jobs anymore.

How does Anthony Jeselnik keep it real?
I constantly compare myself to those around me.

True to this day.

DAVE ATTELL

By Ryan McKee
Art by Joe Gentile
Original Interview: April 2003

Updated Interview: May 2020

Dave Attell is our greatest club comic. I truly believe that and so does *The New York Times*. Just Google that first sentence. I stole it from them.

You'd be hard pressed to find a comic who respects the integrity of joke writing more than Dave. He's done other things in his thirty-year career (*Insomniac, Dave's Old Porn, The Daily Show, Saturday Night Live*) but always in the name of getting more people to come out to his live shows. He obsesses over his act (as you'll read in the interview) and lives to tell jokes.

There's a timelessness to Dave's comedy. He's a pure stand-up comic who could time-travel to different eras and still destroy audiences. Sure, he's too dirty for pre-1970... after all, Lenny Bruce got arrested repeatedly, and his act was clean by today's standards. But if any comic would be able to adapt on the fly and craft perfect jokes for a '50s audience, it'd be Dave.

Both interviews took place over the phone, the first in 2003, when Dave's fame was skyrocketing from *Insomniac* and his album *Skanks for the Memories*. He was everyone's favorite barfly. The second in May 2020. He's been sober over a decade. He hasn't been able to get on stage for two and a half months due to the COVID-19 pandemic. That might not seem like long to a civilian, but for a true New York comic who's used to getting onstage multiple times a night, every night of the week, it's an eternity. I can tell in his voice how bummed he is about not being able to perform and not knowing when he'll be able to again.

Dave seems like the same guy: friendly, humble, and just wants to talk stand-up comedy. We spoke for thirty minutes, and seconds after I hung up, my phone rang. It was Dave.

"Hey Ryan, I forgot a joke for the article. That illustration in the original article… well, I look exactly like that now. A bloated, sad man wearing an inappropriate shirt. That's some kind of a Nostradamus prediction illustration. Okay, please use that one. See you later."

He had to get one last joke in there.

ORIGINAL INTERVIEW

RYAN MCKEE: The first episode of this *Insomniac* season, you're in Amsterdam and your stand-up act seemed to bomb.
DAVE ATTELL: Yeah, I know. It was definitely a translation thing. Also, I don't think I had enough jokes. It was a lot of thinking it up on the spot kind of stuff.

Does *Insomniac* air in Europe?
In London, they have it on Sky TV, or some weird thing there. But they didn't know what we were doing in Amsterdam. I know that.

Sorry, I have to ask the easy pothead question. Were you really smoking pot in that episode?
Yeah, that was pot. "Was I inhaling?" is the question.

Is Salt Lake City considered foreign?
Actually, Salt Lake City has the rep of being the Mormon place, and they really go out of their way to show you that they're not all Mormon. That was a good town.

Did you write many Mormon jokes before you got there?
I've worked there before, so I had a few in my back pocket.
They love the dirty humor.

**One *Insomniac* episode takes multiple nights to shoot. Do
you have to keep putting on the same clothes?**
I usually bring two sets because it gets pretty wet and dirty
out there—a lot of booze and a lot of smoking.

**You're always smoking in photos. Are you the twenty-first
century's Marlboro man?**
I hope not because he died of cancer. I'm trying to quit.

**On the *Insomniac* message board, women keep writing,
"Dave is Sexy."**
Yeah, I don't know what they're doing. I don't go on the whole
thing, but that's great. And hopefully I'll run into some of
these women and hopefully some of these women won't be
married, or with boyfriends, and will be under two hundred pounds.

**These same women on the message board were wondering
about your shoe size.**
Tiny. My shoe is not even a size that says "needs a vibrator"
to get off.

**Lots of comics cite Richard Pryor as an influence. Who
says Bill Cosby?**
I think he's influenced a lot of people. He's the king of obser-
vational humor. I'm thirty-eight years old, so the guys who
were around when I was a young savvy kid were Sam Kinison,
Bill Hicks, those kinds of guys. But Bill Cosby's great. Bob

Hope, I don't know if anybody remembers him? Gotta give him his props. Everybody cries about being on the road, but there was a guy who would stand up to do a gig under hostile fire. Richard Pryor is everybody's thing because he was the first guy to really bring it down and dirty. Plus, his stuff holds up. If you listen to his CDs, they're still pretty funny.

In an interview, Lewis Black told me you write more than any other comic.
I think I rewrite more than any other comic. I'm never really happy with the joke. And I'm always calling a million people to make sure I'm not doing their joke, or that they haven't heard it anywhere before. It's really hard to get an original idea now because everybody's thinking. It's not so much stealing as everyone just thought it up at the same time. That's why it's so hard to do topical humor because the obvious joke is probably being done on network television.

Now that you have a CD out, does that push you to write more?
Yeah, actually it does. That's a good question. I was doing a gig in Boston and people were yelling out the punchlines like it was a concert.

How many months would you say it takes you to put together a new twenty minutes?
I don't know about that. Usually, it's a week-to-week thing, where if you get an idea at the beginning of the week, you can bring it strong on stage by the end of the week. Jokes are kind of like icicles or whatever it is… snowflakes. Each one's different. Some jokes will work one time and never work again. That becomes your Rosetta Stone, and you keep

going back to it hoping that the magic will come back, like the alignment of the stars, or the crowd was sitting a certain way. Those are the ones where every comic goes, "What the fuck happened? I'm doing everything right."

You've been called "The Comic to Watch" since 1992. Was the long climb to the top difficult?
I don't think I'm at the top, and I really don't aspire to be at the top. I think people gave me that title because comics like watching me because they take pleasure in the agony I go through. I bomb a lot, and I say things that really dig me into a hole. I think they enjoy it because it's not them. I'm definitely not the funniest one. I wasn't then and I'm not now. There's always somebody in town who's really on their game.

You said in another interview that drunk comedians are losing cohorts to AA all the time.
I know a lot of guys in the program. I should probably be in the program, but right now I'm enjoying being the liquid adventurer type. But I'm too old to frat-boy-college-drink, yet those are the situations I tend to be in all the time with these guys handing me all these crazy drinks. I say, give them to the people who could really use a shot, like the little kids, or a soldier.

Have you had to pay for a drink since you started the show?
I always pay—either with money or having to sit there and listen to a guy's idea for his own show or have a hot girl talk to me and then introduce me to her boyfriend. There's always payment. And I like to tip big because the bartenders are the ones really making it happen. They really help the show go. They're the ones who first wanted to talk to us and let us in their bars.

Do you have a pornographic video at home that's so dirty you feel guilty after watching it?

I'm sure there's worse stuff out there, but those Japanese anime, crazy, sexual things. It's really weird. Not to be Oprah or anything, but they're really misogynistic, all rape and crazy shit. So those are the ones I try to hide away. Most of my stuff is straight ahead amateur stuff because I like to see the new kids and give them a shot. But I think Briana Banks is super-hot. She's my pick. I read an interview with her, and she said she doesn't drink or do any drugs. That's what sucks when you find out they're normal. It's kind of like catching Santa taking a dump.

Would you ever play the father on a sitcom?

Yes, if I could have sex with my daughter. No, I don't think I could play the father of somebody. I could play the uncle who still lives with the family, living on disability.

The uncle who buys the kids booze and lets them stay up past bedtime?

Right, that guy. Or I could be the owner of a porn store, who's raising a daughter. And every day, she has to come see me after school, wearing her Britney Spears stuff, and all the guys are looking, and I say, "Hey, that's my daughter. If you want a tape of her, that's aisle three." She'd have to mop up in the peep show as her after-school job. Yeah, right. I don't think I will be on *Gilmore Girls*.

How does Dave Attell keep it real?

I tell you it gets harder every day. Doesn't it? Because I'm not a celebrity and I'm not a star and I'm a pretty bad host, so I'm in a weird position where people kind of know who I am, but they know me for very certain things. So, when I go out and drink alone, when I'm just healing my problem, people come up to me thinking I'm doing the show all the time. I never know what to tell them, and they're always disappointed. I'm the fucking rain on their parade. I feel bad about that and I drink more, so it's a never-ending loop. You know, I started the show to get the word out there that I do stand-up, and people come to my shows now. I hope they leave happy because that's what I really work at. And filling up a room is really a good thing. For years I was on the road working for people who had no idea what I was doing. Now it seems to be my kind of crowd. I hope they enjoy it because I enjoy it, and for a man who doesn't enjoy much, that's a big thing.

UPDATED INTERVIEW

Can you tell me a little bit about how you feel looking back on *Insomniac*?
I never really knew the impact of that show until years later when I started meeting the people who grew up watching it. I can't tell you how many times people come up to me and go, "You know, when I was a kid, I would watch your show. And I'd be feeling like shit, like on a lonely night, and I would watch that show, and I would feel like I was out on the bar crawl with you." I realized it was like a touchstone for certain people growing up. People still approach me when I'm at an airport, or at a restaurant or something like that, and say, "Hey, I loved your show." So that kind of makes me feel good.

But for a long time during and after *Insomniac*, it was very difficult for me to do live stand-up shows for people who just knew me from TV. Cause they really just wanted to see the *Insomniac* drinking stuff. And I was trying to do my jokes.

It's crazy to think about now. It's been forever since I drank… even though I'm still chain smoking, I really don't hit bars anymore. I don't even know if that show could work with Twitter now. The cool thing about it, that show was a journey. We didn't set anything up. Twitter would have screwed that up. People would have tweeted out where we were, and the surprise would have been gone, so it really would have made that job harder. And we ran into that anyhow, where people kind of knew what we were doing, and they would follow us around. And, because of that, some places would welcome us, some wouldn't. We would always leave if we weren't welcome and the Twitter thing would have made it less special.

When we spoke before, your debut album *Skanks for the Memories* had just released, and you mentioned people were yelling your punchlines out during shows. How long did that continue?
It didn't happen too long because after you record an hour of material, whether it's an album or a TV comedy special, you gotta do new material. Once I do that material, my job now is to do new material. So within about two or three years, I have a whole new act. I'm not able to turn out an hour as quickly as other people can, but I do try to do the new material more than the old material as soon as possible. Part of the job is to get new material out there.

To be honest, I only did one album and I probably should have done more because I do think comedy is at its best on an album. You know, I grew up listening to comedy. Now you can watch our specials on Netflix and other platforms all the time. But listening to it, especially when you're on a long drive or something like that, that's where I think comedy is at its best.

You brought up Twitter. Do you ever feel like you've had to edit your act because of potential backlash on social media? I'm not really on Twitter, and I don't see any of that stuff as my platform. I see it as like: You want to tell the fans you're doing some shows? That's cool. You want to pay tribute to somebody who's fallen? Sure, that's good. You want to help another comic promote a new special? That's fine. But for me to spend the entire day tweeting back and forth with somebody, that's not my deal. That's not who I am. I'm more of a private person, I guess. I'm too old for that, you know. It's just not my thing.

A lot of funny people have embraced Twitter. I think Anthony Jeselnik is a great joke writer. He's one of the best. And his tweets always stop you. You gotta like, give it a moment. He's hilarious, and it's like he's not for everybody, but he's definitely one of the best. For me personally, I wait to try out a joke in the clubs where the audience isn't allowed to use their phones. That's the safe spot where you can try out jokes, and if you push too far you can pull back.

But I do have a filter up now. I kinda think, you know, is it worth it? Is it right to say what I'm going to say? But I guess that could be because I'm older now. I'm an old sad man, but I'm still not as filthy as people think. And I'd like to think my crowd gets it. They love jokes. They like the idea that I'm going to bring them a lot of material and I'm going to try stuff out, and they're all part of the show. And I think that's the unique thing about the clubs, live entertainment compared to like a Zoom show or whatever, you know.

You mentioned people started following you around as *Insomniac* became more popular. Is that ultimately why you stopped doing the show?

I think that had a lot to do with it. Also, it became harder and harder to find the right town at the right time of year. We were on a small budget. It became hard because you had to keep topping the next one. Like you go to Mardi Gras. What do you do after that? You have to go to Carnival in Rio, and then like, what's the next thing? It became really hard to top the last show. But, you know, I think we did just enough because if it had gone longer, people would've just ended up going like, "Oh, that show. Yeah, I get it. I'm not into it."

And now there's a lot of shows like it, or there were a lot of shows like it. And I think that's good. I think our show was a great example of what a fun travel show could be. The cool thing about the show is that the people involved got it right away. It was a show about regular people, not the fanciest places and the coolest parties. Just people partying and hanging out, regular people doing regular things and having a great time. That's what was cool about it.

In our original interview, we talked a bit about the influence of Richard Pryor versus the influence of Bill Cosby on stand-up comedy. It's tough to have that same conversation today.

I really don't have much to say about that. And since you're trying to make it relevant to today's times, I would say that people always ask about influences in comedy. And at this point, I've been doing comedy over thirty years and can really see a through line from Richard Pryor to now. Richard Pryor was probably one of the best, naturally gifted, organic, no one like him, unique people who has ever taken a stage or done comedy. And that's the truth. Richard Pryor is one of the guys who at this point, people use them as a template and he deserves it because he is that good at what he did.

And as I've been doing this for decades now, I realized that like, comedy doesn't hold up the way music does. And especially now with the way it is almost week to week when you realize what is and what isn't acceptable to say. So, some of this ancient comedy, as I call my act, the ancient times of comedy, when there was no filter, you look back at it and you go, "You know, all right, some of this stuff is offensive." It's considered inappropriate, politically incorrect. But at the end of the day, there are great comics today and comedy is in a boom… up until this incredibly horrible pandemic has hit the world. The only thing that could stop comedy was this [pandemic] cause it was just going up and up and up and up. And it's a shame it might take a year or two years for it to get back where it was.

But truly, comedy is like an important thing now. I mean, like all the great comics who I came up with, Zach Galifianakis, Jon Stewart, Marc Maron, Joe Rogan, these people are important to like the national conversation. And I think that's cool. Even though I'm not up to their level, I'm still a part of that generation of comedy.

So, when you bring up the old comics, you know, all I would say is comedy builds on itself. So what was relevant and important then might not be important now. But you can still see the through line. Like if they hadn't done it, we wouldn't be able to do it now. So, I don't know. That was a convoluted answer to your question.

No, that was great. I know it's a weird question. And here's the last thing I wanted to talk to you about. In 2003, I was doing an interview with Zach Galifianakis for this magazine. And during the interview, you had called him because you had just written a joke and you were trying to make sure he didn't already do a similar joke. Besides Zach, who are the other comics you call to check your jokes?
This question is, I think, an important one. I would say that in comedy, the thing I'm known for is that I do check jokes, and I really feel like it's my job to ask other comics, especially the joke-writing comics, have you heard anything like this? Have you seen it? And I still do it to this day, and it annoys the shit out of them. It really does. Doug Stanhope is a guy who used to call all the time, and I call all the young guys who are out there writing jokes. You owe it to the other comics that you're not hacking their material. So, I always feel that if the joke comes too easy, there's no way I just thought it up, and I have to check.

And now there's so much content, it's almost impossible to check everything. And then you have Twitter, where there's like a lot of people doing jokes on Twitter, you know?

Do you ever just type your new jokes into Google and see what pops up?
I have my web person do that. I'll go like, "Hey, this is too easy. Can you check this out for me?" Not only do you have to check jokes now, but you have to check podcasts. Cause

I think a lot of comics have embraced podcasting as almost like a performance, so you gotta make sure they're not hitting the same topic or hitting the line the same way.

And every time I do come up with something I think is similar, I try to find the comic and go like, "Hey, well here's my joke. What's your joke?" And then see if it's too close. That's another part of it, which makes it even more annoying. So, I do check. I do check.

Let me tell you this. There's boatloads of material that I had to throw away because someone's already doing something similar. It's bittersweet. You see it working for someone else, and then you're like, "Oh, I don't get to tell it."

Well, thank you so much for giving me the time.
Thank you for reaching out to me and doing this. Since it is a new world here, I was just going to say, I'd like to end with one last thing. Everyone is in a tough spot right now. I have no idea when I'll be able to go on the road again. I'm hoping it will be sooner than later. I really do miss it. I've talked to a bunch of comics. We all miss the live performance. We all miss going on stage. And like, I was so lucky I was able to do that every night, a couple of times a night, and I was able to like get on a plane and play a packed house at a club and then do it again and again and again. And I'm really looking forward to when we can do that all again safely. So, I just wanted to include that.

Absolutely. And certainly, from an audience standpoint, we can't wait until you're able to get out and do that again as well.
The Comedy Store in LA has become huge. It's amazing what's happened there, and how just within a couple of years, it's

become the place to be every night of the week. Now I hear they're not gonna open until after the summer. And I'm like depressed about that.

I don't know, buddy. We're going to have to VR our way through this doom. VR, that's the way to go.

Well, I hope to see you at a live show or whatever, you know, when it's safe. And I hope I was able to answer your questions. I know it's been a while since I've actually talked to another live human.

No, you did great. Thank you so much.

SEAN ANDERS

AN ESSAY ON HIS FIRST INDIE FILM

By Sean Anders
Updated Intro by Ryan McKee
Original article: October 2005

Updates: May 2020

Unless you work in the film industry, you probably don't recognize the name Sean Anders, but you no doubt recognize his movies: *Hot Tub Time Machine, Daddy's Home, Instant Family, Dumb and Dumber To, Horrible Bosses 2, Mr. Popper's Penguins, We're The Millers,* and *That's My Boy.* Starting with Sean's first studio film, 2008's *Sex Drive,* his comedies have grossed over one billion dollars. When I first met him in late 2004, he couldn't afford a couple of Sony Handicams. Seriously, he'd just gone to Best Buy to return the cameras he used to shoot his first indie flick, *Never Been Thawed,* and got a refund.

Ron Babcock and I were still living in Tempe, publishing *Modest Proposal* and performing comedy around town, when we met Sean. None of us remember how we connected, but we gave him our magazine, and he gave us a burned DVD of *Never Been Thawed*. That DVD stayed on repeat in our apartment for the next month. Partly because we couldn't afford cable, but mostly because I loved the sheer number of weird characters and jokes they packed into ninety minutes.

Sean had moved to Arizona from LA a couple years prior, after his band, Stone Bogart, failed to get rich and famous. Still wanting to do something creative with his friends, he started working on *NBT* and played its lead character—a collector of frozen TV dinners and the front man of The Christers, a punk band that changed their name from The Reach-Arounds and went Christian because it helped them sell more merch.

We helped Sean set up a screening of *NBT* at our regular venue, The Paper Heart. People loved it. The Christers even started playing at a few shows with us around town.

By the summer of 2005, Ron and I had managed to save up five thousand dollars each and knew "a couple people in the biz." We thought that made us financially stable and ready to conquer LA's comedy scene, so we moved there. Less than a year later, Sean copied us—albeit, in a smarter way.

"We had gotten an agent, so I sold my house in Mesa and used the money to take a shot at living and working in LA," he told me in a May 2020 email. "About a week before that money was gone, John [Morris] and I sold our first screenplay. That was a pretty great day."

I remember meeting up for coffee with Sean a few times before they sold that first screenplay. He seemed pretty hopeless at the time, spending all his time on writing projects that didn't lead to anything.

"It was people asking us to write takes on various scripts and ideas," he said. "That means you spend lots of time basically auditioning to get a writing job. We were not getting any jobs, so we were pretty broke."

Spending all our time at stand-up comedy open mics and hanging at the newly opened Upright Citizens Brigade Theatre, Ron and I lost touch with Sean for a while. Then, in late 2008, he reached out and told us about his first studio film, *Sex Drive*. He'd even convinced the studio's marketing department to pay us to produce some digital videos, featuring a donut costume from the film, as part of a viral marketing campaign. What happened in between hopeless-small-black-coffee Sean and studio-big-budget-latte Sean?

"It started before *Sex Drive*," Sean said. "We were on our last legs, our agents were not returning most of our calls, we were running out of money, and I was sure I'd have to move back to Wisconsin and apply at Jiffy Lube.

"Then, with just a few hundred dollars left in my account, we sold the script for *She's Out of My League* to DreamWorks. Soon, that script was added to The Blacklist: a list of the best unproduced scripts in Hollywood. The script's inclusion on that list really turned things around. We've worked consistently ever since, for which we are very grateful."

Below is an essay about *Never Been Thawed* that Sean wrote for *Modest Proposal Magazine* in 2005. This is before any of us moved to LA. The footnotes are from Sean in 2020, rereading this essay for the first time in fifteen years.

Chuck LeVinus and I sat in my kitchen. We had just watched the first cut of *Never Been Thawed*—the no-budget movie we had been working on for the past eighteen months. He asked me if I was happy with it. I said that I was. I felt awkward saying what I really thought; Chuck said it for me. "I think we might be sitting on a powder keg here." [1]

I had spent the past two months up to my ass in the editing and the audio mixing. Chuck was returning to the project with more perspective, so I was thrilled that he agreed we had created something special.

Later I spoke with John Morris, our other writing partner on the project, and he too felt we might have accomplished the highly unlikely. Three regular guys with no film experience had actually made a movie that people who weren't even related to us would find funny and entertaining—or had we? [2]

---

1   *I remember Chuck saying this and it was very exciting. It turned out NBT was not a powder keg, but more of a tiny spark. It never exploded but it did light a very slow burning fuse that is still burning today. Still, it was a fun moment, feeling good about what we had worked so hard making.*

2   *John is still my writing and producing partner today. John was always so difficult to impress that when John said he thought the movie might be kinda good, it was like anyone else saying it was the greatest movie ever made. He's still difficult to impress.*

Unfortunately, there's no computer program that digitally determines if something is actually funny. By the time a gag is in the final cut, we have written it, re-written it, performed it thirty-five takes in a row, watched each take three times to decide which one is best, watched the best take a hundred times during the editing and a hundred more during the audio mixing. Even the strongest bits lose their luster after the first few billion times. You just keep reminding yourself that this stuff is funny. Then you think of all the flat, unfunny comedy you've seen and how those writers must also have believed they too were funny. And maybe they were. Maybe all of that awful comedy actually is funny, and I just don't get it because I'm the unfunny moron.[3]

I recognize this cycle of insecurity and judgment as a common syndrome shared by many funny people who, despite their sharp wit, are insufferable to be around. They have taken their natural interest in creating merriment in the lives of others and turned it into a ruthless competition that is impossible to win. The only way out of the cycle is to remember this is supposed to be fun.[4]

---

3   *It's a lot of fun to read this because after all this time, it's all the same. You still put your neck out there every time you take a comedic swing. I'd say I'm more insecure now than I was then. I've had a lot of wonderful success, and I've gotten more than my share of laughs, but also many people panning my work, calling me a hack, etc. I wish that added up to thicker skin but... the money sure helps.*

4   *I could stand to heed this advice today. It's easy to get caught up in the pressure of it all and forget how lucky you are to be making movies as your JOB. Duly noted.*

I held the first screening for around thirty of my friends and family in Wisconsin. I expected them to be gracious regardless of their opinion but, as the film went on, their laughter felt more and more genuine. Their relief over not being required to lie to me afterward was palpable. Still, I knew this audience was to be chased with a king-sized grain of salt.

Screening number two was 250 people in a real movie theatre. These were people (and friends of people) who were in some way involved in the making of the movie, so their overwhelming response also had to be taken in perspective. However, a young guy who was working at the theatre approached me afterward, "Hilarious! The projectionist ran down here after about ten minutes and told us we had to get in there and see this!" This kid didn't know us. He watched movies every day. I knew he and his pals were sincere, and I believed it was now only a matter of time.[5]

We sent the film to a friend of a friend who had written and starred in a successful indie film. She told us to get ready for *NBT* to become the dark comedy darling of the 2004 festival season. We high-fived one another and then confidently sent copies of *NBT* to festivals all over the world. In return,

---

5   *Okay, this is the most important part of this story. These young people working at the theatre that night—if any of you are reading this, THANK YOU! Seriously, thank you! I literally owe my entire career and the fact that I'm a homeowner to you guys. Your enthusiasm and your subsequent positive reports to the management started everything. Also, your kind words meant so much because I knew you guys were seeing every movie. Again, thanks!*

festivals all over the world confidently sent us rejection letters. It seemed like every week a new "NO" was in my mailbox. It was like having one of the many girls who wouldn't dance with me in middle school stop by my house once a week to remind me. Remembering that this is supposed to be fun was getting more and more difficult.[6]

Maybe we needed a producer's rep? These are people who, in return for a percentage of the potential sale of the film, use their contacts and knowledge to get the festivals to take a solid look at your film. It was explained to us that fests are so brutally shelled with submissions that, without any stars or someone working it from the inside, your film will be given less than serious consideration. Unknown films are likely sent home with interns who are asked to look at a pile of movies every night. These interns couldn't watch all these movies if they wanted to—and they don't want to as the vast majority of them are beyond bad. Therefore, you are given about three minutes to impress some film student who is comparing your bullshit to their forecasted genius.

This is not our personal observation but what we have pieced together from stories we have heard and read over and over. Perhaps, each time, a crack blue-ribbon panel of judges weighed our film with great diligence before struggling to write us a heartfelt "Dear Filmmaker" letter. Who's to say? One of the letters did look like it had tear stains on it.

---

6   *Yup, this was when all the fun stopped, and the hurt began. In hindsight, taking this so seriously was a mistake. Live and learn.*

So, we confidently sent *NBT* out to every major producer's rep in the business and every major producer's rep in the business confidently told us, in so many words, to go fuck ourselves. The same speech was given over and over, "Yes, your movie is very funny and smart. Hell, I laughed out loud, and my assistant loved it! But there are no real character arcs. Your characters start out losers and assholes and they end up unchanged. We don't think audiences will get it."

But isn't real life like that? A bunch of assholes not learning their lesson? And further, isn't the number one job of a comedy to make you laugh? I thought we all collectively learned from *Seinfeld* that characters could remain self-involved wrecks, and people would love them anyway, as long as it was funny. I guess not.[7]

A few months later, we finally had a letter of acceptance. A small fest in Hollywood where, truth be told, we knew someone on the inside who got them to give us a hard look. We hired a publicist. The publicist got a critic at the *LA Times* to watch *NBT*. The critic raved and the fest gave us a deluxe time slot.[8]

---

7   *I don't disagree with my former self on this, but I have since learned that character arcs and story engines are very difficult to create and pull off. Today I have much more respect for the "hero's journey" style of storytelling. It's especially difficult when you're trying to make people laugh, but it's worth the work and the sweat when people connect with your characters and get more than laughs out of it. I'd like to be as punk rock about it as I was back then, but I have kids now. I'm not punk rock in any way.*

8   *Another person we owe a lot to. A guy named Micky, I think. He got NBT to the LA Times. That good review got us an agent. Major moment that led to many, many other things. Thanks, Micky.*

The *LA Times* called us wickedly funny! Every major distributor in town wanted to see the movie. "But there are no character arcs." Every major distributor in town didn't think people would get it. If only *NBT* had Val Kilmer in it somewhere or a cameo by one of the Golden Girls... anything that Hollywood could sink its marketing teeth into. Alas. Just funny and smart. Not enough.

Today things are going very well. We have a team of smart, ball-bustin' Hollywood agents who are shopping our latest screenplay to the studios.[9]

A couple of solid companies have now made offers to distribute *Never Been Thawed* on DVD and possibly in a limited theater release.[10]

Audiences continue to go nuts whenever we screen the movie. At the end of the day, this is all that really matters. How many people are fortunate enough to take a crack at something in which they have no background or clue and actually have it turn out well? My years of being a mediocre musician has made me hypersensitive to the face people make when

---

9   *That screenplay never got close to development. It was our first real script, and it mostly taught us how not to write. Our next script sold and was later made—*She's Out of My League. *That was the start of paying work.*

10 *A new internet company called Netflix took a chance on us. It apparently did very well for them because I hear they have built it into quite a top-drawer operation today. And we did get a limited run in theaters. Very few people showed up for it outside of Tempe, Arizona, but it was still so exciting to tour with the movie. Plus, I still had all my hair. That was nice.*

they don't really mean the compliment they are paying you. The absence of that expression on the faces of those who file out of the seats is far more than we could have hoped for on a first try.[11]

---

11 *Honestly, we didn't think there was any chance of a future in it when we made* NBT. *I think that's what made it special. It was just a group of friends having fun and seeing if we could pull it off. John and I took it seriously enough to eventually knuckle down and learn how to do it professionally, but it's never since been quite like* NBT. *We had ultimate freedom, tons of laughs and it was a LOT of work. But it never felt like work. Fun to remember what that felt like. Thanks for going there with me for a few minutes.*

EUGENE MIRMAN

—

By Ryan McKee

Original Interview: 2005

Updates: May 2020

In the mid-aughts, Eugene Mirman had the best website of any comedian in the world. Hands down. I have no statistics or science to prove it. Let me instead list all the impressive things on his site: an animated photo of Eugene as a baby that sang popular tunes in a high-pitched voice... And really that's all you need to know. I watched it whenever I needed cheering up, which was fairly often, in the mid-aughts.

It should be noted, however, the bar for comedians' websites in 2005 was set pretty low. Most didn't even have video or audio of their stand-up sets on their sites. But Eugene had an animated photo of a singing baby, funny videos, and a seven-minute audio clip of his stand-up. I listened to that audio clip so often, I could recite it from memory. His jokes were so clever and uniquely written I wanted to dissect them and figure out how to do the same for my act.

I never cracked his code. I'm ashamed to admit it now, but as a first-year comic, I "borrowed" one of his jokes. Word for word:

"It is never funny to pick up a stranger's child… and run… even for a little bit."

I'm pretty sure that's the wording of the joke. I even delivered it in Eugene's unique cadence. It got big laughs. No one in Phoenix knew about Eugene yet. After a couple shows, though, I felt guilty and stopped. Other comics would even ask me why I wasn't doing the joke, and I'd make up an excuse. More dishonesty to cover up my dishonesty.

I never got caught stealing. In fact, the first national company to buy a color, full-page ad on the back cover of *Modest Proposal Magazine*—the most expensive placement—was Sub Pop Records, promoting Eugene Mirman's album *En Garde, Society!* in 2006. Karma didn't punish me for stealing Eugene's joke. Instead I was paid money to promote Eugene's jokes. Is that what white collar crime feels like?

Thankfully, my guilt prevented me from continuing to steal Eugene's jokes. He grew in popularity, and soon people would've noticed and chased me with pitchforks. That is the traditional punishment for joke thievery. In fact, in Mary Shelley's original draft of *Frankenstein*, that is why the villagers chase down the monster, because he retold someone else's joke and claimed it as his own.

Eugene continues to be one of the most unique voices in stand-up comedy. Mainstream audiences recognize his literal voice as Gene Belcher in *Bob's Burgers*. He's extremely admired in comedy circles and beloved for producing live shows that promote the up-and-coming comedians. Much of that is detailed in the recent documentary *It Started As a Joke*.

One final note: In the original interview, I very much wanted to impress Eugene with my "hilarious" questions. I tried too hard. And the resulting questions are not funny. In fact, many are confusing or borderline mean. Sorry. I was still new to comedy. That said, Eugene was patient enough to cleverly answer all of them... not just once, but a second time in 2020.

RYAN MCKEE: Were your parents disappointed when you when to Hampshire College to major in Comedy?
EUGENE MIRMAN: No. My parents were very supportive. One of the reasons they brought my brother and me to America [from the USSR] was so that we could have more opportunities. It's just like in the movies. The kinds of movies where people come from either another country or the past and are really impressed with America. Not the kinds of movies where someone murders you while you're dreaming. We literally came to pursue the American dream.

2020 UPDATE: This remains true. I'd like to say more because we're supposed to comment on stuff, but they remain supportive in the past and also the present.

Why'd you decide to move to New York, where the beans are bad?
For a long time I thought I would wait to move until I got a job in comedy, but then after doing Aspen, *Conan*, and getting

a manager, it became clear that it would be much easier to get work if I lived in New York.

This is also true! In NYC I found an amazing community of comedians and collaborators that I have now worked with for decades. I met Loren Bouchard (who created Bob's Burgers) in Cambridge in the late '90s but then worked with him and the Bob's Burgers cast in NYC for many years. Julie Smith-Clem, who produced our comedy festival (the somewhat accurately named Eugene Mirman Comedy Festival) and directed the movie about the festival, It Started As a Joke, and I still work on lots of things together. Julie and I both now live back in Massachusetts and work on stuff together.

Actually, aren't Old El Paso Salsa commercials the ones that feature horrified cowboys that find out the "salsa" is from New York City, not the beans?
You might be right. Oh well, I really fucked up in my bio. At least you knew what I was talking about, so maybe it's okay.

I don't remember what in my bio this was in reference to (though I understand the gist from the context), but I think it still doesn't really matter? I know I say the opposite in the interview, but I actually believe I must have been joking.

I read in *The Onion A.V. Club* that the crowd at SXSW kind of ignored your set with the exception of one witty fellow who kept yelling, "David Cross!"
The room fit about twelve hundred people, maybe more, so depending where you were, it may have seemed like people were paying attention or not. Most people in the main part of the room seemed to be polite and attentive. I'm sure someone

was yelling, "David Cross," but I never heard them. I do a lot of video stuff, and people rarely yell at it because people know that television can't hear them. Also, you generally know when something goes badly.

I have not remembered more about that show since. But it's true that in a large room at something like SXSW, it'd be very easy to have hundreds of people up front listening and enjoying something and some people by a bar in back not paying attention. I think what is described here very possibly happened, but I think from the stage I didn't know. But yes, don't attend a show and yell anyone's name while another person is on stage. But also, now we won't have SXSW for some number of years, and I'm worried Americans will forget how to high-five or even kiss. And what will we do without weird brand partnerships? If there is no Ford Weather Channel Lounge, where you can win Bluetooth shoes, will love itself fade away?

Were crowds on the Modest Mouse tour receptive to you?
People were fairly skeptical of a comedian, but generally it would go well. Touring was fun, but Florida without your own car is somewhere between hot and boring. Miami may have been one of my worst experiences on stage. In Tallahassee, I fought a tiny drunk girl, and there was chaos. It's more work to open for a band, but it's often worth it in terms of reaching whole new audiences. I do believe though that if Lex Luthor tried to sink Florida into the ocean, to make Georgia more valuable, Superman would probably allow it.

I guess I can clarify that the fight with the drunk girl was shouting based. But also, I remember selling more merch at that show than any other show on that tour. I now rarely open for bands. I tour with Flight of the Conchords, but that's comedy as well. In the last ten years, I've toured with Andrew Bird, Robyn Hitchcock, and do a variety show with Wesley Stace often.

Does Isaac Brock of Modest Mouse return your phone calls now that he's all popular with that floating-on song?
Probably if I called him, he would. I rarely call people to see if they will call me back. Plus, it would be weird when someone called me back and I was like, "Just checking to see if you would."

My guess is he would still return my call, but I haven't spoken to him in a little while. Over the years, I would see him at their shows or various festivals. I hope he's doing well.

How did you hook up with the label Suicide Squeeze?
I have a rock booking agent. She books Modest Mouse, The Shins, etc., which is how I ended up opening for them. She showed my website to the owner of Suicide Squeeze, and he emailed me and asked me if I wanted to put out an album.

This is exactly true. I've since put out several albums on Sub Pop records and might start my own small comedy label with Julie Smith-Clem. I love Suicide Squeeze and David Dickenson who runs it and very much appreciate the chance he took on me.

Elliott Smith has some releases on Suicide Squeeze, and we all know what happened to him. Are you worried?
I believe he was more depressed than I am.

This is still probably the case.

Do you think independent music labels are now more willing to take chances on comics because of Sub Pop's success with David Cross?
I think that's partially it. David certainly did a lot to make people see comedy as sincere, passionate, and popular again. People used to have parties where you'd put on a comedy record and hang out and listen to it. That's since been replaced by getting drunk and complaining about loneliness and the harsh reality of becoming a novelist.

Sub Pop and lots of other indie labels did put out many comedy albums, so the answer to this was yes! Also, Comedy Central put out a lot of comedy albums and they did have somewhat of a resurgence. Not sure if anything was as popular as The Button-Down Mind of Bob Newhart, but there were definitely a lot of comedy albums from a wide range of comedians that came out over the last fifteen years.

Are dogs or babies easier to trick? You wrote in *The Onion* that babies are really easy to trick, but sometimes I'll pretend to throw a ball, but I won't, and my dog will run after this invisible ball and then look at me all confused. It's hilarious.
First of all, I bet your dog thinks you're an asshole. Second, it probably loves you still. (That's the nature of abusive relationships.) I think both babies and dogs are easily tricked. However, as dogs grow up, they turn to crime to stay alive, but babies get jobs. That's why it's better to hire a baby than a dog.

In hindsight my logic is even more true today than it was fifteen years ago.

You described Underdog [a comedy tour with him, Demetri Martin, Leo Allen, and Andy Blitz] as a "cross between The Soft Boys and Neutral Milk Hotel." One group has an album called, *In the Aeroplane Over the Sea*, and another has an album called, *Underwater Moonlight*. Will you guys release an album called, *Skimming over the Water Like a Flat Stone Thrown by a Strong Boy*?

Where did I say that? Wait, you can't hear me and respond (because I am typing alone in a room). Underdog is more of stand-up with group commentary than any sort of seminal rock experiment. However, we have the enthusiasm of "I Wanna Destroy You" and the accordion sounds of "King of Carrot Flowers." I'm bullshitting you. We're more like "Queen of Eyes" meets "Holland, 1945." What specific references! Holy shit! If you get them, that means you know both albums. If you don't, I just wasted your time! Sorry.

Looking back, I do not have anything to add here.

What's on tap next for Eugene Mirman?

I'm working on a full-length DVD with all my shorts. I will probably get married to a bunch of nineteen-year-olds or whatever. Right? Cops are always harassing me to marry a bunch of young adults. I'm like, "Officer, the law allows you to only have one spouse." And the cop is like, "Shut up and marry those teens getting high behind that gas station." It's bullshit.

Well, now all these years later, the DVD came out as part of my first Sub Pop release, but I did not marry a bunch of nine-teen-year-olds. I did get married (and not at the insistence of the police) to a wonderful woman, Katie Westfall-Tharp, and we had a son. She had fought metastasized breast-cancer for the last six years and passed away in January. I'm sorry my answer is so serious. But that is what happened.

How does Eugene Mirman keep it real?

A lot of it is never playing with magic. I'm not sure how real I keep it, but I eat a lot of fish if that's what you mean.

It's true, I still do not dabble in the dark arts, and I eat a lot of fish. I live part-time on Cape Cod, where there is a lot of seafood.

B.D. FREEMAN

———

By Mike Baoule

Original Interview: 2004

Updated Interview: 2020

As a nineteen-year-old kid trying to navigate the LA comedy scene, I crossed paths with primarily bitter, chain-smoking, hack comics. B.D. Freeman, on the other hand, was positive, outgoing toward everyone who crossed his path, and more than willing to share any comedian tradecraft he had learned along his own journey.

B.D. exudes confidence. However, he's also not braggadocious and never belittles others. He is simply proud of his work and all the effort it took to get him where he is today.

It's been sixteen years since I last interviewed him for *Modest Proposal*. Ryan McKee had deputized me as the guest editor for Issue 4. Without hesitation, I knew the first person I wanted to write about was B.D.

Shortly after our original interview, he began playing various characters on *MADtv*, though he often jokes that you can count the number of times he actually appeared in an episode on two hands. The exposure led to better opportunities though. He's done everything from acting in *Degrassi: The Next Generation* and the film *No Stranger Pilgrims* to appearing in so many VH1 shows like *I Love The 2000s* and *100 Greatest Artists of All Time* that it's hard to keep track.

Overall, I'm just happy for my friend and talking to him always makes me feel better.

ORIGINAL INTERVIEW

MIKE BAOULE: Where are your roots?
B.D. FREEMAN: I grew up in a medium-sized town about twenty minutes away from Milwaukee. My father died when I was ten years old, and I grew up in a really abusive home. My mom sort of lost it when my dad died, and it was really hard for her to cope with seven kids. She pretty much became abusive only to me, not to the rest of the kids. That gave me really low self-esteem. To cope, I'd pretend like I was singing a song to an audience, and I would make up little plays that I'd perform all alone. That was my defense mechanism because everywhere I looked, I was taking a beating from school, from a mean teacher, or classmate, or at home.

You're a big guy. I can't imagine you taking a beating.
I was always big, but I was a sensitive big guy.

Why is it that a really dysfunctional childhood makes for a really good entertainer?

I've thought about this a lot. I think you're just constantly looking for that extra hug that you really can only get from a room full of strangers.

Where's Bobby Delerious? [his old stage name]

I killed him a couple of years ago.

That was the cheesiest name ever. All you needed was a bright green plaid jacket to go on stage with and that would have been the best.

He's gone and it's for the better.

KRS-One has the nine elements of hip-hop. Give your three elements of comedy.

Uh, for me I guess it would be number one, commitment. Two would be originality and number three would be rhyme.

The first time I got on stage, you gave me some advice that I can't remember, but that's not important. The cool thing is you took the time to talk to me. Why?

When I left Montana University, where I was studying drama, guys on the road would just never talk to me. I had to learn the hard way about stand-up. When I see someone like you, I'll always take time to talk to them because comedy is like being in the military. You might be in a foxhole with that guy. I would rather give him some tips and then we both can fight better and win.

A lot of Black comics gripe about the TV roles they get. But you really can't blame a guy for taking work, even if it's bad. Be honest, would you do a spinoff of *Homeboys in Outer Space?*

I hope I have the inner fortitude to say no to any homeboy movie. On one side, I don't begrudge a guy trying to make a movie and get a break. But if they make a jigaboo movie or TV show, Hollywood is not very creative and will have a very hard time seeing you for anything else.

There's backlash that *The Cosby Show* didn't represent most Black people because they're upper-middle class. Is that why networks went back to making updated versions of *Good Times* instead of well-written shows like *Cosby?*

Well, you know I was living in an upper-middle class family like the Cosbys. Of course, you know there is no doubt that *Cosby* was a fantastic show, and there needs to be more like it.

Why does it seem *Def Comedy Jam* is filled with old hacky jokes?

I think *Def Comedy Jam*, and let me just say this, I think some of the most brilliant Black comics came up through *Def Comedy Jam*, but I think it's a dumb-downed audience going to comedy shows now, no matter what their race. They want to talk about being on welfare, having sex, having babies, living in the ghetto, living with their mom, not having any money. Cosby said, and I agree with him, "They have to go see a minstrel show." And you see not only a lot of Black dollars but a lot of white dollars going in. Whites might not be hanging on the stage, but they watch it on the TV, which is why the ratings were so high for a while.

How do you keep it real?
For me the most important part of keeping it real is keeping God first. That's where it's at for me. That's where I find my shelter, my relationship with Jesus.

UPDATED INTERVIEW

So is Bobby Delerious still dead?
Absolutely.

When we spoke in 2004, you had all but quit stand-up. Where are you at with it now?
I wanted to really focus on acting back then because that's where my heart was at the time. I've picked up doing stand-up again, but it's still secondary to acting.

What's on your plate now and what's on the backburner for later?
I'm currently developing a new show. And trying to navigate through all the new media platforms. It's a great time for artists to showcase their work. You don't have to rely on the same four networks to make your career anymore.

As far as the future is concerned, I want to maintain good health. You know, I previously lost over two hundred lbs. I physically feel the best I've ever felt, and that's very important to my life.

(He paused and grinned.)

I would definitely contemplate running for public office. I feel like I could help people.

Do you think your voice is heard as a Black man in the boardroom?

Yes, but it's something I had to practice. From the very beginning, I told my managers and agents not to send me out for roles that are drug dealers, pimps, and gangbangers. They told me, "But it'll be great for your career." I knew I had to draw the line somewhere, though.

Are you happy with the roles people of color get today?

I think the problem is you have white writers writing for people of color. So, a lot of the time, the characters they create are one-dimensional characters. Middle Eastern actors are in high demand now, but a lot of them are playing the same part. It's really important for people of color to write their own roles and create their own content so they can be seen the way they want to be seen.

If I gave you a golden ticket that allowed you any job you want, what would it be?

Host of *The Tonight Show*.

You'd steal Jimmy Fallon's job?

Absolutely. You said I can use my golden ticket any way I want.

JESSE THORN

———

By Ryan McKee

Original Interview: 2005

Updates: May 2020

In 2005, this is what I wrote about being introduced to Jesse. Meeting twenty-four-year old Jesse Thorn is what I imagine meeting a young Conan O'Brien would have been like. He's huge, like seven feet or something like that, and exudes a slight cockiness that comes with being intelligent and well-versed in various subjects. He would be intimidating if not for his wide grin and sarcastic wit, which undoubtedly comes from years of besting intimidators with clever remarks rather than violence.

I kinda nailed that. Jesse Thorn is a bit like the Conan O'Brien of podcasting. If you ignore the fact Conan has a podcast now.

Ron and I met Jesse Thorn and his sketch group Prank the Dean (Jesse, Jordan Morris, Lauren Pasternack and Jim Real) while we were all performing at the 2005 SF Sketchfest. Jesse told us about his local public radio program in Santa Cruz, *The Sound of Young America*, where he interviewed a lot of comedians. Jesse and I were brothers-in-arms, producing comedy interviews in our archaic mediums—me with a magazine and he with a radio show.

However, Jesse parlayed his archaic medium into a podcast empire. After being the first public radio program west of the Mississippi to be podcasted, *The Sound of Young America* (renamed *Bullseye with Jesse Thorn* in 2012) skyrocketed up the iTunes Charts.

National Public Radio eventually noticed the success of Jesse's podcast and now distributes *Bullseye* to over 150 stations across the country. After this interview, Jesse moved to Los Angeles and launched the media company Maximum Fun, which now distributes over fifty podcasts. He also started another weekly podcast with Jordan Morris called *Jordan, Jesse, Go!* which has an incredibly loyal following and over six hundred episodes. Jesse's early innovations with podcasting led to *Fast Company* magazine naming him "the most important person in entertainment you've never heard of" in 2011.

Fifteen years later, Jesse seems like the same guy I met. Sure, he's much more successful, is married with three children, and looks more like a friendly Viking (with his shaved head and impressive beard), but I stand by my initial assessment of him.

RYAN MCKEE: **Why'd you name your show** *The Sound of Young America*?

JESSE THORN: I thought a long time about the name. I wanted something distinctive and a little bit ridiculous. It was of course the slogan of Motown records. It's not just something we made up. It's also a canny reference. Unfortunately, we're not the Supremes of radio; we're more like the Marvelettes.

2020 UPDATE: Naming things is so hard. Eventually having an ironic name was too much of a burden; especially because I sound older than I am, and people would assume I was forty-seven. Roman Mars actually came up with the name Bullseye, *which is what it's called now, but it was painful to try and think of anything. The distributor asked for the* with Jesse Thorn *part.*

How'd the show originally start?
As a sophomore at UC Santa Cruz, I wanted to do a show on the campus radio station KZSC. I was Jordan's RA. He and Gene O'Neill were the funniest guys I knew, so I asked them to co-host with me.

I still work with Jordan, doing Jordan, Jesse, Go! *and he's still the funniest guy I know. And I talk to Gene every once in a while. He's still funny and works as a producer on a big reality TV show these days.*

Did you always plan to interview guests?
Early on in the show, we realized that if we booked guests, we wouldn't have to write material. We booked Screech on the show in an obviously ironic move. It was so awful. Dustin Diamond was completely not self-aware and mean, really mean. That was his joke style. Like street jokes about people

in wheelchairs. We said, "Hey, Dustin, maybe you should stick to something from your act?" And he said, "This is from my act." So, we decided from then on, we're only going to book things that we like. Irony is over.

There have been so few shitty guests on my show over the years that this is still my go-to worst guest story. He was really awful. Besides this, it's mostly been the occasional guest who doesn't show or just doesn't really want to be there. But that's maybe once a year. Almost everyone is just as good as you'd hope they'd be. I mean I just interviewed Christoph Waltz, and he was a fucking delight.

How'd the radio show evolve into what it is today?
Well, Gene left when he graduated. And Jordan left when he graduated; I wasn't comfortable on the radio for a while. So, I booked guest co-hosts for a while, but I didn't feel that same social connection with them as with Gene and Jordan. Ultimately, it's just me with guests I truly love and want to speak with.

I was really scared to do the show by myself, so the first summer after Jordan left, I booked guest co-hosts, just local people I knew. Among them were W. Kamau Bell, who has a bunch of Emmys now, and Al Madrigal, who was just second on the call sheet in a Ben Affleck movie. And my first internet friend, an Arizona-based comedian named Nick Adams, who I knew from Okayplayer.com's message boards. He writes on Black-ish now and is still one of my great pals.

How does your show fit with other shows on public radio?
I think there's a hole in public radio right now. It's supposed to be providing a public service, quality in audio entertainment.

It does a fantastic job in many ways. But it has the myopia that it should serve exclusively baby boomers.

Now, it does such a good job, that I think other generations can listen too. I listen to public radio all the time.

You listen to an interview with Carly Simon and she doesn't have to explain herself. But anytime a rapper is on public radio, the focus becomes asking him why he uses the "n" word. That's pretty much the baseline at this point. Rappers shouldn't have to be defending their artform. They should be talking about what they do. And it's the same way with comedy and the same way with indie rock.

My goal for *Sound* is to be that bridge for younger listeners. A show that is fun, with a new angle, and a lot of comedy, but not exclusively comedy. A show that is not stupid and isn't boring. And I'm lucky enough to be on a great radio station that lets me do whatever I want, though they don't pay me. And I'm lucky enough to get in on the early stages of podcasting.

I mean... good job me? Way to mostly get it right? These days, public radio has come a long way. Still relatively few millennial voices, but Gen X is pretty well-represented and there's a lot less cringey stuff. And they're still great at news and important stuff. Besides that, the public service mission and deep experience in audio storytelling ended up working out great in podcasting.

How has the show's focus changed since you started podcasting?
Now I worry less about the Santa Cruz market and think more nationally. That started before podcasting, though.

It started when we expanded the show to the Hattiesburg, Mississippi, public radio affiliate. I program the show for people who like the show, as opposed to trying to not alienate people. At KZSC, my lead-in is *Jazz Kitty*, and she does a great job, but how many people who listen to her show want to listen to my show? With podcasting people actually choose to listen to it.

Man, long time since I've thought about Jazz Kitty. *I mostly think about* Joy in the Morning *with DJ Had-I* and *A Fistful of Soundtracks with Jimmy Aquino.* Community radio is great. The nice dude who put me on the radio in Hattiesburg got fired for being too weird. I hope if he hears me on NPR he goes, "I discovered that guy!" because he deserves it. Even if that and three bucks will get you a cup of coffee.

How did your sketch group Prank the Dean come about?
Jordan and I started it and piloted the ship. Jim is our superpal. And Lauren is our spectacular woman. Whenever we talk shop with another sketch group, they always ask where'd you get that spectacular woman. It seems to be one of the great challenges of building a sketch group.

Anyway, we had Kasper Hauser on the radio show and loved them passionately. We think they're the most wonderful group in the world. We were really excited to talk to them about our improv group. They asked us if we also performed sketch comedy and Jordan said, "Yeah." They asked where we perform and he said, "Ah well, you know, around down here." And then they said they'd help us find some places to perform in San Francisco. We said, "Oh, great!" So, we asked Jim to be in the group, and Jordan knew Lauren from the theatre department from UCSC. Then Jordan and I wrote some sketches and we're still performing those same sketches today.

I am very glad the world is less discouraging to funny women these days. Not quite encouraging, but less discouraging. Lauren owns a huge restaurant in Austin called Bangers now. It's great, and she does Assistant Directing work on the side because she is brilliant and more on top of things than any human being ever. Jim is a very successful scientist, and Jordan is writing a movie for Seth Rogen. So, everybody but me is a big success.

Do you plan to keep performing as Prank the Dean?
Well, our first goal was to write enough material to perform the show that Kasper Hauser had gotten us. Our secondary goal was to get into the SF Sketchfest. When we did both of those, we figured we'd see where it went from there. It just seems like too much fun to give up. However, it's tough since Jordan moved to Los Angeles. We're doing Seattle Sketchfest in September. We don't make any money, but that's okay if you think of it as a working vacation or something.

At Seattle Sketchfest, we slept in a nice couple's backyard prefab garage that they had converted to a bootleg theater to perform episodes of Buffy *in, with an audience sitting in art furniture that they brought to Burning Man every year. There were no windows, so it was pitch black at night, and one night, Jordan woke up and couldn't find the door, so he had to pee in the corner. I really loved doing sketch at weird festivals with my great friends. It was a wonderful part of my life.*

Back to your podcast, what do you think it can lead to?
The reason I got into radio is because I can make a radio show, but I can't make a TV show. I make an absolutely listenable radio show. But I can't do it full time because I gotta pay rent. Even if I were doing a horrible unwatchable cable access show, I'd need six people. I'd like to develop my podcast audience and then maybe stations will be willing to take a chance on something that's a little different.

That's kind of what happened! Also, I had a couple of TV shows. If anyone is reading this and needs a bald guy to host a TV show, I'm in.

What are the biggest problems you foresee?
I'm a passable engineer. We don't have a great phone system. Public radio directors who aren't taking risks might listen to my show and say the quality isn't good. Without a real professional studio, I just can't do that. Terry Gross does interviews over ISBN lines, and I don't have $600 to pay my rent.

Compared to other podcasts though, I should sound a lot better than some asshole with a microphone plugged into his iMac, talking about his dog.

Man, podcasts mostly stank back then. They are way better now. I am about the same amount of good—bad news for me. We rent studios for our guests now, though, and I have the money for my mortgage. So, let's call it a win, overall.

How does podcast king Jesse Thorn keep it real?
I don't. I've got a big head. I bought a used Rolls Royce with pink dashboard covers. My mother has to call me "Mr.

Thorn." I spend most of my time drinking and going on tirades about *Prairie Home Companion*. Podcasting success has made me a different man. Once I cracked the top 100, it's all gone downhill.

Well, the last part is true.

GREG FITZSIMMONS

By Ryan McKee

Original Interview: April 2003

Updates: May 2020

I discovered Greg Fitzsimmons in a different era. No, we weren't sitting around the radio listening to *The Pepsodent Show* with Bob Hope or waiting around the fire for Pa to spin a chucklesome yarn. Still, options were only slightly better.

Today, if you're a fan of Greg Fitzsimmons, there's a steady diet of his content to consume. His weekly podcast *Fitzdog Radio* with nine hundred episodes of back catalog. Frequent guest appearances on *The Adam Carolla Podcast, Joe Rogan Experience,* and *The Howard Stern Show* (Greg also hosted his own SiriusXM radio show on *Howard 101* for over ten years). His hour-long stand-up special *Life on Stage*, plus two *Comedy Central Presents...* specials. His autobiographical book *Dear Mrs. Fitzsimmons: Tales of Redemption from an Irish Mailbox.* And a steady stream of YouTube clips from twenty+ years of stand-up and panel appearances on Comedy Central,

The Tonight Show, David Letterman, Conan, Chelsea Lately, Jimmy Kimmel Live!, The Late Late Show, Comedy Bang Bang!, @midnight, and more.

Occasional appearances on *The Howard Stern Show* first clued me in to Greg. To find more of his content in the early-aughts, I couldn't go to YouTube or streaming platforms or social media. All I could do was buy his CD *Fitz of Laughter* and just hope I caught reruns of his 1998 *Comedy Central Presents...* and sporadic TV appearances.

I was so pumped when Fitzsimmons popped up on Tempe Improv's upcoming events, along with Stuttering John and Artie Lange from *Howard.* I had memorized his CD in the six months since I bought it. I pestered the club's PR rep, Troy Conrad, until he got me this interview.

Greg and I talked in the Improv's lobby while audience members for the 11 p.m. show streamed into the showroom. Usually the club only did 8 p.m. and 10 p.m. shows on Friday nights, but due to the number of *Stern* fans, they'd added a third show. My girlfriend, Chrystyna Golloher, awkwardly snapped photos of us with a stone-age digital camera.

The experience cemented my lifelong fandom. Greg patiently answered all the questions I nervously sputtered out and joked around with me before and after I turned the tape recorder off. (Yes, it was actually a small recorder with an actual cassette tape.)

In the original intro for this interview, I described that night's audience as a cross between an AC/DC show and a frat party with even more booze. Stuttering John opened the show by guzzling beer, doing a whip-it, taking off his shirt, and showing his ass crack. Greg had the daunting task of being the middle act between John and fan-favorite Artie Lange. Even though Greg was a regular on *Stern*, the crowd didn't recognize him and started heckling. To this day, I've never been at such an unruly show and seen a comedian handle it so deftly. Greg alternated between berating the audience and rapid-fire punchlines. They shifted from a raucous middle-school class abusing a substitute teacher to a *Def Comedy Jam* audience from the '90s: laughing, banging tables, and falling out of their seats (though the last one could've been from alcohol). After one of Greg's particularly great punchlines, an ASU bro stood up and pointed to the stage like a referee signaling a first down. I have never seen that response at a comedy show, before or since.

The biggest problem after seeing Greg destroy live at a club, I had to go back to only listening to that same CD and hoping to catch him on *Howard*. You don't know how great you have it, young comedy fans.

RYAN McKEE: When are you going to show your son the articles you wrote for Playboy.com about his conception?
GREG FITZSIMMONS: That's funny because I worry about that. I don't want to fuck my kid up. Especially living in LA, it's an uphill battle as it is. We were at a party, and an agent goes, "I want to represent your kid." Where else does that happen? I called the agent and said, "You got him for one year. When he's two years old, he retires." Yeah, we have some

pretty strong ideas how not to fuck up our kid. Like my wife is pretty cool with rolling with what I say on *Howard* as long as I tell her first, which I respect. I guess with my son, I'll have to have the same boundaries.

2020 UPDATE: I wrote a memoir a few years after this article laying out my insane teenage years (arrests, failing school, and fighting). My kids got a hold of it and throw it in my face every time I try to reprimand them. My daughter once said, "Dad, how can you be mad about that? You got a girl to go to your prom by offering her a gram of cocaine." That book was a mistake.

Also, in those articles, you referred to the rules of comedy. One is "don't bang waitresses at clubs you regularly perform at." What are some others?
Uh, don't eat the mayonnaise in the comedy condo because somebody dunked their balls in it at some point. Tip the staff really well. They ultimately tell the booker who they like and don't like. And… that's it. There's not a lot. Wear what you want. Drink what you want. Show up late. It's cool. You're a comedian.

Do new material. After thirty years I have a lot of the same people coming to the club to see me every year, and they let me know if they have seen the same bits the last time I came through. That means during the weeks I am off the road I need to spend a few nights in the local clubs working on new stuff. It's actually my favorite part of the process.

Boston has given birth to a number of great comics. What is it about that city?
It's like San Francisco, where a lot of comics have also come out of, in that they're both closed communities. Boston never

hired headliners from outside of Boston. They groomed the local talent. It kept us busy, and because of that, you had to compete with everyone around town and be better. You had to have your own voice because everyone watched you and knew if you were stealing, knew if you were being derivative. It was a really good way to come up.

There are so many local scenes now (Denver, Portland, Seattle, Cincinnati, Austin) where comics can get up five to six nights a week. I don't usually bring my own feature because I want to support the locals getting the stage time, and I am always impressed with the level of comics out there now.

But do people stay there after they get bigger?
They do. You've never heard of some of the guys I consider to be some of the best comedians ever: Don Gavin, Steve Sweeney, Kenny Rogerson, Mike Donovan, Mike McDonald—all amazing comics who've really worked on their craft over the years. Nobody knows them, but they make six figures every year for the last twenty years.

*I just recently had the pleasure of having Don Gavin and Steve Sweeney on my podcast. It was hilarious and a little emotional to go through their lives and let them know how much they've always meant to me. Don has a great new CD out (*Live with a Manhattan*) you can get on iTunes.*

The Montreal Comedy Festival turns so many comedians' lives around. Are there people who go there and just bomb and quit comedy?
Like in the movie *Comedian*, people like Orny Adams get too pumped up and think it's all gonna happen and you know

what, you're just fucking rolling the dice. So many factors go into it.

There are so many new comedians now trying to get those spots in Montreal thinking it will help them. In some cases, it does but now newer comics are having more luck just grinding it out on social media and YouTube. If someone is good and they work hard, they don't need that big "break." They build a following slowly and steadily by just showing up with good stuff.

Do you think Orny Adams in *Comedian* gives comics a bad rep, always being so tortured?
We're all that tortured. Those characters in that documentary are the two halves of every comedian's brain. That was the brilliance of that movie. When things are going well and you're in control of your craft, you feel like Jerry Seinfeld. You're in it for the right reasons, and you're just trying to create a better set. Then when things aren't going well, you're like, "It's never going to happen." I mean, obviously, Orny's a pretty fucked-up guy. I know him. He came out of Boston also. Yeah, it makes you kind of sad to see it, but that's just part of it.

Orny is still out there killing it. He, like me, never got on a big sitcom or toured theatres but he loves it. He shows up for every show wanting to kill it, and he usually does. He makes a very nice living and seems much happier.

Did you kiss Rosie O'Donnell when you appeared on her show?
My cousin's a big Rosie fan, so I brought her, and I know she kissed her. Yeah, Rosie wanted nothing to do with me after my performance. I was a little dirty for the show.

Still haven't kissed her.

Editor's Note: Dubbed "The Queen of Nice," Rosie often greeted her celebrity guests with a kiss on The Rosie O'Donnell Show, *which ran from 1996-2002.*

The View versus The Howard Stern Show, which is more difficult to get a word in?
Well, when I did *The View*, it was a one-on-one deal called, "Joy's Comedy Corner." She's a stand-up comic, and she just basically tees up your jokes for you. It's the easiest kind of comedy. And Joy's great. She's there to make you look funny. As for *Howard Stern*, it's a moving train, and you're just trying to get on it.

Since this interview I ended up doing the Stern *show over forty times. Howard gave me my own show on his channel for ten years, and I came to love everybody on that crew. Such a unique niche in show business. Helped my career immensely.*

I read you perform at Midnight Comedy Hour at Lulu's Beehive in LA. One reviewer wrote "at Lulu's Beehive the booker uses LA's notorious lack of mic time to book comedians that deserve much better venues." Is that true?
Who wrote that?

I don't know, actually.
Well, what do we deserve? I mean, you want to go tell jokes in front of a room full of people and here's this great coffee shop filled with people who just got out of an AA meeting, so they're all filled with positive energy. You get a free cup of coffee and some stage time. I'm happy. If I want to make

money, I get on a plane, drive to some godforsaken Midwestern town, and struggle all week long. If I want to go home to my bed every night, that's the price I pay. I'm not going to make much money.

There are tons of little coffee shop shows, but it's sprawled out way beyond that. Shows in laundromats, back yards, living rooms, and if you're lucky enough, Maria Bamford will do a show just for you.

How does Greg Fitzsimmons keep it real?
By doing coffee shops in the Valley.

I just always show up, and I always do my time. No matter how bad it is, somebody out there came to see a show and that's my job.

BRAD ABLESON

———

By Ron Babcock
Original Interview: December 2002

Updates: May 2020

Ryan and I met in an improv group on Semester at Sea (SAS), a collegiate study abroad program on a cruise ship that went around the world. The group started out of boredom. We were at sea for days between ports, there was no internet, and the bar didn't open 'til 9 p.m. None of us knew how to actually do improv, besides our classmate Staci, who'd taken a Groundlings 101 class. She was also an extra in *Austin Powers*, so she was our leader. Soon other students would show up just to watch our practices, which turned into us putting on actual shows. During that semester, we stopped in ten countries: seeing, eating, and doing things we had never done before.

Then we'd come back on the ship and mine it all for comedy. The results of jamming together so many new experiences into one hundred days resulted in incredible bonds of friendship. And that bond extends to anyone who ever went on

SAS, not just your particular voyage. And yes, we do refer to them as "voyages."

Every few months, SAS sends out a newsletter asking for money, spotlighting former students, and asking for more money. In 2002, a newsletter came with Brad Ableson on the cover and included an article about his success as a storyboard artist for *The Simpsons*. I thought, "Hey, *The Simpsons* is a comedy series. We cover comedy! Plus, we all did a Semester at Sea. He has to say yes to an interview with us." Amazingly, I was correct.

A few years after this interview, we visited Brad at Film Roman, the production company for *The Simpsons* and *King of the Hill*. I thought it'd be all skylights and art deco sconces. After all, it's Hollywood! Instead, the offices were in a dank office building. Rumor is there used to be a military morgue in the basement and when the staff would pull all-nighters, some would hear what sounded like ghosts running around.

Despite the lack of skylights and art deco sconces (and the abundance of tortured souls), the atmosphere in the office was bursting with life. The walls were covered in drawings. Artists sat at desks covered in toys and figurines. You could tell Brad was excited to share it with us. Here was this massive *Simpsons* fan who actually got to work on the show he loved. For two guys who had just moved to Los Angeles, it was incredibly inspiring.

Brad worked at *The Simpsons* for close to twenty years and went on to co-create the animated series *Good Vibes* for MTV and *Legends of Chamberlain Heights* for Comedy Central. Most recently, he co-directed the animated film *Minions:*

The Rise of Gru. He's definitely going to make the cover of the SAS newsletter again.

Ron Babcock: Brad, you work for *The Simpsons*. The entire free world is jealous. What's it like?

Brad Ableson: In some ways, it's exactly probably what you're imagining, in terms of it just being funny and wacky and creativity flowing everywhere. Little things that really make it fun is that people draw all over the walls. The management would get angry because it's a corporate-like building, but when you have artists in there, there's going to be some anarchy. It's still a nine-to-fiver in certain ways. The show has been on the air for fourteen years, and it's definitely a well-oiled machine. Back in the day, it used to probably be a lot crazier. All these young artists, amped to have their first job, feeling the success of this new show, working all night long to make it great. Now a lot of those people are married and have kids and want to go home at five. But there's always new kids who keep the energy level up.

2020 Update: This is all still true. And I have become one of the tired, married, jaded OGs.

What got you the job at the ripe age of nineteen?

Oh, I had to sleep with all kinds of people. No, it was between my sophomore and junior year. I had been applying to film school over and over again, and I kept getting turned down. At that point, I'm thinking I'm not going to get into film school, so I start looking into jobs. My dream would be working on *The Simpsons*, so I figured, "What the hell, I got nothing to lose." I called and asked, "What do you do to get a job here?" and they said to bring your portfolio. I didn't even know what a portfolio was. I just brought in a bunch of t-shirts that I designed for my fraternity and stupid shit like that. I walked in and the lady who was in charge of hiring totally laughed at me. What saved me was the fact that I was, and I still am, the biggest *Simpsons* freak you ever met. I know you probably hear people say that all the time, but I was the biggest *Simpsons* fan on Earth. Just being in that building, I was freaking out. I was telling her, "Oh my god, I can't believe I'm in the building where this happens." Her heart went out to me a little bit, and she gave me some pointers on how to put together a portfolio. I don't think she really thought I'd ever even come back. I ran out in a week, did all the stuff she asked me to do and came back with this real polished portfolio. I think she was impressed that I took it that seriously. I definitely was not their first pick, but the fact that I was such a big fan gave me the edge. I struggled like crazy at first. I was pulling all-nighters all the time just to try and keep up. I didn't care. It was my dream job. Then I got the letter from the film school saying that I got in. So, suddenly, I had to choose between the two and the two were both my dreams. That same lady who was so cool to me pulled some strings and worked it out so I could work part-time while I went to school. It was nuts, it was absolute insanity, but I was doing the two coolest things I could ever think of.

Okay, reading this now, I do kind of want to punch "young me." But, man, those really were the greatest years of my life!

Is Matt Groening like a crazy uncle?

Matt Groening is like Mr. Burns, and we're all a bunch of Homers. He doesn't remember any of us. We don't work with him at all. He's the most hands-off guy, and the only time I ever see him is when, once a year, we have a season premiere party, and he'll be there. And every time I introduce myself to him, even though I met him probably eight times, but he never remembers me. Just like Homer and Mr. Burns.

Eighteen years later this is still one hundred percent the same.

What do you do as a storyboard artist?
I get the script and a cassette tape of the voices, which they usually do beforehand. I just read it, picture it in my brain, and sketch it out like a comic book. I'm coming up with the camera angles, the compositions, the cuts, blocking out the basic acting. It's a lot like directing.

A cassette tape, kids, was an mp3 you could touch!

Do you write too, or do you just handle the visual jokes?
The group of writers almost all went to Harvard. They do their thing and send it to us, and we do our thing. They would never in a million years even consider adding a joke that we came up with unless it was something purely visual. And that's something I get to do now and then. If there's an opportunity in the storyboard to throw in a little visual gag, that might make it through.

What is your favorite episode that you worked on?
"Night of the Dolphins" from "Treehouse of Horrors XI." It was a spoof on *The Birds*, where instead of birds attacking Springfield, it was dolphins. The way it works with storyboards is we do one-third of the show. When I do a Halloween storyboard, it's like getting my own complete story. The Halloween episodes are so fun, and anything goes in terms of crazy angles. It'll say, "Dolphins are riding in town square attacking people." It's such a broad idea. That's when

I start coming up with my own jokes, so that is when I really have fun.

Still my favorite episode I ever worked on!

Ever lie about where you work so you don't have to answer questions like these?
Nine times out of ten, I can't wait to tell people because a lot of times it gets a good reaction. In LA, most people don't really care. The farther I get from LA, the bigger a deal it is. I was at this Benny Honda's with my girlfriend at the time, and they sat us with this Japanese family who was visiting. They had this little kid, and I started drawing Bart for him. The mom was like, "Oh, very good, very good." My girlfriend explained that I work on *The Simpsons* and she goes, "Ohh, ohh." She starts freaking out and tells her whole family and I'm not exaggerating, every single one—the mom, dad, grandma, grandpa, the little kids—whips out their own cameras and start taking pictures of me. They ask me for my address and a few weeks later I got this huge package of framed photos, toys, and candles.

"Benny Honda's?" Ha! It was Benihanas!

Are women impressed by where you work?
Very rarely. If I were into thirteen-year-old boys, I'd be doing great, but I'm not.

For the record, I'm still not into thirteen-year-old boys!

Tell us about your movie, Save Virgil.
It's a combination of live action and animation, like *Roger Rabbit*-style. It's about this kid who is born with a birth defect.

It's the normal real world, but this one kid, his birth defect is that he's a cartoon. We got Adam Carolla to do the voice, and he makes it so funny.

Your ulcer almost killed you with all these projects, literally. How you holding up?
I don't know if the ulcer was because of all the shit I was doing, but the shit I was doing didn't help. But it's gone now. I had the surgery where they physically cut it out, so there's nothing. I'm at one hundred percent—ready to destroy more of my body.

I had a surprisingly good attitude back then. That shit nearly killed me!

What's your ultimate goal?
I would love to be a pole at a strip club. Naked girls spinning around me all day, that's definitely what I'm working toward. My ultimate goal is writing and directing comedy movies, not necessarily animation, not excluding animation either.

Classy answer, Brad. SMH

UPDATED QUESTIONS

What are your immediate thoughts after reading this interview?
Aside from being extremely unwoke, I stand by all these answers. I'm actually impressed with how clear my goals were back then and how diligently I was working toward them.

Knowing what you know now, what would you tell "2002 Brad Ableson"?

I would tell him to bend over and let me smack dat young ass! (Okay, I haven't changed a bit.)

Besides the obvious things, what's like, changed for you since then?

Still hustling! But now I'm married (to a woman I met working on *The Simpsons*) with two *Simpsons* babies. I left *The Simpsons* after the better part of twenty years when I sold a couple shows of my own. I'm currently living the dream, co-directing *Minions: The Rise of Gru*. Did I just say, "living the dream"? Yeah, I should definitely be punched.

JONAH RAY

By Ryan McKee

Original Interview: 2006

Updates: 2020

"How to Succeed Without Really Trying with Jonah Ray" is the original title of this article. I'm not sure how we came up with such a "clickbait" title before knowing what the term "clickbait" meant. We weren't knocking Jonah. In fact, I remember brainstorming the angle with him while doing the interview over chicken burritos and Pabst beers in his East Hollywood apartment.

At the time, Jonah liked his slacker vibe. And we all liked it on him. If someone didn't, they were probably envious. The rest of us had to hustle all over LA, doing as many crappy open mics as possible. Meanwhile, Jonah appeared to just scribble some notes on a beer bottle, wander on stage, and get huge laughs at the city's best shows. As a matter of fact, that's precisely what he did on Comedy Central's *Live at Gotham*. He wrote his set list on the back of his beer bottle and admitted as much to the audience. They loved it!

Like many things in life, things weren't as easy for Jonah as they appeared from the outside. His slacker attitude and self-deprecating humor were defense mechanisms. That is, by no means, unique for people in their early twenties. Jonah just did it better than anyone we knew.

"If I only realized that I wasn't chubby back then, I would've had more self-esteem, maybe? Probably not," Jonah told me after seeing the original photo we published of him in the magazine.

Whether Jonah has been working hard or hardly working *(sorry, that's horrible)* over the last fourteen years, it's paid off. He became a writer for *Web Soup* with Chris Hardwick and then a writer for *The Soup* with Joel McHale. During that time, he also started co-hosting *The Nerdist Podcast* with Hardwick and Matt Mira, which got so popular that BBC America turned it into a television show. Jonah co-hosted a weekly stand-up comedy show with Kumail Nanjiani called *The Meltdown*, and that one became such a hit that Comedy Central turned it into a TV show, too. In 2016, Jonah created two seasons of a travel parody show called *Hidden America* for Seeso and the next year became the new host of *Mystery Science Theater 3000*'s reboot on Netflix.

I don't know. Feels like he's been working hard.

———————

RYAN MCKEE: Why are you so lazy?
JONAH RAY: It's weird because seven months in [to doing comedy], I got a writing job on a pilot [*The Offensive Show*

for Showtime]. And things have just kept coming up. Now, I have this weird thought, "If I start trying hard, maybe things won't come as easy." The way I've been doing stuff has worked out okay. If I start working hard, it'll be weird if things don't pan out.

2020 UPDATE: I look back and realize I wasn't THAT lazy. I was constantly trying to make stuff. I just didn't always write for my stand-up set. Also, fun fact about that Offensive Show *pilot, the head writers were Scott Aukerman and B.J. Porter, and the writing staff was me, B.J. Novak, Morgan Murphy, Dan Mintz, Nick Swardson, and Neil Mahoney.*

You bastard. What's your secret?
Hang out, drink beer, and be too open with people. I don't know. I've gotten shit. A couple of comics have told me the only reason I get work is because I'm nice and not because I'm funny. It's a burn, but I don't dwell on it. It freaks me out.

This guy's name was Dan Bailak, and it really did fuck me up for a long time. I felt younger than everybody and was so self-conscious back then that a guy who ran an open mic for two years made me CRUMBLE.

Like the *Milonakis* show…
Right. I got a job as a writer's assistant, and it was a great opportunity. I really tried hard, but I sucked at it, and they fired me. I had turned in some sketches though and they liked them, so they hired me as a writer in the same day. I don't know, though. It's a funny show, but it doesn't prove I can write. When I got the job, my friends were like, "Yeah, you'd

be good at that." And I said, "Why?" They said, "Because you always have half-assed ideas."

What a dick I am here. Slagging a very funny show that was kind enough to take pity on me and have me on as a writer. It just goes on to prove that low self-esteem can make you come off as a piece of shit.

What do you want to do when you grow up?
I just want to keep things fun. When you were a kid and you did video bits with friends, you just did it for fun, not worrying where you'll show it at. In eight years, that will become sad for me to say that though. "I'm just doing it to have fun. Oh shit, I gotta go pick up my kids and take them to my one-bedroom apartment."

WRONG, BITCH! Keep it fun and everything you want will happen! I own a house and got a vasectomy!

What would make you work hard?
Maybe the thought of my memoirs when I die: *What If I Tried? The Story of an Unknown Comedian.*

That was something B.J. Porter said to motivate me.

Did you move to LA because it's the ultimate slacker town?
I said I never would move here, but I wanted to take classes at Groundlings. I wanted to be a sketch comedy guy because growing up the fat kid, I thought I'd be a Chris Farley type. I went to one audition, decided it was the shittiest thing ever, and then just sat around on the porch for a year drinking beer in San Pedro and going on tour with bands.

"I went to one audition, decided it was the shittiest thing ever"
... Let me try to "uncool" this phrase. It was the shittiest feeling
to me because it wasn't EXACTLY like how I thought it was
gonna be. So, like any young, scared kid, I called it stupid
because it was hard. But yeah, living in San Pedro was the
best year of my life. Still friends with everybody down there.

Then you just…
Looked up an open mic in *LA Weekly*. It was at the Ha Ha
Café. I was doing pretty well until I did a bad joke mention-
ing incest, and some guy in front stood up and said, "Are
we going to keep listening to this guy? He's fucking creepy!"
And everyone else started yelling, "Yeah, you fucking creep!"
It was the scariest thing ever, but at the same time it was so
invigorating. I started going up four nights a week for the first
year. Well, let's say the first six months. That's more realistic.
Now, I get on stage maybe twice a month.

My friend Ronn Benway, who ran the record store I worked
at, really pushed me into finally going to an open mic. I owe
everything to him. Once I started doing open mics, everything
else seemed like an inevitability.

Me playing down how many times I got onstage is another
classic example of me trying to act like I didn't care. I would
diminish everything I did back then. Maybe I still do? I'm glad
Jeselnik won't read this.

Do you ever sit down and write jokes?
That's when I write my worst jokes. When I'm out and about,
talking to my friends and I think of an idea, I write it down,
and they always turn out way better. I know workhorse comics,

like Anthony Jeselnik. They're like Mormon people, who think that their next kid might be the messiah. So, they have as many kids as they can, hoping the next one will be the messiah. Those kids are like their jokes. Most are shitheads, and a few are really awesome jokes. My style is different. When I'm on stage, I'm like that asshole at the party talking to you: some stories, a few jokes, and some whimsical phrases.

I still don't. But I've gotten better at prepping ideas to take on stage.

How do you keep it real?
5 p.m. chicken burrito with avocado and a forty-ounce beer. Then I work my way on to the evening.

What a god damned wonderful life I had.

UPDATED QUESTIONS

What are your immediate thoughts after reading this interview?
I realized I was leaning so hard into the "slacker" esthetic that people really thought I was lazy and didn't do anything.

Knowing what you know now, what would you tell yourself in 2006?
BUCK UP! YOU SAD SACK ASSHOLE!

What's the biggest difference about starting comedy now versus when you did?
When I started in LA, there were maybe one or two booked shows worth trying to get on, and maybe one halfway decent

open mic a night. The clubs were terrible. Now, there are multiple booked shows EVERY NIGHT that are worth going to, and the clubs have great lineups all the time.

Besides the obvious things, what's like... changed for you since then?
I drink better beer and fake chicken burritos. Everything else is the same.

KULAP VILAYSACK
& VAL MEYERS

———

By Ryan McKee
Original Article: 2006

Updates: 2020

"Alternative comedy" is a relic of the late nineties and mid-aughts when the term really meant something. Acts who earned the label were the ones who took risks, explored new formats, broached untouched topics, and differentiated themselves from typical stand-up, sketch, and improv comedy.

Wyatt Cenac (*The Daily Show, Wyatt Cenac's Problem Areas*) used to play a character who claimed to be a "featured artist" in all of hip-hop's biggest hits. Onstage, a song would role, and he'd reenact the part where a guy gets shot in the opening verse. Track after track, he'd yell "No, nooo!" (GUN SHOT) and fall back into the curtain. Then he would just lie on the ground and improvise bits through the rest of the song. Audiences loved it.

When Ron and I first moved to Los Angeles in 2005, *Comedy Death Ray* at the UCB Theatre was *the* alt-comedy show. It eventually evolved into a terrestrial radio show, then a podcast, and finally a multi-season show on the IFC Network called *Comedy Bang Bang*. Before that, the weekly showcase featured established comedians like David Cross, Bob Odenkirk, Zach Galifianakis, Paul F. Tompkins, Janeane Garofalo, Marc Maron, Louis C.K., Dana Gould, Maria Bamford, and Sarah Silverman. The *Death Ray* gatekeepers—Scott Aukerman and B. J. Porter—also tapped a select number of younger comics to perform: Anthony Jeselnik, Morgan Murphy, Wyatt Cenac, Jonah Ray, Harris Wittles, Jen Kirkman, Nikki Glaser, and many other highly regarded names today.

Garage Comedy at El Cid was *Death Ray*'s younger, punk rock sister. Every week, we didn't know what to expect: childlike singalongs, sword-swallowing, stage combat, nudity (exclusively male). I once saw Jonah Ray and Neil Mahoney go shirtless on stage and slap their bellies along to the music. It got to the point where their stomachs were bright red. There was no structure or actual punchlines. It was just silly and weird, and it absolutely *destroyed*.

The show's producers—Val Myers and Kulap Vilaysack—made sure any performer with unique ideas got a chance onstage. *Garage Comedy* didn't spark a comedy revolution, but the show's regular performers are involved with many great TV shows and movies today: Wyatt Cenac, Josh Fadem, Paul Rust, Neil Campbell, Johnny Pemberton, Charlyne Yi, Amy

Seimetz, Mikki Ann Maddox, James Adomian, Pat Healy, DeMorge Brown, and more.

Kulap has gone on to write, direct, and produce the series *Bajillion Dollar Properties* and the film *Origin Story*. Her IMDB page is longer than a giraffe's neck.

Val goes by Valerie May now, and she's writing an epic Netflix Special because she has "masochistic optimism" about Netflix someday asking her to do a Netflix special. She and her husband co-own the restaurant Cafe 50's in West LA, which she also does the marketing for, and they have a nine-year-old daughter named Minnie, "Who is very serious, all business and will not participate in jokes of any sort."

Val and Kulap recently looked back at our original interview and gave some updates in the footnotes.

––––––––––

One of Los Angeles' most popular weekly comedy shows doesn't allow stand-up. Actually, *Garage Comedy's* only rule to get booked on their show is, "no traditional stand-up." You can do a sketch. You can juggle. You can swallow knives. You can play a naked Nazi. All of which I've seen. However, you cannot do stand-up.

"When we started the show, I was so bored of straight stand-up," says Val Myers, co-founder of *Garage Comedy*. "I would just see people doing material to showcase with, not doing anything new or taking any chances. They weren't doing it for the love of the live performance but literally just to cash it in. By not allowing stand-up, we've taken that 'showcase mentality' out of the show. Now people write stuff for the fun of doing our show."[12]

Val, who is also the co-host for the TV show *Junkin'* on the Turner South channel, started doing stand-up at eighteen years old in Seattle. Over the next five years she worked her way up to being a feature act and decided to move to Los Angeles.

"I came down here and couldn't get a set," she said. "It's such a popularity contest and I'm socially awkward. I don't talk to people very well. I'm a freak."[13]

Val didn't freak out Kulap Vilaysack when they met while taking Second City classes. The two started doing sketch comedy together and talked about producing their own show. Val wanted a place where "people like her" could get stage time.

Kulap had been helping with the stand-up-heavy weekly show, *Comedy Death Ray.* One of the most elite shows in LA, its regulars include Zach Galifianakis, Louis C.K., Paul F. Tompkins, and Patton Oswalt to name a few.

---

12 *Valerie: Wow! I had a lot of opinions and anger about stand-up! Yikes. I really just wanted to have a show where I could do my weird bits. At the time the only type of show was stand-up, and I couldn't get sets anywhere because I was too "theatrical." But I might have gone overboard with the whole "people not taking chances" thing.*

13 *Valerie: I was lying about being socially awkward. This was way prior to the MeToo movement, so I didn't want to say the real reason I couldn't get sets which was… men ran comedy! I was relentlessly hit on, and if you aren't into it, they hate your guts!*

"One night at *Death Ray* I had this realization that I'm never going to be on *Death Ray*," said Kulap.[14] "Where am I going to perform when my mind isn't 'stand-up-y.' There were booked stand-up shows and open mics and that was it. Individual sketch groups would do shows, but there wasn't a place to just to put up a sketch or do a character. *Death Ray* would do characters, but where do you go to get good enough to get booked there? We just wanted a place for us to perform where it wasn't cliquey, and where you didn't have to kiss ass to get on."

So, on March 7, 2005, *Garage Comedy* did their first show.[15] To get booked, you didn't need to "know someone." You just needed to email them your performance idea. It quickly became a haven for nontraditional, quirky, creative acts. Already a Mecca of alternative comedy in New York City, the Upright Citizens Brigade Theatre decided to open a location in Los Angeles. When they did in July 2005, it was no surprise that many of their initial shows were by *Garage Comedy* regulars.

"With the UCB opening, the scene has really become a lot better over the last six months," Kulap said. "Now there's also the *Tomorrow Show* at the Steve Allen Theatre and the Fake Gallery has opened back up. Good places where you can do different stuff. And people have told me that *Garage* has had a part in that."

---

14   Kulap: *At the time, I meant as a stand-up because I'm not one. However,* Comedy Death Ray *then* Comedy Bang Bang *became more than a stand-up show, too.*

15   Kulap: *Whoa, I had forgotten. That. Was. Some. Time. Ago.*

"And I'm seeing stand-up comics doing a lot of great stuff too," Val said. "I definitely feel it's time to go back and do a good stand-up show now. We're going to start one up soon as soon as we find a good venue. I think, definitely think, stand-up is getting back to the art form it was before the '80s killed it."[16]

Now that other shows in LA have opened up with similar formats as *Garage Comedy*, are the ladies worried about their attendance?

"We're all young and hungry," Kulap said. "We all need to go full-force because we're figuring things out, so the shows will stay exciting. And the afterparties this summer will be even better. If you don't know this by now, we like to party."[17]

"No one appreciates audiences in this town," Val said. "So, when we throw a party, it's a thank you for getting off your couch and coming out on a Monday night, which I know is hard. I really appreciate audiences."[18]

---

16 *Valerie: I am completely full of shit here. Also trying so hard to sound like a big shot. "We" are going to start a stand-up show. Oh really? "We" are? Hmm, just hung up on finding a venue, huh? Also, WTF "the '80s ruined" stand-up? Just for the record, I love stand-up comedy. I do stand-up comedy. In fact I am immersed in it now more than ever. I really can't wait for the world to open up again!*

17 *Kulap: Memories are flooding back about the afterparties. Sometimes they were more elaborate than the actual shows!*

18 *Kulap: I love this. Valerie: Thank you. It's funny because IF live shows ever come back post virus, I think all audiences will be appreciated.*

So, stayed tuned this summer for more *Garage* parties, juggling, sketches, and naked dudes. And the girls also plan to take *Garage Comedy* on the road, too. Check their website for dates near your town.[19][20]

---

19   *Kulap: I think the only town we went to was Phoenix with you! I can't believe you originally misspelled my last name, Ryan. Absolutely butchered it. I recall you said that the extra L stood for LOSER. So savage.*

20   *Valerie: I got a LOT of shit from a lot of people, Not just Erik Charles Nielsen, for this article and the original title, "The New Comedy" "Oh so you've invented a NEW kind of Comedy? What? Comedy that's not funny?"*

TOTALLY FALSE PEOPLE

———

By Teresa Aguilera
Updated intro by Ryan McKee
Original article: January 2003

Updates: May 2020

Since its inception in 2002, SF Sketchfest has grown to become one of the largest and most prestigious comedy festivals in the world. Reading through the past lineups is like reading through a who's who of the best sketch, stand-up, and improv comedy performers of the last thirty years.

In 2005, Ron and Ryan (my comedy duo with Ron Babcock) performed in the festival. Still relatively small at the time, their audiences were some of the most intelligent and enthusiastic I've seen. Quite honestly, that might be why Ron and I never amounted to much as a duo. We could never recreate that same high.

The festival creators—Janet Varney, David Owen, and Cole Stratton—couldn't have been nicer or more accommodating...

really, they set bar too high... and I'm realizing my failures as a performer are their fault. Anyway, in January 2003, when we were putting together our second issue of *Modest Proposal Magazine*, my friend Teresa Aguilera pitched us an interview with the sketch group Totally False People who founded the festival. We didn't know anything about it then, and neither did she, but she had recently moved to San Francisco and wanted something to do.

Janet, Cole, Totally False People's fourth member Gabriel Diani, and Teresa provided updates to the original article in the footnotes.

This is the most important event I've ever attended in San Francisco. Of course, I've only been in the city about three months. But no matter, an evening of comedic entertainment awaits at the Second Annual SF Sketchfest. The cabbie says he's never heard of the Eureka Theatre. He must be new to the city, too. But he takes me to the intersection that's scribbled in my notebook.

Arriving at the modest two-hundred-seat theatre[21], I flip hastily through the slick program, seeing Fred Willard[22] and his Hollywood Players, mugs of the Upright Citizens Brigade[23] and fourteen other bios, before finally spotting Totally False People, the group behind it all.

---

21 *Janet: Which is now run by 42nd Street Moon and is called The Gateway Theatre*

22 *RIP*

23 *Janet: We've had the UCB every year since this one!*

With more than one hundred years of collective life experience and a combined weight of over five hundred pounds,[24] who else could be more qualified to conceive of a sketch comedy festival in San Francisco?

Of course, Gabriel Diani, David Owen, Janet Varney, and Cole Stratton, the three latter of whom are producers of Sketchfest, admit they didn't pull it all off on their own.

"There's a lot of local groups, kind of a burgeoning scene," said Cole in a group interview at The Holding Company, the "Official Bar of SF Sketchfest."

For last year's event, they rented a theater for a month, got together with five other local groups, and called it a festival.[25] Three of those groups (plus TFP) came back for more this year, happy to have a local venue worthy of the sketch format.

"There aren't a lot of places, especially for sketch," Cole explained. "There are places where you've got to walk across the stage to get to the bathroom, so in the middle of your act people are walking across. We thought, why don't we get an actual theater where we can really present this well?"

The concept caught on, and in its second year, the month-long Sketchfest has graduated from the eighty-one-seat Shelton

---

24 *Janet: I shudder to do the math now... Gabriel: Honestly, we were probably closer to six hundred pounds even then.*

25 *Cole: It's been DIY from the start, and that hasn't changed. The scope is much bigger, but the sentiment is still the same.*

Theatre to the Eureka and grown from six Bay Area groups to nineteen nationally and locally recognized acts.

"So next year, 145 groups," Cole forecasted enthusiastically.[26]

"It'll be a three-month-long festival," joked Janet. "It'll only be a couple of years before it's year-round."

It's a good thing they all enjoy comedy so much.

"I just know that I have a better time in life when I'm around people who know exactly how to make me laugh," said Janet. "And that's really the reason I got involved with it. Because I wanted to be around people who have a good time."

"So, why did you stay?" Gabriel demanded.

"Yeah, have you found those people yet?" asked David.

Declaring that her cohorts are a "black hole of non-comedy," Janet explained that although all four attended San Francisco State University, she didn't meet these guys until after they graduated.

"I was hired as the token girl," she laughed, referring to an ongoing gag in that night's set.[27]

---

26 Cole: I thought I was exaggerating for effect. But it's an understatement now. The sheer volume of performers we bring through every year is staggering now. Big props to our travel and artist hospitality teams who help us with all that!

27 Gabriel: I'd like to go on the record and say that Janet was never the token girl.

"Yeah," said David. "She'll be getting a raise soon."[28]

Despite such group successes, all four pursue interests outside sketch comedy. Janet does some acting and modeling on a national scale,[29] while Gabriel has an award-winning[30] one-man show called *God Complex*, among other writing credits. David wrote, co-directed, and starred in the feature film *Stuck*, which recently screened to good reviews at the San Francisco IndieFest. Cole also picks up acting gigs here and there, crossing paths with the likes of Betty White and Mark-Paul Gosselaar (Zack from *Saved by the Bell*).

"[Gosselaar] does a lot of crosswords," said Cole. "I have to name-drop now. [I've worked with] Don Johnson. And puppies. I've worked with an elephant."[31]

"That's not name-dropping," asserted Gabriel. "That's elephant-dropping."[32]

"That's noun-dropping," Janet corrected. "Elephant dropping? I don't like where you're going with that."

---

28 *Teresa: Have I really become such an SJW that this line immediately makes me think of the wage gap? Sigh. Sometimes I miss the simplicity of the aughts. Janet: Same!*

29 *Janet: Oh god, I really hope those weren't my actual words.*

30 *Gabriel: Best Solo Male Comedy Performer. It's a highly competitive category.*

31 *Cole: That elephant still won't return my calls. You think you know somebody…*

32 *Gabriel: Oof. I just really wanted to participate in the interview I guess?*

With all that fame and fortune, what keeps drawing Totally False People back to sketch comedy?

"The format itself is just short little funny plays for people with short attention spans, so it's one of those things where it's fun to write sketches," said Cole. "You get to work on your writing and your performing and, you know, the comedy, all in one little thing, without investing all your time and energy on a major thing like a play or a film."

"You can explore ideas and characters without having to go the extra mile. We've all done stuff like that."

"And it has more mainstream appeal than doing a play," Gabriel said. "It's like a band or something that you want to see." He adds with extreme bravado: "When you hear the waves of laughter rolling up toward you, you can't help but take a breath and say, 'My God, that is wonderful!'"[33]

Then again, everyone agrees, sketch comedy is not always this easy.

"Who knew it would teach more humiliation than anything else I've ever been a part of,"[34] Janet said, "I can't think of anything that's harder than getting up on a stage, making an ass out of yourself, and then not having anyone laugh at you. And it's not anybody else's material. It's yours. It's yours and the group's. You've directed it, you're in it, you've

---

33 Gabriel: God, I really hope this was some bit I was doing that didn't translate to the page.

34 Janet: But then I moved to Hollywood!

decided to orchestrate it. There's no one else to blame. You're one hundred percent responsible for what you do, and if it doesn't go well, it's totally humbling."

Cole agrees: "It's either so much fun, or it's like dying a thousand deaths on a bad night, but it gives you the extreme high and the extreme low. That's why I like the format. It's an adventure."

Apparently, there's no excuse for bad comedy—only for bad art.

"If you're doing a play, and people don't laugh, you can be like, well, it was art," explained Gabriel. "But sketch comedy, if people don't laugh, it doesn't look good. It made you think, yeah."

In that case, what prevents an early stage death?

"You learn by just making mistakes, you know?" David said. "We've been doing this for three years, and we learned that we gotta edit, keep cutting, keep cutting, just focus on what is really funny, and, you know, we're still learning how to do it."

"Most of those sketches [performed at Sketchfest] went on much further," admitted Janet. "Like, Gabe actually shit on the floor several times in one."[35]

---

35 *Janet: Can a person cringe themselves to death?*

"Sketch endings are just, so tough," Cole said. "There's also really a concern about brevity and keeping it short so it doesn't wear out its welcome."[36]

Keep it short. Yet another thing journalism and comedy have in common. Despite public opinion, though, we don't shit on the floor.[37]

---

36 Cole: *This has not changed in the slightest. Takes a lot of time to come up with a good button and out for a scene, and to try to get it all done in three pages or so. I've since moved to directing sketch, and it's interesting to look at it from that perspective.*

37 Teresa: *This would have been stronger as an editor's note, but I think I just wanted to say "shit" twice.*

HENRY PHILLIPS

———

By Ron Babcock
Original Interview: 2005

Updates: May 2020

When Henry Phillips walked on stage at the Tempe Improv carrying a guitar, I didn't want to like him. You weren't "supposed" to like guitar comics in the aughts. *It's a crutch, man!*

"Well, Ron and Ryan," you may ask, "didn't you use musical instruments in your act?" Yes, but we at least had the decency to not know how to play them.

All that went out the window as soon as Henry started. His understated delivery of sincere ballads with sadly absurd lyrics made me totally forget to not like him.

"I have one foot in the music door and one foot in the comedy door," he said. "So, I'm not getting anywhere. I'm just sort of humping the wall in between the two doors."

After the show that night, we befriended both Henry and the opening act, Chris Fairbanks. A few years later when we moved to LA, we invited them to one of our first shows. It was at this hip bar in Silverlake with white upholstered cushions for walls. We didn't think they'd come. Comics almost never go to a shitty bar show that they aren't booked on. But in walk Henry and Chris. They said they came to lend support although the most supportive thing they did was not comment on how bad we bombed that night.

A few months later, Henry headlined our monthly show at The Paper Heart back in Phoenix. When Ryan reached out to him about updating his interview, he commented on how many good memories he had from that trip, but he apologized for spilling beer down Ryan's back. Ryan joked that he didn't even remember. That's probably because it didn't happen to him, but to me. Here's my journal entry for that night:

02-21-2006

After the show we moved down to Bikini Lounge where we started drinking like Prohibition was starting tomorrow. I have never had as much fun there as I did on Saturday night. Henry poured beer down my butt crack...

The joke's on him because later in that same entry I wrote: *We got home in the middle of the night, after a six-hour car ride, where I learned that I apparently heavily fart in my sleep.*

Before falling asleep during that car ride, I opened up to Henry. I was very self-conscious about being a virgin in my mid-twenties, even though I joked about it on stage.[38] He was so kind about it. He just said, "Ron, don't worry. You are going to have so much sex in your thirties. You won't believe how much sex you will have." And you know what, he was right. Well, he was mostly right. It depends on what your definition of "so much" is.

Since pouring beer down my butt crack, Henry has released multiple comedy albums, earning him a Critic's Choice in *Billboard Magazine*. He also made the semi-biographical film *Punching the Clown*, which received the Audience award at the Slamdance Film Festival, and the sequel *Punching Henry*. They are the best examples I have ever seen of a comedian translating their act to a different format and making it even better.

He has also appeared in HBO's *Silicon Valley* as the ponytailed uber low-energy IT guy and on Comedy Central's *Drunk History*. His YouTube series *Henry's Kitchen* has millions of views and is quite simply one of my favorite things on the internet. Plus, Moby once said he was "disconcertingly funny." I can't think of a better review.

RON BABCOCK: Is the road taking its toll yet?
HENRY PHILLIPS: It's exhausting. The problem is those two days in between gigs where you're sitting there going, "What the hell am I doing?"

---

38 *If you want to learn more, listen to "The Virginity Story" on Ron Babcock's stand-up comedy album* THIS GUY. *on Spotify.*

2020 UPDATE: Surprised I didn't mention the two full days of plane travel that bookended those trips. Your flight gets delayed, so you try to compensate your body by stuffing your face with Pizza Hut and Cinnabon. Those days took years off my life I'm sure!

So, is this what you wanted to be?
I fell into it by accident. I wanted to be a heavy metal guitar player in a rock band.

Looking back, I'm glad I entered comedy instead of rock music. Rock musicians appear to have a tougher time thriving through their later years because they are tied to youth-oriented fan bases, whereas comedy is something you can keep finding fresh ways to do throughout your lifespan.

What bands made you dream of that?
Black Sabbath, Iron Maiden, Triumph—that one didn't really fit in there, but I thought the guitar player was so good.

Hell yeah, still love those bands. I should add Queen and AC/DC, and everything in between.

Do you still listen to Triumph?
I have two of their records in my car as we speak.

Yes, mostly for nostalgic reasons. Trying to play some of that stuff to a fresh listener would not be easy.

Did you ever actually play heavy metal?
I was in a heavy metal band in high school that literally went through all the garbage that other bands go through in a twenty-year period within about six months. Our name was Abyss.

I'm still pals with the members of Abyss. It's a dark childhood secret that we have all kept from our loved ones. We share a common bond, similar to the kids from It, but Abyss was way more embarrassing than the clown.

Triumph would be proud of that name.
We went through the one guy getting a girlfriend and breaking up the band to reforming. Then one guy got into drugs, so we used the term "solo project" for him because he got kicked out of school for dealing drugs. We also used the term "photo session," which meant that the drummer's mom would use her Polaroid and take pictures of us for a flyer.

These are already way too many confidential details about the Abyss days, so I'll stop it at this.

How much shit do you get for being a guitar comic?
I only get shit if people haven't seen it before. I started out playing in music clubs—being considered a musician who wasn't taking music seriously and getting shit for that. And then I moved to comedy clubs—being a comedian who was using a prop. Some comics are like, "Well I don't want to follow a guitar act because a guitar act is going to kill doing 'Wasting Away in Diarrheaville.'" But a lot of comics note that I'm not hard to follow because I'm basically just doing stand-up comedy bits to music. Doug Stanhope is the perfect example. I was friends with him for three years, and he purposely avoided seeing my act because he said he was afraid I was going to suck, and he wouldn't want to hang out with me. But when he finally did, he started bringing me on the road with him and touting me as a good comic.

This is pretty telling of the times. I only really hear older comics complain about guitar comics nowadays. Doesn't seem like younger people are keeping that stigma alive from what I can tell. Maybe because there have been a lot of great musical comedians: Bo Burnham, Lonely Island, Flight of the Conchords, and many others. I think it's more acceptable if the act is original, but that counts whether you have a guitar or not.

Why did you cut your flowing rock star glam locks?

Sex. I wanted to have sex more. It just isn't appealing to hang onto your youth. I could show you a picture of what it looked like toward the end, and somebody needed to put that hair down. It had had a long happy life, but it was time to say good-bye.

This holds up. Now, if you're FAMOUS and have flowing glam locks, that's a different story. But I wasn't.

How do you keep it real?

I don't make promises I'm not going to keep. If somebody says to me, "Hey do you want to be involved in this project?" I'll say, "Yeah, but only if tomorrow when we wake up and I'm sober, I don't have to talk to you about it ever again."

There are exceptions. But learning how to honestly tell someone you're not interested in what they want you to be involved with never gets easy. But it's a necessary skill. Otherwise you'll find you have no time to do the things you love.

JEFFREY BROWN

———

By Brandon Huigens
Updated Intro by Annie Worth
Original Interview: 2006

Updated Interview: May 2020

"Cartooning will destroy you; it will break your heart," said *Peanuts* creator Charles Schulz. That attitude has been shared with many artists alike. And yet, when *Modest Proposal* interviewed Jeffrey Brown fourteen years ago, he seemed less like a bitter Charles Schulz and more like a heartfelt *Peanuts* comic strip itself.

If feelings had a beard, you would have Jeffrey, who brings moods, honesty, and wit to his work. First, imagine a Midwestern boy drawing comics of toys and cartoons who then grew up and walked away from an MFA program in painting to pursue an original enthusiasm. Not only did cartooning not destroy him, but it pushed him to self-publish a book in 2002. His first book, *Clumsy*, quickly built him a devoted following because of its scratchy, candid drawings that had the ability to capture small meaningful moments.

Through the 2000s, Jeffrey Brown self-published dozens of comics, many of them autobiographical, while maintaining his childhood penchant for making comics about his life and toys. *Modest Proposal* caught up with him in 2006 because Brandon, one of our contributing writers, knew him from his days at a comic book store. You will see from his original interview that at that time he already had some notoriety. Since then, he has published several successful graphic novels in his original autobiographical style as well as best-selling children's books and mainstream fiction. He's done two *Star Wars* series, *Darth Vader and Son* and *Jedi Academy*, and won back-to-back Best Humor Publication Eisner Awards for the books *Vader And Son* and *Vader's Little Princess*. He also co-wrote the 2012 film *Save The Date*, starring Alison Brie, Lizzy Caplan, and Martin Starr.

Modest Proposal reached out to Jeff for an update on how the last decade plus has been treating him. He re-read our original interview and answered some questions about his life since we last saw him.

ORIGINAL INTERVIEW

BRANDON HUIGENS: Has making comics about your ex-girlfriends made them contact you to tell you what they thought?
JEFFREY BROWN: Yes. Of course, this being a family magazine, we can't print what they had to say here.

Do you find girls more or less interested in you because of
The Girlfriend Trilogy?
Yes, I do find them more or less interested in me. I think it's
better to have met a girl who didn't really know about the
trilogy before meeting me.

**Do you now intend to stay away from making comics
about relationships?**
I think I've done enough whining about girls breaking my
heart, so I'm moving on to other parts of life. I'm particularly
interested in tiny, inconsequential things that in context
become more meaningful.

Have you ever made comics specifically to impress a girl?
Never. But I have created elaborate schemes with my friends
to appear as though I were a wealthy heir in order to impress
a girl in high school. But then she found out, and she left me,
not because I wasn't rich, but because I had lied to her. In the
end, though, she realized she loved me, and I loved her, and
that was all that mattered.

**Have there been any changes in Marvel's stance not to
publish the Wolverine story you did?**
No, they still don't want to publish it. I took too many liberties
with the characters. I mean, if Wolverine is a character who
also cuts himself, how are they going to convince Pepsi to put
him on their cans and bottles when $X3$ comes out?

*Editor's Note: Jeffrey self-published a twenty-page comic book
called* Wolverine: Dying Time *and submitted it to Marvel
Comics.* Wizard *magazine named it one of the best Indie books
of 2004, but Marvel refuses to publish it, due to the dark content.*

If you stopped drawing today, how many years would you be able to fill with your unpublished work?
Only one year. One year where my massive twenty-five-thousand-page magnum opus of unpublished work comes out.

Are French girls empirically hotter due to their accents?
My girlfriend was with me while I was there, actually. She's empirically hotter because she tolerates all my nonsense.

Have you been able to quit your day job yet?
I still work part time so I can have insurance.

What projects do you have coming up?
Every Girl Is the End of the World for Me will be out in April, and later this year my expanded gag collection *I Am Going To Be Small* will come out. I'll continue contributing to the Fantagraphics *MOME* anthology. We'll see what else I finish and get printed. Also, out around April will be an animated music video for *Your Heart Is an Empty Room* by Death Cab for Cutie, part of their Directions project.

Which *Back to the Future* sequel did you like best?
I think it was *Part II*? Not the cowboy one.

UPDATED INTERVIEW

What are your immediate thoughts after reading the interview?
I have seen both *Back to the Future* sequels, and I liked *Part II* better, because *Part III* is the cowboy one. It's funny to see me mention my girlfriend at the time because now she's my

wife, and we have two kids. Also, it's very weird to read an interview with me without a single mention of *Star Wars*.

Knowing what you know now, what would you tell yourself back then?

Nothing. If I had to get through it all without knowing any better, why should young me get to have the benefit? Actually, snark aside—it is hard, because if things had gone any differently, I wouldn't be where I am now, and I'd rather have the sure thing of a pretty great life than risk messing it all up.

What's the biggest difference about being a cartoonist now versus the early 2000s?

The book market and the kids' market. There are way more mainstream and traditional publishing avenues to get work out there, and there's way more interest in comics for younger readers. Scratch that, the biggest difference is that people no longer ask comic book cartoonists if they aspire to having a strip in the newspaper someday.

Do you miss anything about self-publishing?

I miss lots. The freedom, and the creative exploration. Not having the expectations that come with bigger publishers and sales and marketing and all that. It pays the bills better, but there are way more limits on the work I'm making, even though I've managed to carve out a big chunk of being able to do what I want.

Would you say you've achieved all your hopes and dreams?

Pretty much. At least all the childhood ones... I've drawn *X-Men* and *Star Wars*, published books, gotten both critical acclaim and bestselling status. I think the only one left is creating the art for a Tolkien calendar some year. That's not to say I'm creatively satisfied. That's a never-ending dream.

What's a new dream you might try?
I don't know. All the other dreams I'd have are pretty much unachievable, but I think that's okay. Have to have something to do when I'm asleep, right?

RITCH DUNCAN

———

By Ryan McKee

Original Interview: April 2003

Updates: May 2020

At first, I hated *Jest* magazine and its editor Ritch Duncan. I ignorantly thought *Modest Proposal* was the only magazine being written by comedians (despite Ron and I barely being comedians at this point). Suddenly, I learned we weren't the *only* one and we weren't even the *best* one.

When Ron interviewed Chelsea Peretti about her website BlackPeopleLoveUs.com, she mentioned she wrote for another comedy magazine *Jest. What the fuck? A competitor?* I angrily found stamps, wrote a check, mailed away for copies of *Jest*, and waited weeks just to hate-read it. That's what we had to do back in 2003.

Upon arrival, I realized *Jest* was on another level. They were the NBA and we were the Guam Basketball Association. They had full-color printing, something we only dreamed about.

Their articles were smart and so funny. I even thought their ads were hilarious (which, as you'll read later, proves my humor tastes weren't exactly distinguished).

How were they so awesome? I started to internet-stalk *Jest*'s editor-in-chief Ritch Duncan for clues. I learned he lived in New York City, worked as a stand-up comic, and wrote for *Weekend Update* and *Tough Crowd with Colin Quinn*. That sounded like a life I wanted! I couldn't hate him. That would only be hating myself.

Ritch agreed to an email interview, and I did my best to craft the funniest, most-interesting questions my twenty-four-year-old brain could muster. He humored me and wrote better answers to every question.

Check out the original interview with Ritch's updated responses and stay tuned after the interview to find out what happened to *Jest*.

ORIGINAL INTERVIEW

RYAN McKEE: Is the *Jest* office just your apartment?
RITCH DUNCAN: Well, I like to phrase it differently. I'd say that the *Jest* office is just south of the *Jest* TV room and about twenty feet away from the *Jest* kitchen. Keep walking south and you'll find the *Jest* bedroom, a stately pleasure dome currently piled high with the *Jest* dirty laundry. In the corner, you'll find the *Jest* houseplant, which is dying. We're currently looking for real office space.

2020 UPDATE: Every answer was a joke, but this is accurate. Jest never acquired office space until after I left in 2004. I did all my work over email and on (gasp) the phone, and we held writers' meetings in bars, specifically at a place called SHADES OF GREEN on 15th Street near Union Square. We picked that spot because they had a big lounge upstairs, and it was centrally located.

Have you resolved your past-due balance and amended your credit report?

Long answer (evasive): In the premiere [*Jest*] issue, where, because I had no real "Letters to the Editor" yet, I answered my junk mail and letters from collection agencies. A collection agent named Kayleen sent me a letter, and I pretended that she was hitting on me, instead of hitting me up for cash. I have spoken to her on the phone, as they won't stop calling me, and somehow got my cell-phone number. I didn't mention that I published her letter.

Short answer (direct): No.

Happy to report that after Jest, I was hired as a digital writer/ blogger by truTV in 2008, came on full time in 2013, and was eventually promoted to Senior Writer before AT&T bought Turner Broadcasting and laid off forty percent of the company in 2019. So, my credit is fine. You know, currently. But then again, I currently don't have a full-time job anymore, and there's a global pandemic on, so maybe check in with me next year?

Do the magazine's contributing writers also write many of the ads in *Jest*?

No, but we have encouraged clients to be irreverent in their advertising as an attempt to get noticed. The publisher, David

Fenton, and his sales agents work with the clients to try to get something good out of them. David used to be a stand-up, so he writes a great deal of them. I believe, by and large, the clients have been very happy with what he's written.

I was being very political with this answer. The ads in Jest *were written by the publisher and his ad sales team, and I absolutely hated them, almost without exception. But, as part of our deal, he had the final word on the ad copy, and I had the final word on editorial. The ads were crass, would regularly include nudity, and the humor was almost exclusively shock value. They made me crazy because they pulled focus from the editorial and weren't funny, which I felt hurt the brand. One of them, as I remember, was an ad for a local furniture store that they had captioned "Furniture You Can Fuck On," which I just absolutely hated. Still, "I believe, by and large, the clients have been very happy with what he's written" was a pretty deft misdirect, and I wasn't lying.*

Did you do any magazine writing before *Jest*?
I took a shot at humor writing for magazines when a friend of a friend became, briefly, the editor of the "Shouts and Murmurs" section in the *New Yorker*, which has its moments. I didn't get anything published, but I did write a lot of pieces and got valuable feedback from him on several of them, which was fun.

He soon left the magazine to edit Steve Martin's book, and I was out of luck on that end. I still like the *New Yorker*, but that humor section seems to be religiously devoted to pulling up just short of funny. Whenever I read it, I see these great ideas carefully tailored to be JUST clever and amusing enough to allow an Upper East Side socialite to nod in bemusement while their tea steeps, but it's certainly nothing that will cause their teacups to rattle in their saucers.

Man, I really had it out for "Shouts and Murmurs" back then. But then, as now, comedy writers can criticize The New Yorker *until they are blue in the face, but I can't think of a single one who wouldn't be thrilled to be published by them. Recently, I had a humor piece published in the really well-run comedy magazine* American Bystander. *It felt good.*

Have you made a dime off *Jest* yet?
Not really enough to live on, but I also do a fair amount of stand-up on the road.

At the time, I was also working at the late, great Reel Life, an indie video store that used to be on the main drag of Bedford Avenue in Williamsburg. The owner went on to be one of the guys behind Nitehawk Cinema, which I really hope makes it through after this pandemic. I also had epically cheap rent, which is truly the key to pulling off a DIY, artistic lifestyle.

How many of the *Jest* writers also do stand-up?
I'd say about half. Of course, we went from about thirteen people interested in submitting to over two hundred, seemingly overnight, but our core writers are either stand-ups, improvisers or sketch artists that I've met and enjoyed over the past eight years.

All the core writers I had at the time I knew from my connections doing stand-up in the city. Folks like Dan Cronin, Andres DuBouchet, Bob Powers, Kyria Abrahams, Dan

McCoy, Victor Varnado, Jon Corbett, Christian Finnegan, Chelsea Peretti, Julie Klausner, Sean Conroy, Adam Felber, Justin Tyler, Liam McEneaney, Michael Bernard, Rusty Ward, Karen Sneider, Dale Goodson, Frank Lesser, they were all around. Now I feel bad that I'm leaving people out. We had a very vibrant scene, and lots of folks went on to have pretty impressive, award-winning careers. Or barring that, went to work for truTV.

A comic told me that comedians go to New York to get better at stand-up and go to LA for TV and comedy writing opportunities. Any truth to that?
I bet he also told you that it's important to do crowd-work to get the crowd on your side early, and that a strong opening joke that really builds your "character" in the view of the audience is crucial. Also, I bet he said that while performance is important, you really aren't going to get above a certain level without writing.

Comics love to come up with bullshit philosophies and theories, but bottom line, nobody knows the answers. If you do stand-up every night, you'll get better at it. You can do that in New York. I've never been to LA myself, but I'm told there are far fewer spots to get stage time. I've freelanced for three comedy shows here in New York and got a staff job on another one, so who knows. I think I've been lucky.

I can't believe I admitted I'd never been to LA. I've been since then. It's nice, and there are plenty of places to get stage time. Comedy is much more popular now than it was in 2003. You know, I'm told.

Are comedians like rappers and get caught up in that whole West Coast vs. East Coast rivalry?
I had a friend tell me once that if there was any truth to that "East Coast/West Coast" rivalry, they'd have taken out Woody Allen twenty-five years ago. That friend now lives in Los Angeles.

New York seems to be about embracing the fucked-up suffering, and LA about embracing the fucked-up cure. If you come to New York, I think you can kind of float around and suffer for a couple years, and people will think you're working. Do that in LA, and you could end up fucking Tommy Lee.

My main takeaway here that I now object to is my assumption that having sex with Tommy Lee would be the result of poor life choices. With the benefit of age, I now feel like whoever you are, if you lived a life that led to you having sex with Tommy Lee, at bare minimum, you were saying yes to the world, which is hard to criticize.

What are your favorite jokes that you've written for *SNL*?
Here are two of my favorites that actually got on, both from "Weekend Update." The first one was read by Colin Quinn, a number of years ago, and the second by Tina Fey last season.

"In anticipation of the release of his film, *Primary Colors*, John Travolta met with President Clinton this week and harshly criticized the German government for their treatment of Scientologists. An outraged German official rebuffed his statements by saying 'Look, we're Germans! When we're religiously persecuting you, you'll know it!'"

"This weekend, White House Officials said that President Bush meant no disrespect when he referred to the Pakistani people as 'Pakis.' But just to be safe, White House staffers canceled his trip to Nigeria."

Two pretty strong jokes. What I notice about them now is how in the '90s/early 2000s, pulling off a joke that included "edgy" topics like genocide/racism/PC Culture was a lot more in. Comedy has lightened up a lot since then. Lots more funny faces, comedy songs, and silly non sequiturs. I'm not saying one way is better than the other, but it does feel different now.

Does anyone in New York watch *MADtv*?
Not me. My friend Bryan Tucker wrote on it for a season, and he's very funny. I didn't see anything he wrote though. When is it on?

Bryan Tucker: now at SNL, *still funny.* MADtv *had a bad reputation back then, but in retrospect, there are a lot of folks who worked on that show that were so good. Key and Peele came out of there! Alex Borstein! Andrew Daly! So many more. I think it was also fashionable back in the early 2000s to crap on bad comedy. A ton of the alt rooms would have performers who would do entire acts making fun of "hack" stand-up comedy, to the point that it actually became hack to make fun of hacks. People were so mad at Carrot Top! It makes no sense to me now. I try to be less critical of other people's comedy these days. There's a huge difference between classifying someone else's work as "not being your cup of tea" as opposed to just pronouncing it "bad."*

With everything going on, how does Ritch Duncan keep it real?
By living constantly in denial.

That sounds about right. Thanks for giving me the opportunity to revisit this!

UPDATED QUESTIONS

How long did *Jest* last and why did it ultimately shut down?
I started discussing creating *Jest* with the publisher of the magazine in the summer of 2002. I was the editor-in-chief, and he ran the business. I knew his parents had passed away; he lived in a giant Brooklyn apartment and didn't seem to have a job. I didn't know where the money was coming from, and I didn't ask. We published our first issue, a test issue with a limited run in November, and the first official issue came out in December. It was a Christmas issue, and featured George H.W. Bush and Barbara Bush under the Christmas tree, opening a gift box from George W. Bush that contained Saddam Hussein's severed head. That was four months before the invasion, and a year before Saddam's capture and eventual execution. So, we were a year early on that one.

Jest lasted (for me) through August of 2004. We tried to publish an issue of original, New York-based comedy writing every month, and to provide a non-Ivy League pool of comedy writing talent that TV shows could draw from, and we were mostly successful.

I always wanted the slogan to be "*Jest*: Almost Monthly," but the publisher wouldn't let me do it, citing that admitting we weren't always hitting our deadlines might get advertisers jittery.

I can't speak to why it ultimately shut down, but I left in August. The publisher and I had very different ideas of what was funny; we fought about the direction and editorial tone of the magazine constantly, and the straw that broke the camel's back came when we were putting together that August issue, and he wanted a certain article published. I felt it wasn't ready and said no. He went behind my back, went into our internal website, had our designer lay out the article, which was unfinished, and put it in the magazine without my knowledge. I was paid practically nothing to be the editor-in-chief. I think I might have been making $700 an issue or something, but what made it worth it to me was total editorial autonomy. I was already dangerously close to burned out, and when he crossed that line, I knew was done.

The magazine kept going for, I think another three or four issues and went through at least two other editors-in-chief before it ultimately folded. I can only assume because it must have been tremendously expensive to publish a glossy, full color, sixty+ page print magazine every month. Oh, and yeah—the internet was starting. Not exactly the dawn of a great era for print.

What are your biggest takeaways from your time at *Jest*?
When working with comedy writers, respect their talent, let them know constantly how much you appreciate and respect what they do, and pay them. The amount is less important than the gesture, but I wanted them all to know that we were doing professional comedy writing, and that means writers get paid. We all came out of this alt-comedy scene in New York in the late '90s, early '00s, and it was commonplace that performers in the city were rarely, if ever, paid. I didn't want to do that, and it created a loyalty and dedication that showed.

Also, who you work with matters. At the end of the day, if you go into business with incompatible people, you'll have an unpleasant outcome. I knew going into this that working with this publisher was going to be hard, but the opportunity to create a magazine in the vein of *Spy* and the original *National Lampoon* with the young comedy writing talent I was surrounded with at the time was too appealing to pass up. Ultimately, it wasn't arguments with the publisher that led to an incompatible relationship. It was that we'd have the same arguments, over and over and over again. I believe Tony Hendra, when talking about *The Lampoon*, said something like "In any creative collective endeavor, at some point, the people involved are going to want to strangle each other with their own intestines." I knew there would be conflict because everybody cared about the quality so much. But when you have a conflict, solve it, and then all of a sudden, next month, you're having the same fight all over again, it eventually becomes unsustainable. So, I try to carry that with me going forward, and really try to only work with good folks (unless, you know, I really, really need the money).

MICHAEL RAYNER

———

By Ron Babcock

Original interview 2006

Updates: May 2020

We just bombed so hard that I threw my bongos down backstage and broke them, an act that Ryan still makes fun of me for to this day. "Hey, remember when you threw your bongos?"

Our duo act had won a contest and the prize was performing in Las Vegas! Our big show was on the outdoor stage at the Fremont Street Experience in downtown, which is known more for its laser light shows than stand-up comedy. Our concern though was how the stage was next to multiple casino entrances full of noisy slot machines. The only good news was the drunken crowd was standing room only, but only because there were no chairs. It was also Halloween.

That show fell under the category: comedy vs. everything.

I remember hearing "you suck" quite often in addition to a shockingly stern, "Watch yourself when you get off the stage." After a quick rage toss of some bongos, we did what young comics do to make themselves feel better—go watch other comics bomb.

Then Michael Rayner hit the stage like a desert windstorm balancing a wheelbarrow (a freaking full-sized wheelbarrow) on his face. Michael demanded people stop walking by and watch. Imagine if Jack Black juggled and mixed that with classic Steve Martin. That gives a good idea of Michael Rayner's post-modern vaudevillian show. It's inspiring to watch a performer sprint toward a situation you dread.

At one point, he brought children from the audience onstage (what were children even doing there?) and made them jump for dollar bills while yelling, "Dance for it! DANCE!" It felt like we were watching a fight, and Michael was clearly winning. He got people to stop, watch, and even stop sucking on the straws from their three-foot-tall frozen margaritas to actually laugh.

The extremely short-lived Las Vegas Comedy Festival had produced that awful show. We'd earned a spot on the fest, after only six months into performing comedy, because we entered in the "Props" category. We qualified because we used instruments we didn't know how to play in our act. Since this was 2003 and not 1985, there were very few prop comedians, and we won our category.

It's painful to think back on how bad our act was at the time, but Michael was supportive. People made fun of us for using "props" but watching Michael made us realize using props doesn't just mean Carrot Top. Before watching him, we would meekly say "props" when people asked us what we won. After watching him, we continued to say "props" but with an in-yer-face attitude.

Fast forward a few years and we're talking to Michael at *Garage Comedy*, a former comedy show, in LA, telling him how we don't have enough money to publish the next issue. We never had enough, but this time we were really short. Michael asked how much, and we told him $800.

"You need $800? I'll give you $800." And then he gave us $800.

"You guys are going places, so I'm going to grab onto your coattails now. Remember me when you get your shot at TV," he said.

Michael ended up being a bigger shot than we did. His signature trick, spinning a McDonald's cheeseburger on a parasol, earned him appearances on *America's Got Talent, The Late Late Show with James Corden* and *Sesame Street*. That and his other tricks have garnered over two million likes on Tik-Tok. It's nice when good things happen to talented and kind people. Maybe this time around, Michael can spot us for a new set of bongos?

RON BABCOCK: Did you know that I used to have a crush on your wife when I saw her as Mo[39], the referee on *Nickelodeon GUTS*?
MICHAEL RAYNER: Is that true?

---

39 *aka actress/writer Moira Quirk*

2020 UPDATE: Of course, it's true. I've now had dudes tell me they masturbated to her. Where do I go from there? It's weird. She now has a younger demographic because she's done voices on several popular video games.

Absolutely. I just wanted to say congratulations.
Okay. (kinda awkward silence)

No more awkward silence. I mention it in my shows now as a point of pride.

So, whenever you wanted sex and she said no, would you say, "Whatsa matter, don't you have the guts?"
No. (full blown awkward silence) But when we were dating and I would do a kid's birthday party, the parents and the kids would all talk about *GUTS*. I would say, "I'm dating Mo from *GUTS*." And the parents would just shake their head and go, 'No she's on TV juggleboy. That's a lie.' And then it became sad, and I kept saying it, and then it became weird.

This happens at shows now, and I pull out my cell phone and we call her and have a Q&A and then I slam my phone back in my pocket triumphantly.

When you moved out to LA, what was your low point?
There was a pilot for UPN for a game show called *Man O Man*. Women pick the guy they like the best. If a model kisses you on the cheek, that means you are still on the show. But if they push you in a huge pool of water that's behind you, that means you've been voted off. Being shoved by models. It was like a big replay of my entire high school and college years.

Weird. This question is so much more loaded now. I was doing quite well. I have regular venues, a house in the valley, a kid in college, and no DEBT! And savings. And then COVID-19 struck. Fuck! Shit and Fuck. I was going to have a sweet ass savings by August 1, 2020. And just like Kevin Spacey's career... GONE! One hundred twenty shows gone. But Man O Man *is still the low point. I'll get through this. I'm married to Mo from* GUTS. *Did I mention that?*

What was high school like?
I couldn't look people in the eye 'til I was eighteen—ultra, ultra-introvert.

No update there; except people follow me on Instagram that were the popular people in high school.

What brought you out of your shell?
The epiphany moment was this—everything in life is about sex. You want to maybe have sex someday. This girl that I liked down the street said, "Yeah, this guy, he can juggle." It infuriated me, so I learned how to do a few tricks, and I just started learning more. About a year later, a computer friend and I went to a country fair and they said, "You got any talent?" and I did five minutes of tricks and won and got $25. I just screwed around for five minutes and got $25. The fact that I remember that...

Seems true still. But my new fear was TikTok, all the cool kids doing dance moves. My daughter said I should do it. It's like high school all over again. I did a few posts wrong, and then she explained how it worked. I went viral. One went onto Reddit and then Ellen *paid for one of my videos. What brought me out of my shell this time was fear of not embracing a new thing. Because of TikTok, I have new fans that hopefully will come out to live shows when those happen again. Plus, I now have a social media agent who sells my vids to internet shows.*

The fact that you went to a "country fair" with your "computer friend" …
He would write programs that would make the letter "O" turn into an American flag.

No more country fairs for me.

Will you go to your high school reunion?
I despise my hometown. I'm super white and I was considered a minority. That's how Klannish my town is. If you carry your books close to your chest like I did, you were obviously gay. Anything out of the normal was gay. Just living in California makes you gay. When I left, it was rated the worst city to live in America.

Michigan went for Trump and armed militia stormed the capital. I cleave to California like a baby to the breast. And that breast can be from a man/woman/gay/lesbian/bi/trans/+/ gender-fluid/ person.

(The next question was "How much shit have you gotten for using props?" But I didn't even have to finish it for him to understand what I was asking.)

How much shit...
Tons of it. The thing is Steve Martin, who is the grandfather of modern comedy—everyone loves Steve Martin—he was a prop comic. In a weird way, Andy Kaufman, who was another huge influence on me, was a prop comic just doing weird stuff with

bongos and impersonations and whatnot. Why do comics care so much? I was talking to Maria Bamford and she said, "If you're doing something fun and people like it, why does it matter?" There's this weird thing against anyone who uses any kind of prop.

Patton Oswalt said nice things about me on stage at Frank Conniff's Cartoon Dump Show. *Kristen Schaal and Kurt Braunohler have me on the* Hot Tub *show, and I'm a regular at* The Tomorrow Show *with Ron Lynch. I make money, I do my shit, and I'm married to Mo from GUTS... did I mention that? So, I'm not as sensitive about that anymore. Why? Did you hear someone talk shit about me?*

Do most people change their mind when they see you?
Some do. Even my wife, we met at an amusement park, and when she found out I did juggling tricks, she was like, "I don't want to see that." And then she came inside, and she liked it.

Most people seem to now, but one douche said some shit on his podcast about me. I was pissed for a minute because I've had so many cool experiences in LA with celebrity types who dig what I do. Probably one of my favorite moments, I was doing a show in Riverside, California, and Ice-T and Coco are in the audience losing their shit because they dig my mojo. I used Coco in a bit, and she was spectacular. On the way back to my hotel, they get in the elevator with me, and Ice is quoting my show back to me. We get out and take a picture. So, did Ice and Coco want to see me? Probably not. But they had a good time.

You met Mo at an amusement park?
We both worked at Universal Studios Florida. I was doing a show there, and she was working on *The Murder She Wrote* show.

Correct.

That sounds horrible.
Now it's the *Harry and the Hendersons* show...

That show is probably gone by now.

That sounds even more horrible. Do you think comedy is in a better or worse place than it was five years ago?
I think comedy is fine. I think audiences aren't. There is so much comedy, they demand so much more, so *Jackass* becomes comedy. Steve-O shooting bottle rockets out of his ass with a string tied to another guy's dick—outrageous becomes comedy.

Comedy always evolves and I love it all. I'm a fan. I love this project and the history of all the performers in Modest Proposal. *Never too much comedy.*

How do you keep it real?
I've actually read many of the *Modest Proposals* and most people do the whimsical, funny answer. But this is actually the real answer. I took my child to Ikea to play in the ball area, and then I watched her rat out the other kids who were throwing balls around aggressively. I raised a rat, and I'm proud of that because when she sees somebody holding the crack, she will rat them out. That's how I keep it real.

I still practice new tricks and bits. And my older daughter will still be the rat. My younger daughter will hold the crack. And that's how it should be.

BLAINE CAPATCH & MARC EDWARD HEUCK

———

By Ron Babcock

Original Interview: December 2002

Updates: May 2020

A good entertainment journalist enters an interview with a carefully crafted list of thoughtful questions. A skilled interviewer can make the entertainer look good, which, in turn, makes for a more engaging article. I was not a skilled interviewer. I wasn't even a journalist. Honestly, I wasn't all that interested in learning about the comedians I interviewed for the early issues of the magazine. I just wanted them to like me. And you know what makes great comedic interviews? Neediness. My goal was to have the interviewees hang up the phone and think, "Wow that guy was really cool. Too bad he doesn't live here. Otherwise we'd hang all the time."

I first attempted to win approval from Blaine Capatch and Marc Edward Heuck from the Comedy Central game show *Beat the Geeks*. If you weren't a comedy nerd in the early aughts, you probably missed this show. Think *Jeopardy!* but fun. I'm not saying *Jeopardy!* isn't fun. I'm saying no one on *Jeopardy!* looks like they're having fun. They're all just concentrating really hard. It feels like watching a job interview. *Beat the Geeks* felt like the exact opposite, an over-the-top campy riff of the game show format.

The show had contestants face off in trivia matches against resident "geeks." Blaine was the effortlessly quick-witted and deft host while Marc played the Movie Geek with his limitless database of esoteric film knowledge.

Since our interview in 2002, Blaine has been a staple of Hollywood writer rooms working for *@midnight*, *Web Soup*, and various *Comedy Central Roasts*.

Marc is still writing for the *New Beverly Cinema* blog, along with his *The Projector Has Been Drinking* blog. He's also done BluRay/DVD commentaries for Shout Factory, Vinegar Syndrome, Code Red, and other labels, and his hands can be seen in *Once Upon a Time in Hollywood*.

Here is my first attempt at playing it cool with Blaine Capatch and Marc Edward Heuck of *Beat the Geeks*.

———————

ORIGINAL INTERVIEW

RON BABCOCK: Are film students annoying?
MARC EDWARD HEUCK: As a former film student, I can vouch for the potential of annoyance.

BLAINE CAPATCH: I think they're annoying as fuck. And you can quote me on that. F-U-C-K, annoying as.

(We laugh heartily at their expense.)

MARC: There's definitely a dangerous Trekkie mentality, especially in our current generation of film students, because they've surrounded themselves in this pipe dream of becoming filmmakers, but they're badly uninformed. They tend to think there were four movies made before *The Godfather: Gone with the Wind, Citizen Kane, Wizard of Oz, Casablanca.* That's it. They're not doing their homework. You've got to start digging. The shit you think is really innovative, it's been done before. No, really it has.

BLAINE: You know what else? I don't want to watch your diary entries from tenth grade for an hour and a half. I don't care what happened to you at the coffeehouse. There better be a Corvette flipping over onto its roof at some point. That's all I know. There better be talking dogs; I want talking dogs; I want a Corvette flipping onto its roof, and a guy hitting another guy in the head with a bat.

MARC: And I want tits.

BLAINE: I'm going to get some this afternoon. I'm getting a row of them down my back, like a stegosaurus.

What happened to the last host [J. Keith van Straaten]?
BLAINE: He spiraled down into a void of sex and drug abuse.

MARC: Actually, a mineshaft[40] of shame and self-loathing.

BLAINE: I wouldn't say self-loathing. I would say just loathing in general. I think Comedy Central went in a different direction, but either way, he's a great guy.

Blaine, did you "geek yourself out" in the audition?
BLAINE: Yes, I started rolling *Dungeons & Dragons* characters.

How did you jump from stand-up to writing for *MADtv*, *The Martin Short Show*, and *The Jamie Kennedy Experiment* to hosting?
BLAINE: It was good that I did stand-up seventeen years. When I started writing for shows, I still did stand-up at nights. It kept me in shape for the show, so I could be that interface between the contestants and the geeks. It's not hard. Comedy's fun.

Marc, how did you ascend to geek status?
MARC: Pure dumb luck. I had been working a job next door to a video store, and when they were putting the prototype together and trolling for geeks, they called the proprietor of the video store because he had a lot of obscure titles. He wasn't interested and he recommended me.

---

40 *Marc: I want to say that I had said "miasma" but because of the phone connection it sounded like "mineshaft"—ultimately, either word is funny. I'll leave it to you to choose what to go with because while I do regularly use the term "miasma" it is definitely a five-dollar word and probably makes me sound, as Blaine would say, F-U-C-K, pretentious as.*

Life is a battle between geeks and meatheads. What has *Beat the Geeks* done for our cause?
MARC: I think it's proven that we've got some muscle, metaphorically speaking.

BLAINE: It shows that just because your knowledge isn't practical, it doesn't mean you're not a good person.

What's the best way to sneak into a movie theater?
BLAINE: I usually walk up the front and hand the guy $20, and he looks the other way. It's expensive, but it's smooth.

MARC: I pay for my movies. I don't have my friends go in with a full ticket then have them go *(at this point, he took a deep, angry breath)*... I'm not going to continue because I don't want to legitimize this sort of thing because I had to bust these clowns. *(more angry)* Because it's all fun and games. "Oh yeah, we're stickin' it to the man." But if you wonder why certain movies get made that are such crap, it's because the good movies don't make any money because people pull stunts like this.

(The following was said out of fear.)

Totally understandable, very cool perspective.
BLAINE: Also remember, if you're going to sneak into the movies in the trunk of a car, make sure it's a drive-in.

MARC: And that your friends actually like you.

BLAINE: And never let them tape your mouth shut.

MARC: And if they've done it to you before, they're going to do it to you again.

BLAINE: No matter what they say. Remember Charlie Brown never kicked a football in Charles Schultz's entire life.

Blaine, I found an intensive website about you by one of your fans. Is that kinda creepy?
BLAINE: She's very sweet, that girl. But I've got a couple of creepy stalkers. I had one guy track me down in my hotel room at 3:30 a.m. and just kept calling and calling. Though, if people are stalking you, it means you're doing something right. Just as long as nobody comes up and stabs me.

Marc, how about producing one of your nine screenplays?
MARC: Oh, I've been thinking about that all the time. No one else is thinking about it. No one else is thinking about giving me the money to do that sort of thing. It's not like I'm sitting here at home thinking, "Hmmm, shall I let somebody do this or not?"

Who has been your favorite guest star geek?
BLAINE: Dana Gould, the *Planet of the Apes* geek because he's a buddy of mine, and he's one of the most brilliant comics there is. He's one of the producers on *The Simpsons* now.

MARC: When I was growing up and watching Dana Gould do stand-up, he was just someone who consistently made me laugh. To think that one day, I would be on the same stage as him, being accorded the same level of respect in terms of geekdom, that was a pretty big moment for me.

BLAINE: My favorite thing with Dana Gould was that nobody challenged him on the show. The producers made me ask him a question so he could show off some geek knowledge. The question was "What did Charlton Heston say at the end of the movie and who wrote the screenplay?" Dana listened and he looked very thoughtful and said, "You know, Blaine, that's a very good question that you've asked and I think it's a very important thing that we should address, and I think the answer to your question is Dog Penis." It was flawless, and of course we didn't use it.

What are some of your favorite comedies?

MARC: *The Fortune Cookie, Animal House, The Party,* a '40s movie called *Hellzapoppin'* with the comedy team of Ole Olson and Chic Johnson, which breaks the fourth and possibly fifth wall in terms of all the gags it does. It is, for some obscure legal reason, horrendously impossible to get on video. There are so many gags done in this movie. I have yet to see that stuff attempted today. All these ideas we think are original have been attempted before.

BLAINE: *Young Frankenstein, Blazing Saddles, History of the World, Part I; High Anxiety, Vacation, Caddyshack, Stripes, Airplane, Top Secret!* and *The Jerk.* I noticed that every time I go over my comedies, they're always these really stupid, over-the-top slapsticks.

MARC: But they're all carefully crafted slapsticks. People are trying to copy them today, and they can't do it.

BLAINE: It looks like there's idiotic shit going on, but it's actually a ballet of shit.

MARC: There's choreography. There's character development, as opposed to a lot of comedies that are being made today where, "Oh, let's do something outrageous. Let's do a big shit joke. Let's do a big testicle joke."

BLAINE: My attitude with comedy movies is the same thing with comedians. I like funny. Anything that's funny is fine with me. I don't compare. I don't contrast. Comedy is so subjective. There's no way to quantify it and say, "Well, you're wrong if you don't think this is funny." If you like it, you like it. If you don't, you don't. I love laughing.

MARC: I agree with Blaine.

BLAINE: It's a good attitude to strike when you're a comedian too because sometimes you're in a room with bad comedians. I got to find something to get me through the next hour and a half. I'll try to laugh at it.

UPDATED INTERVIEWS

BLAINE CAPATCH

What are your immediate thoughts after reading this interview?
The first thing I thought was, "Did I get coronavirus when I went to Vons yesterday? I touched the card reader when I entered my PIN. Oh God! I got coronavirus at Vons oh God! Oh God! Oh God!"

I remember doing this interview with Marc, who I love and am still in touch with through my lawyers. I remember trying to make him laugh, so the film student-hating thing was probably just for show. But yes, I still feel every movie should have an exploding Corvette in it. I feel that very strongly.

Knowing what you know now, what would you tell yourself in 2002?

Your mother and all your cats will die, and you'll get cancer. But you'll also write for *Mad Magazine*, so it works out!

What's the biggest difference about starting comedy now versus when you did?

Comedians and writers have instant access to visibility. Everyone can tap into it. You don't even really need clubs to do comedy anymore. I mean, I love the clubs, but dot dot dot. You know what Rodney Dangerfield always said, "Adapt or perish." I've always had a lot of respect for that, a lot of respect.

What trends in comedy do you miss?

I miss some friends who died. Sorry if that's not a joke. EYE ROLL.

Besides the obvious things, what's like… changed for you since then?

I have a wife and a little boy—*at the same time!*

MARC EDWARD HEUCK

What are your immediate thoughts after reading this interview?

I'm legitimately sorry I came down so hardass on the movie sneaking question. I should have just said, "Pass," or asked for a sidebar and explained my fractious employment situation where I was afraid that anything I did publicly would bite me later in my then-job as assistant manager at Nuart. Thank the fates Blaine immediately served up some comedy to riff on and took us back to jocularity again.

Knowing what you know now, what would you tell yourself in 2002?
Marc, get some therapy NOW. Don't wait until 2013 to start. It'll be too late then.

Besides the obvious things, what's like... changed for you since then?
This is where I'm supposed to be calm and gentlemanly and talk with perspective about the fleeting nature of fame and luck, the importance of finding small victories and validations, and being true to oneself—no matter how often it feels like an increasingly indifferent world is stripping it all away. Considering that there's no way that I can truthfully answer this question without publicly acknowledging an awful lot of humiliating details that I am still attempting to reckon with, let's just pretend that's what I said.

CHRIS FAIRBANKS

———

By Ryan McKee

Original Interview: 2005

Updates: June 2020

On a Thursday night in late 2004 or early 2005, I showed up to the Tempe Improv ready to hate whoever walked on stage first. Sarah Silverman was headlining that week. I'd been a fan since she began appearing regularly on *Late Night with Conan O'Brien* in the late '90s. As soon as I saw her name listed on the Improv's upcoming events, I pestered the club's manager Dan Mer to book our duo act, Ron and Ryan, as the opener.

We'd been working at the club regularly, opening for everyone from Patton Oswalt to *Police Academy*'s Michael Winslow, and I felt confident we'd hit it off with Sarah. Unfortunately, she brought her own opener from LA, which meant Ron and I had to hate that person.

Less than a minute into Chris Fairbanks's opening set, I completely forgot to hate him. He dressed like a skater with a huge mop of curly hair and delivered his jokes in a rapid stutter-like fashion. I remember Ron, never good at maintaining petty hatreds, looked at me and said, "This guy is awesome!"

Later, we befriended Chris and booked him to headline our monthly Paper Heart show multiple times. In addition to being a hilarious comedian, he's also a talented artist and contributed illustrations to *Modest Proposal's* later issues.

Even though I've seen Chris perform countless times, I'm always excited to see him perform. In fact, his brad-new special *Rescue Cactus* is so good, I've watched it three times in the last week. Also, check out his podcast *Do You Need a Ride?* where he and Karen Kilgariff shuttle their guests to or from the airport, somewhat dangerously, in a '08 Honda Accord mobile sound studio.

———————

RYAN MCKEE: Why'd you move from Montana to Austin?
CHRIS FAIRBANKS: I followed a girl. She asked me to. I didn't just simply follow her. We made arrangements, and then I moved. They also have a pretty famous stand-up scene, and I wanted to start doing that. This was '99.

2020 UPDATE: *Followed a girl? I clearly had just watched* Good Will Hunting. *Also, a famous stand-up scene? I'd absolutely heard nothing about Austin's "scene." Was I trying to sound cool? I already don't want to read the rest of this interview.*

I thought musicians moved to Austin, not comics.
Yeah. They call Austin "The Live Music Capital of the World," but that applies mostly to a lot of cover bands and dueling piano bars. Some good music too. Austin really does have a healthy comedy scene.

What? Jesus. Okay, I have no business saying it was "mostly cover bands." There were just a few bars near the Velveeta Room comedy club with bad blues music, so I guess that's what I was referring to. But Emo's was also right there, and I saw a bunch of great rock shows there. I have great memories from that place. Also, there I go again, trying to defend Austin's comedy scene, calling it a HEALTHY one. Not so famous now, just healthy.

Why is Montana called The Treasure State?
Because of the old, lucrative mining days in towns like Butte. They had a million people striking it rich in the early 1900s, and they built all these fancy houses there. Now, Montana is the poorest state in the country. Those houses in Butte are empty, the mine is a cancerous pit of death, and everyone drinks and punches each other in the face. Beautiful, apathetic country.

Again… what? I mean, there's drinking sure, but "everyone punches each other in the face"? Okay, I was trying to sound like I was tough and from the Wild West or something. My dad has fighting stories from his childhood, and I was pretending it was me. Also, no idea what I'm saying here calling Montana the poorest state: West Virginia, Arkansas, Mississippi all have higher poverty rates.

That's still true about Butte being the historic epicenter of a mining boom though, and the Berkley Pit being carcinogenic. It's a major Superfund site.

What's the biggest misconception about people who live in Montana?

That we are dumb. I didn't start meeting all these dumb people until I left Missoula. I grew up in a pretty, artsy, liberal town of writers and intellectuals. People there are Smarty Pantses. They just like to fight and drink, that's all. Like Canada.

I was defending Missoula specifically here because it's a liberal arts college town, and I'm proud of it, but there's plenty of dumb people in Montana and every state, clearly. Look at our current situation.

Also, there I fucking go again with this fighting thing... clearly trying to sound tough. Weird. I mean kids did drive around and get in fights when I was in high school, but it's way different now. I clearly was going through some phase where I felt I had to prove myself to some nonexistent challenger. Maybe I WAS dumb!

What's the last skateboarding trick you learned?

I just relearned late back foot flips. That's my crowd pleaser. I like switch heelflips because, for the life of me, I cannot do switch kickflips. I also like frontside bluntslides... only on little, short ledges, I'm afraid.

I'm forty-five now, and I had a hip replaced like three years ago. But I'm skating again, after years of rehab. I could maybe do these tricks today, but they'd be slow and sloppy. I've been having a blast skateboarding through this quarantine though. I'm really happy to have it back in my life again. My new hip feels amazing.

What's the last stand-up comedy trick you learned?
Inverted mic grabs. I stick those every time.

Wow, good answer, idiot. It's also a dumb question that was looking for that answer.

You skateboard, draw, crack jokes, and have the ability to legally purchase alcohol and cigarettes. You are a rebellious teenage girl's dream man. Aren't you?
I really don't think that's what teenage girls like. They like weed and nice cars. I don't have those.

Did someone's grandpa suddenly barge in and submit this question? "You crack jokes?" Also, even back then, I was thirty and had zero business being a teenage girl's dream man. "Legally purchase alcohol and cigarettes?" No more questions outta weird dirty grandpa!

When drawing pictures for the textbook company, do you ever try to put any subliminal messages in the drawings?
I put a hand-job in the back of a bus for one illustration for a fourth-grade aptitude test. They caught the discrepancies and circled them and sent them back to me. I was ashamed.

This is untrue and requires immediate explanation. I used to do illustrations for a company that published the TAAS Texas aptitude test. It was a sweet little freelance drawing gig. When they'd send me art instructions, I was given a very detailed description of the drawing they wanted. I remember this math word problem called for "a teacher and student in the back of a bus, going over homework." I didn't do it on purpose, but my boss circled the teacher's hand in my drawing because the activity looked questionable, or at least unclear. Of course, I didn't do it on purpose. I really wanted to keep that job AND was trying to be funny with this answer.

How did you get booked to open for Cyndi Lauper?
A girl who acted in a short film with me works for Verizon Wireless. They put on the show. I hope my set didn't get her fired. It did not go well.

All true—I still hope she wasn't fired.

True or false, Lauper's crowning achievement was the album, *A Hat Full of Stars*?
False. The correct answer is the *Goonies* theme.

This is the only question in this embarrassing interview that I would give the same answer today.

Finally, how do you keep it real?
That question makes me a little nervous. It reminds me of the fist pound the kids do at the end of handshakes these days. I guess I don't keep it very real.

Fifteen years later, my nervousness has transformed into anger. I am actually mad at this question. Bring that grandpa back in here. He was better.

JAMES KOCHALKA

By Brandon Huigens

Updated Intro by Annie Worth

Original Interview: 2006

Updated Interview: May 2020

More than anything, James Kochalka's professional career can be described as the ultimate tale of ambition fulfillment.

His beginnings didn't start with getting bitten by a super bug or being born on a mystical planet, like a telltale hero but did include drawing over two thousand pages of comics and completing a first graphic novel as a kid in the 1970s. He is revered, in an iconic hero sense, and has become a prolific artist who incites devout followings.

There is no one else in the world like him. James is the first *cartoonist laureate* of Vermont, a lead singer in the band James Kochalka Superstar, and a proud father and husband. He writes for and is adored by children and young adults. He continues to turn out trippy, heartfelt, and insatiably cute art, all while exuding just the right blend of both genuine and celebrity vibes, and without missing a beat.

When *Modest Proposal* spoke to James in 2006, he was busy traveling around the world to appear at comic book conventions while also creating tons of comics and music. He had released the *SuperFuckers* series, which was adapted into an animated series starring the voices of David Faustino, Maria Bamford, and Jaleel White. As if that wasn't enough, he had nine albums with his band and created Plunger the Dragon for Nickelodeon.

To say the least, *Modest Proposal* was stoked to interview him.

ORIGINAL INTERVIEW

World renowned, badass cartoonist. Sex idol rock star. Beloved husband and father. Drunken bike race champion. Kochalka's life's greatest influence? His cat, Spandy.

"Spandy sort of turned me from an angry punk rocker into someone who loves kitties. It was an important step to take before becoming a dad. The images kind of soften a bit."

Despite her awesomeness, Spandy's love for James can turn into a bitter (yet nonviolent) jealous rage. Example: the cat's boiling animosity for the Kochalka's new son.

"She's been really mad at me ever since we had Eli," James explains. "For like two years, she's been totally pissed off at me. Now, she suddenly likes me again."

So just when the fate of the Kochalka family hangs in the balance, Spandy shines true, like the power of Greyskull. Or does she?

"She still doesn't like Eli," Kochalka says. "Anytime he's awake, she's hiding."

Eli holds no apparent grudge against the bitter kitty. James and his wife Amy help the situation by not dressing their smallest family member in humiliating, dumb ass outfits.

"Cats hate that," James says. "Dogs will put up with it, I guess. But they don't really like it, though."

Kochalka's take on creating art and music is one being embraced by new, untrained artists (and those of us who really suck ass at drawing or singing or being a comedian in any capacity). He's inspired hundreds—perhaps thousands—of aspiring comics and music creators, thanks largely to his revolutionary daily autobiographical comic, published daily on AmericanElf.com. His perspective on the subject of craft incites monumental motivation to anyone striving creatively.

"I have a few ideas on craft," begins Kochalka. "One, you don't need any great skill to make a great work of art. What you need is a lot of energy and drive. You have to have the ability to open yourself up and explore things that other people just can't do. It's sort of magic. What you need is magic or some spark of genius; you don't necessarily need to have any technical skill to have that magic or spark of genius.

"And then there's the second part, which is, somehow, and I've seen this happen again and again, the better somebody gets at the craft of whatever they do, the worse they are. It's really clear in music. For instance, some band's first album: awesome. They barely know how to play, and they make an awesome album. They start to play, learn a few more chords, and before you know it, their songs are just a mess, and they're no good. Sometimes, you do better work when you don't know that much."

So how does Kochalka, a prolific comics artist AND musician for nearly two decades, keep from sucking?

"I have to try to purposefully draw myself a little off balance or try and push into new directions and hope I'm not turning into one of those lame old guys," he responds.

Musically, Kochalka surprisingly says he didn't receive any negative criticism for the song, "Show Respect to Michael Jackson," which he did with his band, James Kochalka Superstar.

"Most people just think it's awesome. It's a song about how he's great, and that he deserves respect. It was written before we were pretty darn sure he was a child molester.

"He's not a great songwriter, but there's something special about him. Whatever he has, it's amazing."

Searching deeper into Kochalka's advice to stay fresh and how it applies to him, he says he's not very interested in trying out his left hand at cartooning.

"I'd rather draw drunk than with my left hand," he says.

Speaking of getting drunk, new father Kochalka hasn't been defending his title as "Greatest Drunk Cartoonist Bicyclist" since the inception of his son, but he hasn't given up entirely on alcohol.

"The funny thing is, now I'm kind of drunk on one beer."

Kochalka had a busy 2006. iTunes now has an exclusive EP available for download featuring new and old Kochalka material. Included is the old favorite "Hockey Monkey," the title song for FOX's new sitcom *The Loop*, which Kochalka says features neither hockey nor monkeys but is delightfully wonderful. June will see the release of Kochalka's superhero parody *SuperFuckers*. This summer, *American Elf Volume 2* will collect daily strips—what Kochalka considers will be his most relevant comics legacy from 2004 through 2005. Like The Beatles, Kochalka doesn't plan on a sprawling US tour until he has a #1 hit.

UPDATED INTERVIEW

BRANDON HUIGENS: What are your immediate thoughts after reading this interview?
JAMES KOCHALKA: Now, I'm sad all over again that my cat Spandy is dead. I have a little box of her ashes, though… which we play with or talk to every once in a while. And we have three other cats now: Nooko, Wendy, and Hermie. Nooko is the last one that I got to name, and then the kids named the two with more normal names. When I name a cat, I prefer to pick a brand-new name that never before existed. Oh, and I must have done this interview before my second son, Oliver, was born.

Knowing what you know now, what would you tell yourself back then?

Well, the me in the interview seems to be doing all right. His career is cranking, his family life is great. I'd try not to mess anything up for the dude.

What's the biggest difference about being a cartoonist now versus the early 2000s?

There's lots more women in the comic scene, lots more people of color. And their work is great! As I knew it would be. Also, all the really big mainstream book publishers either have or are starting up graphic novel lines.

Of course, now we're in the middle of the coronavirus pandemic. I have no idea what the comic book industry is going to look like even one year from now. I'm trying to prepare for various scenarios.

Do you miss anything about self-publishing?

I only ever really self-published one book, *Magic Boy and the World of God*. That was done at a real printer, back in the mid-90s. Unless you mean making homemade photocopied mini comics, which I did much more of. Yeah, I miss making mini comics.

I did make a bunch with my kids when they were younger that most people probably don't know about, but we sold them at the comic book store in town here and sometimes when I'd go to a comic book convention. There's a great one Eli drew when he was three or four called *Two Dead Ninjas*. So, I do miss making comics with them, but they've grown out of it. Eli is almost seventeen now.

Oh! I just started serializing a comic on Patreon called *Moon Book Prototype*. So, I guess I *am* self-publishing, on the web at patreon.com/kochalka.

Would you say you've achieved all your hopes and dreams?
Having achieved a dream is awesome, but that doesn't mean I've done that thing. I've had dozens and dozens of books published, but I dream about making even more! I've made animated cartoons—*SuperFuckers* with Cartoon Hangover and *Plunger the Dragon* with Nickelodeon—but I'd still like to make more!

And I'd still like my books to find a bigger audience. To that end, I recently signed a three-book deal with Scholastic for my new series, *Banana Fox*. Scholastic is probably the largest graphic novel publisher in the United States. Their reach is just gigantic. They're a juggernaut.

What's a new dream you might try?
I'm trying to put together an album where I collaborate with a bunch of my famous musician friends. I just got Greta from the band Frankie Cosmos to sing on three songs, and it was wonderful. I hope to use that as a seed to grow the project bigger.

I'd like to try writing a prose novel someday. The only reason I haven't is because I'm so busy drawing graphic novels and writing and recording music. I keep waiting for my comics career to stall out so I have more time, and I can put a bunch of time into writing prose.

But if I don't find myself with *more* time, I'll have to try just cranking something out in between other projects or in my spare time. Write it all rough and loose and cool.

ADAM FERRARA

———

By Ron Babcock

Original Interview: February 2003

Updates: May 2020

Interviewing is a lot like driving. At first you think, how hard can it be? I've been watching people drive my entire life. But when you finally get behind the wheel and start backing out of the driveway, you realize you don't know what the hell you're doing.

I *cringe* at how dickish some of my early questions seem now. I was just trying to be funny, but I wasn't yet. And when you're not funny yet, you just say mean stuff thinking it's funny. And you think it's okay to say because you're saying it to a comic (see *Love Boat* question).

On top of not knowing how to interview, I didn't even know who to interview. I remember watching Adam Ferrara's stand-up special on Comedy Central and thinking, "He's funny, let's interview him." That's the entire amount of thought that went into this interview. And because the internet hadn't exploded yet, Adam didn't fact-check that Ryan and I were two virgins[41] who didn't know anything about anything. So, of course, he agreed to the interview.

Now Adam is still funny and much more successful. Since *The Love Boat*, he's been in FX's *Rescue Me*, HBO's *Nurse Jackie* and co-hosted the US version of *Top Gear*. He's still as nice a guy as he was when I originally interviewed him.

RON BABCOCK: When in public, are you recognized most as:
a) Adam Ferrara, the stand-up comedian
b) Adam Ferrara, that guy with Denis Leary on *The Job*
c) The Olive Garden commercial guy
d) The young doctor on NBC's *Scrubs* because seriously the physical similarities are uncanny.
(he laughs)

ADAM FERRARA: I get the stand-up thing a lot.

2020 UPDATE: And I still think Zack Braff is a very handsome man.

True or false: The highlight of your career was guest starring on *The Love Boat: The Next Wave*.
(At this point, he made a sheeesh/fart sound with his mouth) False.

---

41 *Okay, only one of us was a virgin, but I'm not saying who. Fine it was me. Happy?*

I'm not familiar with the sheeesh/fart sound. Any similar sound made on my part is purely coincidental.

I'm sorry, did you say false?

False, but I did make dental. You have to make a certain amount of money in television, so the union will pick up your healthcare. I did *The Love Boat* and got my cavities fixed.

Just an update, the teeth are doing fine. I cannot over emphasize the importance of flossing.

You've been nominated for best stand-up comedian of the year at the American Comedy Awards, twice, and haven't won. Does that piss you off?

Nah, it's nice to be nominated. I get to bring my parents out to LA. You ride in a limo; you see your friends. The guys who won were great comics. Brian Regan won one year, and Schimmel won the next year so just to be in that caliber is fine. The pricks.

You travel the country more than a train hobo. What's the worst city there is?

There is really no place in Mississippi you should ever go. Everyone was surprised at Trent Lott's racist comments. He was the senator of Mississippi. You didn't see that coming?

I was wrong, I have since been back to Mississippi, and they're wonderful people... it is my understanding Trent Lott is from there too.

When you started as the class clown in high school, did that help you meet girls, or did that make you just a friend?

You know everyone says I want a guy with a sense of humor, and it's bullshit. Bullshit. They like those foreign guys with the long hair and the accent, "I will make love to you. Your orgasm will be so intense you will see dead relatives." That's the kind of shit they want. They don't want "knock, knock." So, what's going to get a girl hot—that or two Jews walk into a bar?

When doing sitcoms, is it difficult to relinquish the Machiavellian control that you have as a stand-up comedian?
I didn't have a lot of input in the first two pilots I did, and that was kind of troublesome, but then you're just hired to do a show. You're hired to do a job. When you're in stand-up, you're in control. You're the pope. You're the writer, the producer, the performer, the editor. The only one you really have to answer to is the audience. If the audience doesn't laugh, you can blame them only so much before you have to go back and start looking at the joke.

Did Denis Leary ever ask your opinion of *The Ref*, and if so, did you ever cough politely and excuse yourself from the room?
Nah, *The Ref*'s a great movie. I love *The Ref*. You didn't like *The Ref*?

It's a personal preference I guess, but no.
The Ref was a great film, made me laugh. There's a line in there where all the police cars are showing up, and Denis is looking out the window and under his breath, he goes "Holy shit, it's not like I shot Kennedy," which was fucking hysterical.

Still makes me laugh.

How long did it take before you knew you were going to be successful in this?
I still don't know. This is the only gig I've kept the longest, so you just keep going. I started out on Long Island in 1988, and at that time bar owners found that comedy was very cheap to produce. You just needed a microphone and a light, and a lot of the times they didn't even have a light. You would just go to these different bars and fight to get and keep people's attention. A big gig for me was when you would see the word "comedy club." You were thrilled because they were coming to see comedy. This wasn't just a bar that had a comedy night. That was the big step for me. "Look I'm really in a comedy club."

Any tips for beginners?
If you want to work comedy clubs, don't start out at a comedy club. Start out in coffee houses. Start out at other places. Don't be brand new at a comedy club because that's their first impression. Get yourself on your feet, get a good five minutes together. It's like magic. You don't want to see the magician shoving the doves into the suit.

(I said "uh-huh," but really had no idea what the last line meant. I still don't. Write me if you do.)

My apologies, it means nobody wants to see how the trick is done. Just show them the magic. I'm here if any further clarification is needed.

The worst interview question you ever heard?
True or false, the highpoint of your career was doing the new *Love Boat*.

Oh man, that guy's an ass.
You asked.

What are you going to do now, like right now?
Immediately after this I gotta go do my laundry.

You don't have someone to do your laundry?
I'm in the struggles, trying to get some papers.

UPDATED QUESTIONS

What are your immediate thoughts after reading this interview?
My name is spelled fifty percent correctly, so the glass is half full.

AUTHORS NOTE: Turns out it's "FERRARA." Ferrara.

Knowing what you know now, what would you tell "2003 Adam Ferrara"?
I'm glad you got your cavities taken care of, young fella.

Besides the obvious things, what's like, changed for you since then?
I send out my laundry.

LEV

———

By Ron Babcock

Original Interview: 2005

Updates: May 2020

Out of all the people we featured in *Modest Proposal*, Lev is one whose career I've most enjoyed following.

He is the San Francisco-based creator of *Tales of Mere Existence*, a quirky animated series born in 2002 that is still very much alive and well. The animation is simple and low-tech. His videos consist of a series of images with additional lines appearing as if being drawn by an invisible hand (although you can kinda see his hand through the semi-translucent paper). The technique was inspired by the French documentary *The Mystery of Picasso* (1956), which makes it sound extra fancy.

The tone of his work is slightly pessimistic, slightly sarcastic, and definitely dejected. It still manages to be extremely accessible though. Every time I start a new office gig and we do that ritual where we ask, "Hey have you seen..." I always pull up a video by Lev for group approval.

As someone who has found a home working in animation, his "jeez-even-I-can-draw-this" animation style is inspiring and refreshing in its simplicity. You don't need a million-dollar budget to make something interesting. Lev claims each episode costs less than four dollars to make.

"When I was in school, I was aware of how iffy this path was," Lev said. "So, I said to myself, 'If I'm going to be stupid enough to go to Art School, I had better at least be smart enough to work cheaply.'"

Since we interviewed Lev in 2005, he has self-published *The 7 Habits of Highly Negative People* (2006) and *Sunny Side Down* (2009) through Simon & Schuster. His work has been viewed over fifty-three million times on YouTube with over 280k subscribers. Through it all his visual style has stayed the same. And while his latest work isn't chock full of positivity, it is slightly less depressing than before. Here's a guy who found a unique voice and grew right along with it.

RON BABCOCK: How did you get involved with *Jump Cuts*?
LEV: To the best of my knowledge, they found me. I didn't know that sort of thing ever really happened. I was in a show in New York, and I think a member of the Uprights Citizen Brigade was there, and they told Comedy Central about me. I'm not sure who it was, and I'm not even sure this is true.

Since Jump Cuts *did not go to series, I may as well explain that it was a compilation show on Comedy Central. I can't even remember how many episodes they made, but I think I was in all of them. I didn't have Comedy Central when it was on (I still don't), so I went to watch the show at the local bar on Clement Street.*

Before that, did you ever send out your stuff?
I had actually sent a lot of stuff to MTV and got rejected so many times. Eventually this guy said, "Look man, we really like your stuff, but this is just way too intelligent for our audience." I was bummed at first, but I eventually figured I should take that as a compliment.

This may still be a compliment, but now I can't make up my mind for sure.

Is the character in *Tales of Mere Existence* autobiographical?
That character is really an aspect of me. It's the little part of me, the little part of anybody—the defeated part of your personality that will creep up and make you feel like not bothering. Sometimes you can control it, and sometimes you can't. Sometimes it's very easy to fall into that kind of thinking, and sometimes I catch myself thinking in that certain way, and I find it funny, and that's pretty much where the whole angle of the series comes from.

I have moved a little away from it being all about self-doubt, but a lot of this is still relevant.

What makes animation such a popular way to tell stories?
It makes the subject matter slightly more abstract, so you can be a little more outlandish with it. For my particular project and

the simplicity of what I'm doing, I just think it takes any kind of pretension out of the picture. The stuff is so simple, almost so that a ten-year-old can draw it. If the visuals were more complicated, I think it would take away from the actual message.

My view hasn't changed much, except that I now get much more obsessed with facial expressions and body language, even though I still use the low-rent technique.

Did you go to art school?

Yeah. Almost immediately after I got out, I thought I don't want to be part of the art world because that's exactly what it is. The art world is this very, very small community. I was much more interested in average people—people who would not normally go to any sort of art show.

I may believe this more now than I did back then. I wasn't bullshitting on this one.

Do animators have any hack moves?

When a cartoon character says, "Well, I'm just a cartoon character," I have a tendency to tune out.

I am keeping my mouth shut here.

How did the comic book get started?

I had shown a lot of the shorts around town and in a bazillion little festivals. Then I started to get wise to the fact that it was very much a dead end. I didn't want to go the route of getting on my hands and knees and attempting to do a half-hour standard television program. The competition for that would be ridiculous, and I didn't have any ideas anyhow. I got the idea of trying to get to the next level because I realized there was a unique position to take that character and put him in comic book form. Naturally, profit was not my original motivation.

This wasn't a good answer. It not only doesn't make a lot of sense, but it's also wrong. I started drawing the comics because I wanted something to sell when I screened at festivals. I didn't think people would buy an independent DVD, but they would buy an independent comic book WITH a DVD. Being able to make a little money off my work was part of the idea. Eventually, the comics became as important as the animations, so I am glad I did that.

What's the grandest compliment you've ever received for your work?
(actual eighteen-second pause) This kid wrote me saying that I was defining his mood and difficulties that he was having in adolescence, and that made me feel pretty damn good. It means that a lot of this stuff has got this adolescent twinge to it. It's like a part of me stayed in arrested development and never really got over the sorts of things that most people dealt with in their teenage years.

(Another twenty-three-second pause before I began typing) This is still true. I have been getting a lot more mail since the pandemic began, and mail like this means a lot to me.

Consequently, what's the worst critique of your work?
It was so poorly spelled I didn't care. (eight-sec pause)

Hello?
I'm still here, I'm just... (seven-sec pause) I don't care if somebody really, really hates it, but when people are completely

indifferent to it, that's definitely the most difficult thing to deal with. Being lavished with somebody pouring some hate on you, at least it affected them. But when somebody's indifferent and unmoved whatsoever, that's a little bit bothersome.

Bang on.

How do you keep it real?
I've been asked a couple of times, "Have you ever done anything that you thought was too embarrassing to put out?" The only time I've ever been really embarrassed about a piece was when I tried to second-guess what the audience would respond to instead of doing what I thought. As soon as I start to make something I think people will like, it totally sucks.

This is even more so now than it was then. When people say to me, "Don't ever change," I think, "Hey man, I seriously don't fucking know how."

SCHADENFREUDE

———

By Ryan McKee

Original Interview: May 2003

Updates: May 2020

"It's the closest a sketch comedy show can be to a rock concert, with the music and the energy," Sandy Marshall said when asked to describe Schadenfreude's show in 2003.

In 2020, he added, "...for those times when you happen upon rock concerts in forty-five-seat black-box theaters."

2003 Sandy's description is closer to my experience seeing the group. Arizona State University flew the Chicago sketch group out to perform on campus, and they rocked a four-hundred-seat theater, packed with students. They seemed like rock stars to the twenty-four-year-old me.

Just to have a solid turnout at ASU is a feat in itself. I saw Zach Galifianakis perform in a near empty auditorium. I watched seminal hip-hop group Blackalicious do an outdoor afternoon show along with thirty other fans. Mighty Mighty Bosstones and Reel Big Fish, at the height of ska-punk popularity, played on the football practice field for a scattered bunch of underage drunks.

After the show, we convinced them, along with ASU's student comedy group, to party at our house. We staged a flip-cup drinking game tournament between sketch groups and *Modest Proposal* won—definitely our proudest moment of 2003.

Schadenfreude just celebrated their twentieth anniversary with a round of sold-out shows in Chicago.

The ensemble is spread out across the country. Adam Witt is in LA, Kate James lives in Brooklyn, Sandy Marshall is in Toronto, and Stephen Schmidt and Justin Kaufmann still live in Chicago.

"Even though we are not in the same place, Schadenfreude continues to produce new and works on various scripts and projects," Justin wrote.

This original interview took place by a hotel pool, hours before the aforementioned show. Nic Wegener and I conducted the interview, and at the time, Schadenfreude had a sixth member, Mark Hanner.

RYAN MCKEE: What's your regular show like in Chicago?
MARK: We call it a party with a show before it. Watch the show and stick around for the party afterward.

ADAM: It used to be five bucks and a free beer for a long time.

2020 UPDATE

SANDY: *Before the show was five bucks and free beer, the show was three bucks and free beer. We'd take turns getting cases of Miller Lite and your Red Dog for the audience each week.*

ADAM: *I cannot drink a Miller Genuine Draft to this day.*

Are you scared of rednecks and cowboys out here in Arizona?
ADAM: I'm from Ohio. (they all laugh) Kate is from Michigan. (more laughter, confusion)

STEPHEN: I'm from Minnesota (more laughter, more general confusion)

JUSTIN: Illinois has plenty of cowboys. Chicago is a big city in a really shitty state.

ADAM: Ohio has the market cornered on hicks.

ADAM: *That's back when we called hillbillies "hicks." It's tough to read now.*

Did you join a sketch comedy troupe to feel like you're in a rock band?
ADAM: Uh, no. I started a sketch comedy troupe because this is like my fourth one. And this is the only one that didn't suck.[42]

---

42 Adam: *I'm trying to impress the kids. This is unfair to Not Found in Nature, Pocket Change Theater, and Apocalypso.*

SANDY: I got into it because Adam asked me to and didn't want to go through all the audition processes other places.

JUSTIN: There's an element to it that is a late-night kind of party. But I don't think anybody got into it because of that. But when we're doing an improv festival, or any festival in New York or LA, we're treated like rock stars.[43]

MARK: The ladies don't look at us like they look at rock stars. They look at us like fat comedians.

Wait, you're a sketch group, and you headline improv festivals?
KATE: They always ask us. We never really fit in. But we all came from improv, and we know that community, and they sort of honored that because they know that's how we write a lot of our stuff.[44]

JUSTIN: A lot of reviews would call us improv and they saw the show. A lot of reviewers[45] don't really have an understanding of the difference, so we'd just get lumped in with that community.

Do the Chicago comedy communities, sketch, improv, stand-up, mix very often?
JUSTIN: Sketch and improv do because most of the people who do sketch are improvisers. Chicago just started doing

---

43 Justin: I don't even know what this means. Who treated us like rock stars? Idiot.

44 Adam: While Kate scratches her chin about why we don't fit in at the Improv Festival, picture a gospel choir, dogs dressed as tigers, and the music of a live bagpipe band.

45 Justin: Ha what's a reviewer? Also, remember when critics actually reviewed comedy shows? Also, what's a critic?

a sketch festival, and they boast thirty-some sketch groups in the city. There are not thirty sketch groups in Chicago. What it is, is a lot of improvisers saying, "We'll do sketch for a show."

KATE: Yeah, there's a lot of controversy[46] with that.

MARK: Stand-up doesn't cross over at all. That's its own community.

JUSTIN: Yeah, we did a stand-up festival last year, and it was really strange. Because we were the only group, first off, and it was a weird crowd, a whole different crowd.

JUSTIN: That's code for saying we bombed.

ADAM: Code Translation: They were all there to see Doug Stanhope.

Where do you think live comedy is headed?
SANDY: More sketch groups are popping up here and there. I think people want to show that they write as well as improvise. In Chicago, where everyone is an improviser, the good part is you can get a lot of great stuff. The bad part is that it's totally oversaturated.[47]

---

46 *Kate: Pining for the days when I used to think things like this were "controversial."*

47 *Adam: Improv was oversaturated in 2000. This sentence is adorable.*

JUSTIN: Improv was hot like five years ago, and I'm sure it still is. However, we're not in it anymore. We're always working, so it's hard to get a pulse on things.[48]

KATE: What I think is interesting, also, is the whole reality sketch idea with Jamie Kennedy and *Jackass*. They're taking this curve of reality TV and putting it to comedy.[49] I think it'll double back. At least, I hope.

JUSTIN: Two or three years ago, all these sketch shows came out on TV, and they all tanked. That's when The WB put out *Hype*. America then thinks, "Ah, that's what sketch comedy is." Then they see a Schadenfreude poster on the street, "Oh, sketch comedy. It's probably like that show *Hype*.[50]" And they won't go see it.

KATE: We were in Los Angeles when *Hype* came out, and what this agent said to us was, "I feel like your next couple of years are going to be made or broken on whether or not *Hype* does well." And he had a great point. It's the one sketch show that gets through to mainstream America, and it tanks. So, people are like, sketch sucks, but now sketch seems to be coming back.

---

48 Justin: *Sketch kind of died out in Chicago. There used to be a scene with a couple of groups, but once you realized that you could just do a "one-man sketch show" (code for SNL audition piece) the scene died off.*

49 Kate: *This is how we now describe the government. So, guess I blame Jamie Kennedy and* Jackass?

50 Justin: *Haha* Hype! *Great reference. Wasn't Frank Caliendo on that show? Doing Kramer impressions?*

ADAM: But now it's all talent driven, like Dave Chappelle, Ashton Kutcher. They trust the star to draw the audience more than they have any concern for sketch comedy.

JUSTIN: I don't know the national scene, but not a lot of groups out there will stay together for long periods of time to perfect the art because the way to make money in this business is to go to LA and try to make it. Like Bozo over there (he points to Nic Wegener who has finally shown up to help with the interview).[51]

ADAM: *We were approached by representation around this time. The future of sketch comedy was hilariously dependent upon Hype, a thoroughly forgotten show even in the week of its airing. Cut to fifteen years later: We're all drinking together at a Chicago Old Man Bar. And what do I find underneath my Old Style? A coaster advertising Hype.*

I was reading an old interview that said you guys spend so much time together, you can imitate each other taking a shit. Still true?
JUSTIN: Yeah, it's true, look at us.

KATE: They can't imitate me, nor can I imitate them.

JUSTIN: Kate doesn't take shits.[52]

JUSTIN: *Our theater in Chicago had a backstage the size of a bathroom. So, when someone had to go to the bathroom, we all had to go outside into the alley and wait it out. So yes, this is accurate.*

---

51 *Justin: Still true! Nic is still a bozo.*

52 *Kate: Still accurate. It's problematic.*

Has it been difficult changing your comedy to fit radio?
KATE: It's retraining our brains because we're so visual. We'll be reading through something for the fifteenth time and we'll say, "Oh, we forgot to say that she's the mom."[53]

JUSTIN: It's a different thing. It's not like when you can just write whatever and put it on. There're themes to each show. Each thirty-minute show has to stand on its own. In a month's time, we wrote probably 180 sketches. And we thought that would be the hard part, but the hard part is picking the seventy that are going to go. Then, rehearse it, record it, edit it, and mix it. We're the director, we're the producer, and we're the editor. So, yeah, we have to be together seven days a week, it sucks. (he laughs)

JUSTIN: We ended up doing sixty episodes of that show. So much work for a collective audience response of "meh."

ADAM: Where's your radio show Hype?

You tried to get Balki (Bronson Pinchot) into one of your acts, but he turned you down. Why?[54]
KATE: How did you get that information?

JUSTIN: He was in town doing some popular one-man show. And there were these great stories about how he would party

---

53 *Kate: Oh God, I had to use "Mom" as my example? I wish I could update that to "crazy girlfriend," or "elementary teacher," or "chamber maid in sexy chamber maid outfit."*

54 *Stephen: I still don't know why we stopped trying. This is the guy to get. I'm picking this up for 2020. We all have the time now.*

next door at the bar, just out of control drunk all the time. So, we're like, Balki Bartokomous, cool. We wrote a letter to him saying that we wanted him to be in a video with Mark, and they would be in bed together. He called me back and left a message on my machine, (here he mimics a boozy Balki) "Hey Justin, this is Bronson Pinchot, and I got your tape and letter. I'm looking at it, and it looks like you guys have a lot of fun. But I don't understand what you're doing." We've been turned down by a ton of people. Bernie Mac didn't even call us back.

KATE: We did get Colin Mochrie to be in bed with Mark.

MARK: Yeah, that got a big response.

JUSTIN: And John Lithgow was in our video, and Taye Diggs (everyone laughs and repeats the name Taye Diggs here. I don't know why). And David Cross. We've been trying for years to get Mayor Daly, the mayor of Chicago. He only does a number of public appearances, like he has a quota of five a year. But, if he doesn't make an appearance at your event, you'll get one of three: a letter saying he won't do it, a video tape thing of him, or he'll send you a letter endorsing your product. The Improvfest got the endorsement letter, and they got huge boners[55] over it.

ADAM: They laminated it.

JUSTIN: Ha, this was the rejection of the week. Schadenfreude was really good at asking. We ended up getting Barack Obama (then Illinois Senator) for a radio bit not long after this. And

---

55 *Justin: Huge boners? I'd say small boners.*

Rev. Jesse Jackson. And our biggest claim to fame was roasting Mayor Daley at his retirement party. That was probably the scariest show I ever did.

(It's time for Nic's questions and he does an exaggerated, "Ohhh, oh, yeah.")

ADAM: (mimicking Nic) Why you guys gotta be like that? (Everyone laughs except me. I think it was an inside joke from the party the night before that I didn't attend.)

ADAM: I wouldn't trust anything I say. I may have sustained a concussion walking into a closed sliding glass door at that party because I was wearing mirrored aviator glasses to be cool.

NIC: All right, who were your influences coming up?

ADAM: When I moved to Chicago, I would never miss a Second City set for like the first year. I would take the bus down to Second City. It was free, and I came to Chicago for comedy.

JUSTIN: I'm fascinated by the days of John Belushi. The early '70s when he was at Second City.[56]

MARK: A book that we've all read is… (He's caught off guard as an attractive brunette woman does a half-way inverted flopping kick-out into the pool, which looked painful. Everyone looks at the pool until she starts to climb out. They all begin

---

56 *Justin: That lasted two weeks. I was reading* Wired *by Bob Woodward on the plane.*

clapping and cheering. The woman, as if she expected this all along, does a ninety-degree bow.)

The Attractive Brunette Woman: Are you laughing with me?

Schadenfreude: Yeah, of course.

(Satisfied, she walks away.)

KATE: *This whole chunk of the article feels very "early aughts" to me. Can we track down this woman and apologize? God forbid she try to take a swim without seven men commenting all at once. On the record, nonetheless. (This is fun! I love busting chops over things that happened decades ago!)*

KATE: (imitating the Schadenfreude men) *Yeah, we're guys and you're wearing a string bikini, we're laughing any way you want us to laugh.*

JUSTIN: *I was truly worried about her safety.*

SANDY: Other influences are politicians, people who infuse the real stuff into the comedy. One of my comedic heroes today is Larry David. His show is one of the most brilliant shows I've ever seen.[57]

ADAM: Got to give props out[58] to *Mr. Show, Monty Python.*

---

57 *Sandy: True to this day!*

58 *Adam: "props out"—Gotta fit in with these fellow teens by using their own words.*

SANDY: And lately I've been paying more attention to the olden days of radio. I listened to *War of the Worlds* like a month ago, and it's unbelievable.

What about *National Lampoon's Radio Hour*?
(collective agreement)[59]

ADAM: *Fireside Theater* also, you know they have that back on NPR. Oh, and the '85 season of *Saturday Night Live*, when they had Christopher Guest, Billy Crystal, and Harry Shearer.

NIC: That whole '85 cast hated Harry Shearer.

ADAM: Well, he's hateable, I guess.

ADAM: *Well, we're wrapping up; anyone want to shit on a legend before we go?*

---

59 *Stephen: To this day, I've still only seen the movie.*

DAVE ANTHONY

——

By Ron Babcock

Original Interview: 2004

Updates: May 2020

One of Dave Anthony's best traits is that he is an alarmingly frank and honest performer. You can hear this on his popular podcast, *The Dollop*. On the show, Dave takes a little-known event in American History and reads about it to his co-host Gareth Reynolds—like how the creator of Kellogg's accidentally made corn flakes in his attempt to create a flavorless diet in order to suppress lustful thoughts (Episode 46). We experienced Dave's alarmingly frank honesty when we gave him a copy of our magazine. He said nice things, but then he also said that absolutely no one in the industry in LA would care about *Modest Proposal*. We were shocked and heartbroken. Later that night, we got very drunk and convinced ourselves that Dave didn't know what the fuck he was talking about.

Of course, Dave very much knew what the fuck he was talking about. When Ryan and I arrived in LA, we would lay the magazine on the desks of powerful people with a large "ahem," only to have it picked up and moved to the edge of the desk, just shy of falling off into the wastebasket. It took Ryan and me an embarrassingly long time to realize what Dave had already known—that show business is just that, a business.

But we have a plan that'll really show him what's what. We just published an anthology based on the print magazine he said the industry "wouldn't care about." There's no way the industry isn't going to care about re-packaged content from over fifteen years ago. And this is better than a magazine. It's a book. Everyone knows the heavier something is, the more important it is. Take that, Dave, and your super successful podcast!

RON BABCOCK: Do any comics openly admit to doing dumb comedy?

DAVE ANTHONY: There are people out there that'll admit to it. "Yeah, it's not my thing. I do whatever." But most guys think, "I'm the next Bill Hicks" and then they talk about tourists. Or they are angry at toast. Those guys are great. "I put bread in the toaster, and it's bread. And then it's not toast, it's hard bread. Fuck you, toast." Those guys are awesome. You've got to have that guy in Arizona who's just screaming about stuff that doesn't matter.

Denis Leary was the beginning of those guys. The first hack was trying to be like Seinfeld, the second hack was trying to be like Bill Hicks, and the third hack is trying to be like Dave Attell.

2020 UPDATE: After Attell it became C.K. Now I think they are trying to be Bill Burr. This is just a cycle that's not ever going to end. But there are really some amazing comics working today, like Stewart Lee, Rory Scovel, Kyle Kinane. I was clearly more focused on the negative then.

What's the fourth hack? People trying to be like Dave Anthony?

Well, there wouldn't be a lot of clubs because no one would want to go out on the road and they would get really lazy and stop caring. So yeah, that could happen.

It was definitely Louis C.K. I was not lazy as much as I was beaten down by the business. I never wanted to go on the road because I thought doing clubs was bad for your act. I still do. Jake Johannsen told me that early on and then I told that to Mitch Hedberg. Years later, Mitch told me it changed his career trajectory, but it was just knowledge passed down from comic to comic.

Is this the type of thing when you're a kid and you're really good at basketball and your dad wants you to play but you don't want to? Did your dad make you do stand-up?

My dad started making me do stand-up when I was three. A lot of poo jokes, today I mean. Back then, not so much. No, I always wanted to do it, and when I did, I really liked it, and then the business part of it pretty much killed my desire.

That was a really bad joke I tried to tell there. Cringe worthy. My father used to give me what he called "wit training." He would talk to me quickly and try to get me to respond fast with humor. Totally normal thing to do as a parent. Hard to believe he was an alcoholic.

What can I expect from being a comic?

You can expect some wonderful asshole club owners and managers, horrible bookers, people who have no talent succeeding amazingly while people with talent stand on the sidelines going, "I don't understand what's happening." All that stuff just gets to you after a while. When you get to LA you realize it's not really about being funny. It's just about if you're a commodity to them.

Ah, dark sad guy. You can also expect to have nights where you're so jazzed from killing that you can't sleep for a while, hanging out with comics making each other laugh until early morning, and the exhilarating feeling of coming up with a new bit that you know will kill. Comedy is an addiction for a reason.

Did you start on the tail end of the stand-up boom?

Exactly when the boom was ending was when I was starting.

Looking back, I think this was actually good for my stand-up development. It's really great to not be performing in front of huge audiences before you are ready. A lot of stand-ups in the '80s got big super-fast or were just pushed to headlining before they were ready and that makes your act worse.

Was that when alternative comedy started happening in San Francisco?

Alternative comedy is a strange term because comedy was so shitty that it was actually just people being themselves. A club I always performed at made you try to make the other comics laugh because there was not going to be any audience. You always had to have a brand-new set. So, it created this atmosphere with you really trying to be unique and yourself as opposed to other places where you might try to copy guys or conform to what the audience wanted. And then all those people moved to LA, and they started the LA alternative scene. Not me, I went to New York.

Shitty comedy is my term for stuff that has no meaning. I don't know why people do comedy if they don't want to say anything, but there are also plenty of audience members who aren't interested in hearing a point. They get to have comics too. Just not me.

Were you in the alternative comedy scene in New York?
I tried to shy away from it foolishly. I went to New York to be dirtier and cater to the audience and that messed up my act for a while. The reason I don't like stand-up is I've made some bad decisions over the years.

I had an open invitation to do alternative comedy in New York. I would do it occasionally, but I focused on the Comedy Cellar, The Comic Strip, and Caroline's. I was also intimidated by the alt scene in New York. The number of amazing alternative comics meant I felt I really had to bring my "A" game.

So now you make a living at writing screenplays?
Yeah. Writing screenplays is like what doing stand-up was when I was an open-micer. I was just doing it because it was what I liked and there were no people telling me what to do or how to do it. Unless you're a headliner, you can't make a living doing stand-up. You really can't. I'm sorry.

This is funny to read now. There are so many people telling you what to do when you are writing in Hollywood. I started booking a lot of commercials after this and did that for a while, which I really liked. Then I wrote for Maron and recently Deadly Class. But it's all people telling you what to do. Finally, I'm just doing podcasts, and no one has told me what to do in years. And I think podcasting is more rewarding than any of the other things. It's weird that's the thing that got me performing in theaters. (Though my experience on Maron was pretty amazing.)

You mentioned you have a half-hour of just shit jokes?
This really is quite an honor and something that all comedians should strive for. I was known as "the shit guy" in San Francisco. I can take a subject like George Bush for election and somehow turn it into a shit joke. That's called political comedy, guys.

I really did have a lot of shit jokes. I have zero problem with going low as long as you are also doing something interesting.

So, really, you can do thirty minutes of all shit jokes?
Nick Swardson probably comes close. He has a shocking number of diarrhea jokes.

Still true.

Ever do comedy in England?
Greg Proops is a friend of mine, and I keep asking him to take me to open up, but I think he's scared of my power. He's successful over there for the exact reason that he's not successful here. He does really smart comedy, and he doesn't low-brow it for the people here. In England, you get an audience for doing that and here people are kind of baffled, and they want you to be like Henry Cho.

Weird to read. Proops and I are no longer friends due to poli-
tics. Changing times in America. This has changed. It's easier
to find a smart audience due to the internet and podcasting,
etc. Since this, I did a one-man show at the Melbourne Inter-
national Comedy Festival, and I loved it. For a while I was
actually bigger in Australia than the US, which is largely due
to Aussie comedian Wil Anderson, who boosted me down there.
So, I guess he was the Proops I wanted. I think it's important
to help out and champion comics who are below you and you
enjoy. Patton Oswalt is great at doing that.

**Is there any reason audiences in America are less apt to
pick up smart humor?**

I think smart people are in this country. I think they have been
driven away from comedy. And I think they are coming back;
David Cross gets big audiences as well as Nick [Swardson] and
Zach [Galifianakis]. But years of watching Henry Cho and people
like that drove the smart people out of the clubs. So now you
have people coming in like, "I'm going to see comedy," and they
think it's going to be happy and stupid and fun. There's room
for everybody, but if you're smart, you don't want to see shows
that are dumb. And I need those people because I do shit jokes.

This has definitely changed. If a comic doesn't want to do clubs
anymore, they don't have to. You can book your own shows in
bars and rooms all over. I think that would have really changed
my trajectory, but I'm pretty happy with how things turned
out. Not the path I expected but all good.

How do you keep it real?

I don't know how to keep it real. I just get annoyed with
people all the time.

Right after this final question, Dave said, "That's it? It seemed like a boring interview. Did I not bring it?" Which goes to show that deep down, he still cares.

Yeah, I always cared. And I still get annoyed with people. Come to Twitter and say something to me, and there's a fifty percent chance I block you.

DO BANDS OR COMICS HAVE IT HARDER?

By Ron Babcock
Original Article: 2006

Updates by Ryan McKee and Mishka Shubaly: 2020

Both roads to music and comedy careers are littered with broken transmissions, bad whiskey, and belligerent crowds.

But which journey is harder?

We asked three comedians and three musicians about their experiences on the road and learned that both have sweated it out. At least when musicians sweat, it's sexy. When comics sweat, it's creepy.

As for who won the title of toughest path, we realized that when it comes to a "whose pile of shit is bigger" contest, there is no winner.

Editor's note: We reached out to everyone in this interview for updated comments, but we were only able to get responses from Mishka.

MUSICIANS

MISHKA SHUBALY

2006: Covered in tattoos and filled with whiskey, Mishka is a one-man music machine that sounds like his body needs a new transmission, but it still works. This singer/songwriter is a reliable vehicle for powerful ballads, entertaining banter, and good stories. Sounds like Johnny Cash getting punched in the face by Tom Waits.

2020: Mishka just celebrated eleven years of sobriety and has been incredibly prolific over that time. He's written six best-selling Kindle Singles, the memoir *I Swear I'll Make It Up to You* published by PublicAffairs, and the Audible Original *Cold Turkey: How to Quit Drinking by Not Drinking*. He continues touring internationally, performing music and more recently comedy. His album *Never Touring Again* went to #2 on the iTunes Comedy charts. When not on the road, he teaches at the Yale Writers' Conference.

SEAN BONNETTE & BENJAMIN ORA GALLATY FROM AJJ

In the years since we used to hang out with these guys around the downtown Phoenix scene, they've released seven albums, built a dedicated fanbase both nationally and internationally, and are cult heroes within the folk-punk genre. Their songs have millions of listens on Spotify, with hundreds of thousands of new listeners every month.

JOSH MALERMAN FROM THE HIGH STRUNG

The High Strung are still touring together and have released eight albums since this interview. Their song "The Luck You Got" appeared on the Showtime series *Shameless* and has over five million listens on Spotify. Josh Malerman is the true success story though. He's published eight novels, the most popular being *Bird Box*, which Netflix adapted into a film starring Sandra Bullock and became a breakout horror hit in 2018.

———————————

RON BABCOCK: When you are on the road, how much money do you budget for yourself in one day?
SEAN: I just close my eyes and hope for the best.

JOSH: $10 a day. No exceptions. That's the plan we've been on for some time now. Money is like Zeus to me, some incredible myth from a bygone era.

MISHKA: $10 a day for food, drinks and "'entertainment." I've spent as little as $4 a day while saving up to buy a porno mag. I've tipped bartenders in change, bought drinks for minors for money, stiffed bartenders completely (they usually take one look at me and understand) and eaten out of the trashcan (but it was in Miami and I saw naked boobs on the beach later, so it was worth it).

MISHKA: Wow, I'm so glad I'm $100k in debt from getting a master's degree in writing so that I could write "naked boobs." What a fucking caveman. But also, do you remember porno mags? Man, I miss porno mags.

Do you stay in a hotel room or your van?
MISHKA: When I'm out by myself, I stay in the van. In ten months of solo touring, I got a motel room once for $33. I still have those towels.

JOSH: We've played twelve hundred shows in the past four years and we've stayed in twenty-four hotels. We stay in so many parking lots that it's gotten to the point where we prefer this hotel's lot to that one. What the fuck is that?

MISHKA: The High Strung was the band that put the evil idea of living on the road into my head. Still, I recall feeling maligned when this article came out because The High Strung outdid me at every turn. Thank God Josh Malerman never went on to do anything great like write a horror novel that became a movie that became The Biggest Netflix Thing Ever.

Tell us your worst "I'm totally fucked" situation.

MISHKA: I was driving into LA from Las Vegas (summertime, no AC, wearing just my cut-offs, which felt like a big wet diaper) and the shocks on my van finally and conclusively bit the dust. It was like trying to pilot a boat. I had about two dollars in change and a full Subway card. I waited as long as I could to eat, 'til I was literally shaking, and then pulled off and found a Subway. This sullen girl made me the biggest, most beautiful, raunchiest roast beef sub heaped with jalapenos. When I handed her the card, she told me that they no longer accepted "Sub Club" cards. I could have wept. I went to McDonald's, ate two gray hockey puck burgers and got back on the road. I pulled into LA around seven. Fortunately, I found a garage that was still open maybe six blocks from the club. I dumped my van there, grabbed my guitar, my amp, and my bag and started hiking. It started raining. When I got to the club, the bartender didn't know anything about my $50 guarantee and said I only got two free drinks. I was playing with two punk bands and a goth band. When I got on stage, I said, "Ladies and gentlemen, if you like one single thing about the show tonight, please buy ten CDs. I am totally and utterly, no, wait," I dug the last of my change out of my pocket and threw it on the floor, "Now I am totally and utterly broke. Please help me." I drank for free all night, got fifty bucks from the bar, sold five CDs, and went home with a forty-four-year-old stripper. No lie.

MISHKA: Oof. In hindsight, this night was a low point that inspired me to make massive changes in my life, honestly to reinvent myself from the ground up, which is to say I no longer eat meat.

Most expensive part of your car (or van) that had to be fixed while out on the road.

JOSH: The transmission. We pulled into a gas station in Peru, Illinois, and heard this tremendous CRASH! And we came to see that the bottom had just fallen off the car. Seriously.

Sketchiest place you slept?

MISHKA: Sleeping in my van is pretty fucking sketchy. But I've stayed at people's houses where I've gotten up in the middle of the night and told that person, "Oh, I gotta grab my toothbrush from the van," and then just split.

SEAN: On the bed of the Snake River at the crack of dawn.

JOSH: Man, one time we played in Minneapolis at the 400 Bar, and it was the middle of winter. We had nowhere to sleep, and the bar owner (bless his heart) told me we couldn't sleep in the basement. The word "hotel" sounds as luxurious to us as "yacht" and about as monetarily feasible. The solo guy we opened for tells us that we can't sleep in the parking lot because we'll get towed. This is when I expected him to tell us we could just sleep at his house, which he sort of did. He said we could sleep in the "driveway" of his house safe from any tow truck. I'm not the sort to believe we deserve this or that, but it was eighteen below zero. We decide there's no fucking way this jackalope is going to stick to his guns. The drive to his house was forty-five minutes, and we pulled into his driveway. I already had my sleeping bag in hand ready to head inside. But he just didn't ask. He came to our window and bid us a happy goodnight. I wanted to pull his teeth out with piano string.

Sketchiest person you hooked up with?

JOSH: One time I made it with a girl who I later found out was called the "Rock 'n' Roll pin cushion." That scared the piss out of me.

MISHKA: One night in Denver I hooked up with a girl who took me to a sex shop to buy condoms and then totally ditched me there. I'd been drinking the way I normally drink, but at high altitude and was like "stumbling around in traffic" drunk. Then this girl re-appeared... with two big yellow rocks of crack. We smoked it out of a tin can and then tried to have sex. I drink enough that I don't really need a drug that makes me not able to fuck, you know? To be fair, she was kind of a sweet girl and bought me a lot of drinks and breakfast the next morning, to say nothing of the crack. And lest any women out there feel I'm maligning them, I'm going to come out and say that out of 99.44 percent of the girls I've met on the road, I was the sketchier one.

MISHKA: Hey, What's-Your-Name, I miss you. Please call me, baby, let's work things out.

Biggest "I shouldn't buy this, but I'm going to anyway" splurge?

SEAN: Three words: Amoeba Fucking Records.

BEN: I bought a Japanese telecaster in Portland, and I think that I'm still paying off my credit card.

JOSH: I bought *Dracula*, a book that I already have five versions of at home, just because the cover was so cool on this one. I blew sixty percent of my earnings ($10 of course) and wasn't able to eat that night. Something about that is ridiculous. A lot about that is ridiculous.

Worst crowd response?
SEAN: The Knitting Factory in LA. The only member of the audience left when she found out it wasn't comedy night.

BEN: Kimberly, Idaho. We had a crowd of forty-year-old cowboys in our pocket until they saw our incredibly satanic T-shirts. They turned on us real quick.

JOSH: San Diego. I didn't realize that the place was only frequented by sixty-year-olds. I plugged in and played one stinking note, not even a full chord, and an old man at the bar hollered, "Turn it down!"

How many times the thought, "Why am I doing this?" comes into your head while on the road?
SEAN: Cartoonists create their own pornography.

JOSH: Absolutely never. A militant optimism is necessary to survive five years straight on the road. I assume I'd just have to remember my last job if I needed to answer that question.

MISHKA: How many angels can fit on the head of a pin? Dick.

MISHKA: *What's funny is that in 2006, I thought I was at the end of suffering on the road, haaaaaaaaa.*

COMICS

JOE KLOCEK

Joe continues to be a staple in the San Francisco comedy scene. Ron and I first saw him perform at the end of Punch Line Comedy Club's Sunday night showcase. After a marathon on young comics, Joe destroyed the previously comatose audience with his energy and crowd work. We were in awe. Joe let me open for him a few times on the road, for which I am eternally grateful to him because every night he had to dig his way out of the hole my twenty-minute set had left onstage.

EDDIE GOSSLING

Before we ever saw Eddie perform, we knew his legendary road status. Other comics would tell us how Eddie worked the road so much that he lived in his car for years. Since this interview, Eddie seems to have settled down with his wife (comedian Megan Mooney) and children in Los Angeles and worked for years as a writer/producer for *Tosh.o*.

NICK GRIFFIN

Nick has been working as a stand-up comic for over thirty years and seems to have no intention of slowing down. He's a staple at the world's most prestigious comedy club, New York's Comedy Cellar, where he recorded his 2019 special *Nick Griffin: Cheer Up* for Amazon Originals. Nick appears often on late night TV, including eleven performances on *Late Night with David Letterman* and multiple times on *Conan* and *The Late Late Show*. If he's not performing at a comedy club near you soon, just wait, he will.

When you are on the road, how much money do you budget for yourself in one day?

JOE: Budget? I practice denial.

EDDIE: Budget is a funny term to use as I usually spend what I have, then ask for an advance, then borrow a little and then steal.

NICK: After eighteen years on the road, I don't have to budget myself. It just happens automatically. Something in my head just clicks. *"You can't afford that, you pathetic fuck!"*

Do you stay in a hotel room or your automobile?

JOE: In the early days of one-nighters, I really did park at rest stops and sleep in the car. Nothing was more depressing than climbing in the back seat with a tattered old blanket that I knew would not keep me warm enough through the night. I would turn the engine on every few hours to warm up and then turn it off because I was worried about running out of gas.

EDDIE: For a while, when people got into the passenger seat of my Taurus I would have to say, "Sorry my kitchen is a mess."

NICK: Usually a hotel room or an apartment that has cable television and a coffeemaker and not much else except the sexual remains of every comic that has ever slept there.

Tell us your worst "I'm totally fucked" situation.

EDDIE: I was six months into comedy and opening for Gregory Hines in San Antonio. I watched the crowd arrive in tuxedos and knew this was not my crowd. They weren't and I am still to this day banned from performing at Trinity University.

NICK: I once drove from Minneapolis to Ocean City, Maryland, stopping only for gas. Only to arrive at the club and find out it had closed permanently two nights previous. No one called me.

Most expensive part of your car that had to be fixed while out on the road?

JOE: My sister's husband gave me a piece of shit old Chevy van. The winters had rusted it out, and it had blacked out windows in back. It couldn't have looked more like a stalker mobile if I had monkey bars on the roof instead of a luggage rack. The transmission gave out somewhere in Washington. There was no way I could fix it, so I made the choice to "baby it." At a gas station I put in the high-octane fuel and changed the oil. That was the best I could do. I forgot to lock the hood down so when I got up to speed on the highway, the hood flew up and cracked the wind- shield. It didn't break, but it now had this concentric circle of spider web-like cracks in the center of the windshield. I could see it heaving in the head wind. I stuffed a blanket that happened to be bright pink, another gift from the sister, between the dashboard and the windshield and really babied it. At a stop light in Yakima, Washington, I started to pull away and second gear was not there anymore. When I parked that van at the Red Lion, where I was opening for some hack asshole, I knew that van was not coming with me.

Sketchiest place you slept?

JOE: Take your pick of the bartenders who always would say, "Dude, you can crash at my place. You just have to know…"

EDDIE: Condo @ Zanies in Nashville. It was Halloween, I carved a pumpkin, a crackhead stole the candle.

Sketchiest person you hooked up with?
JOE: I have loved a lot of cocktail waitresses in my time.

EDDIE: Hands down, managers and agents.

Biggest "I shouldn't buy this, but I'm going to anyway" splurge?
JOE: POT! Being out in Montana, not having enough for gas to the next gig and a guy after a show saying, "I know where we can score." Dumb.

NICK: Something illegal, white, and powdery. And no, it wasn't Gold Bond.

Worst crowd response?
JOE: Getting my ass kicked by skinheads in Idaho.

EDDIE: Little Rock, Arkansas. Did forty-five minutes to silence. Got off stage and the waitress said to me, "How does defeat feel?" I said, "Not sure, I'm in Little Rock."

NICK: All my bad shows morph into one and haunt me on a weekly basis, but who cares? I have no boss and the coffee is free.

How many times the thought, "Why am I doing this?" comes into your head while on the road?
JOE: Almost always. It's like a mantra. Checking into the shitty hotel. Seeing the "stage" for the first time. Hearing "what works" from the bartenders. Seeing that sadly demonstrated by the opening acts. Getting the tiny paycheck where I am seeing almost no profit.

NICK: Less often than ten years ago but at least a couple times a week. But I've been consumed with doubt my whole life. I'd have second thoughts giving CPR to baby Jesus. It comes with the territory.

MACHU PICCHU & CHARLYNE YI

———

By Amy Seimetz, Charlyne Yi & Miki Ann Maddox
Art by Miki Ann Maddox
Original Piece: 2006

Update: May 2020

The sky is overcast and the sound of bells from the tamale man accompanies the noise of cars passing Machu Picchu's palace in Los Angeles. Machu (Amy Seimetz) combs her hair with an ivory-tooth comb as she tells Picchu (Miki Ann Maddox) how to kill an African elephant. Picchu eats spoonsful of vanilla icing as she listens. SUDDENLY, Paul Revere rides through the Machu Picchu Palace and yells "Charlyne Yi is coming! Charlyne Yi is coming!" and then he and his horse leap into the refrigerator portal disappearing to another historic event.

Machu and Picchu run to the window and see Charlyne Yi shoot out of the Hollywood sign, running through the air, leaving a trail of rainbow. She puffs away at ten cigarettes. Her smoke is like clouds from a coal engine train. Though her mouth is full of tobacco products, she is not prevented from chanting "Chugga, chugga, chugga, next stop Machu Picchu Choo Choo Palace." When she lands, she spits her cigarettes out and they all perfectly land in an ashtray. Then the interview begins...

MACHU: What's important to you?

CHARLYNE: Cash, money, and dollar signs.

MACHU: What's the difference?

CHARLYNE: (punches the wall) What difference does it make? Cash is this... (she slaps both Machu and Picchu with one swift move of her buff arm).

MACHU: Ow!

CHARLYNE: Shut up! This is my interview. Hey! Stop staring at my bulging veins! (She flexes and her veins spell out "STOP STARING." One vein pops and squirts blood in Picchu's left eye.) Better get a test, babe. I think I'm posi...

(Picchu grows fangs.)

CHARLYNE: POSITIVELY A VAMPIRE!

MACHU: Generally, vampires are very old. How old are you?

CHARLYNE: Raaaaaaaaaah!

(Machu is writing down Charlyne's answers in a notepad. Charlyne stands up over Machu's notepad. Charlyne then pees through her jeans onto the notepad, causing all the ink to run.)

CHARLYNE: Take that!

MACHU: Oh, uh, I didn't need that anyway.

(Machu tosses the pee-soaked notebook to the floor and begins writing the interview on her leg. She is not wearing pants.)

MACHU: What's our next question?

CHARLYNE: Ask me how much money I make.

MACHU: How much money do –

CHARLYNE: 1 2 3 4 5 6 7 8 9 10 11 12 13 billion dollas! Cha-ching cha-ching!

PICCHU: My blood feels warm.

(Picchu's eyes have turned red, and she is now floating in the corner of the room. Her fangs are really sharp now.)

CHARLYNE: Cha-ching cha-ching...

PICCHU: Let's get to the guts... (She says this in a British accent and is starting to look a little like Brad Pitt from *Interview with the Vampire*.)

MACHU: When did you start doing comedy?

CHARLYNE: I used to perform when I was little for school in little things. And for my parents and my little sister and her friends. Oh yeah and in my head. And to my mirror and walls too. In kindergarten during recess, I was shy, and so I would stand by this tree and spit at it and sing and talk to it in weird voices, not because I hated the tree but because we were friends. And two girls would watch me, and they became my friends, and soon they spat at the tree too. And I would make them laugh with my friend, my hand Jimmy, he tells the greatest jokes...

Oh! But um... My first open mic was October 14, 2004. I remember the date. It was at the brewery near my house [Fontana, California]. That's where I met Dan Bialek [comedian]. He was like (in a gruff man voice) "You gotta go to LA. There's these guys with glasses and mustaches, and you'd fit right in." Probably because I have glasses and a moustache. Oh yeah, Dan Bialek was talking about the Pretty Okay Ho-Hum Spectacular on Ice guys [Josh Fadem, Pat Healy, Chad Fogland, Danforth France].

MACHU: Do you have big goals?

CHARLYNE: HUMONGOUS GIGANTIC ONES! I also want to get really buff, you know cause I'm probably gonna look like Elijah Wood when I grow up, weird looking with a big head, and no one is going to want to use me anymore. So, I am going to get big muscles to even out my big head, and I'm going to be buff, and it's going to be awesome. Yeah, I have my whole thing planned out.

MACHU: You graduated from high school not that long ago, right?

CHARLYNE: Hell yeah, the summer 2004! And then I went to college for two quarters, but I couldn't afford it. But I snuck into the theater class for about three more months.

MACHU: Your teacher asked you to keep coming. I think you told me this before.

CHARLYNE: Why don't you shut your face and listen okay? Alright. Well… sneaking into that class was really cool. I felt like, I felt like I was in a movie, and I totally felt like a badass too. I used to be all nervous, and all these theatre people confident and scary, and then I was like, "I don't care what they think anymore, I'm a badass now." Yeah… breaking the rules just came naturally to me. Erik Charles Nielsen [comedian] argued with me once and told me what I do isn't stand-up and it's very close to sketch. I don't think it's sketch at all. I mean I've done sketches before, but what I usually do, I would not call sketch.

MACHU: Yeah that's like us. We don't know what to call our stuff, so I call them creations.

CHARLYNE: Yeah, I call them doo-dahs.

PICCHU: So, you got second place in the Kaufman awards in New York recently?

CHARLYNE: I really loved New York. Yeah, the first night of the show, I felt like I did really bad. No one was laughing. I mean not laughing isn't bad; the thing that bothered me was that there was no reaction at all. It felt like they weren't even listening. Dead silent. The night of the finals was amazing. The audience laughed a lot, and they were scared. Cause I did this thing where I was just staring and my nostrils were flaring and I looked at this woman in the audience and she whispered, "Oh, she's so scary." I was like "Yes! HAW HAW HAW!" I met Andy Kaufman's brother and he was shaking everyone's hand when they were getting off the stage and then when I got off he hugged me and went (she breathes in deeply with her eyes closed), and I thought he was going to cry and he said "Andy would have been proud." I felt like I was going to cry too.

MACHU: In your performances, you make the audience play like kids. Especially when you bring them on stage and make them do this dance or hold hands or once you made every single audience member come up to the stage and say their name in the mic so you could thank them... Charlyne: Oh yeah, I did that at *Garage Comedy*. I was so happy when it worked. It felt like Christmas time in my stomach. When I do something that doesn't work, I get kind of sad, but I mean, when I first started out people would be like "Arghh! What are you doing? Fake magic? You don't belong here. That's not stand-up!" But I would still do it. My friend said he tests things out at three different places, and if it doesn't work, he'll never do it again. I told him, "No! That's dumb. I've bombed for a whole month straight, but I kept doing it."

MACHU: Yeah, we continuously get people saying, "You guys are weird."

CHARLYNE: Yeah, me too. And I'm like, "This is just how I am."

MACHU: Me too. They've said it to me my whole life, but I still think "Really? I really don't think I am that strange."

CHARLYNE: This woman came up to me after a show and was like, "That was really weird... I mean I like weird but that was really weird." (She laughs) Once after a show some lady came up to me and was crying and was so happy and she said, "Oh my god you just made my day. I had a really shitty day, and it made everything so much better seeing you perform." And that made me happy because I felt like I made a difference. I don't know... for me, I have to perform... this might sound dumb... but I feel like a superhero when I perform. I feel like that if I can capture their attention and affect somebody's life in the slightest way, even just for that moment, that's an amazing thing.

I was talking to my comedian friend the other day, and it was telling me it felt like it was ready to give up and quit comedy forever. I told it how at one point in life, I really thought about giving up too, and I told it the same thing my acting professor told me, "It doesn't matter if you don't perform again because no one cares. And that's the truth. No one cares. You have to make them care. YOU have to care..." And he's right; god dammit he's right. If you don't care enough to perform, how could anyone else if you don't let them see what you see?

Machu Picchu is crying now. Picchu curls into a ball on the ceiling and covers her head with the vampire bat wings she's grown. Machu's tears drip onto her leg, smearing the notes she wrote on the skin of her thigh during the interview.

"I gotta take a minute," Charlyne says taking a deep breath and pointing her finger toward the bathroom. "I'm gonna go powder my nose."

Machu and Picchu sniffle. Then they hear pee trickling into the toilet, then the faucet turning on, then the shower, then the bath—when Charlyne comes out of the bathroom, she sees the entire Machu Picchu Palace is flooded. Machu and Picchu are on a large pirate ship, looking at Charlyne through a telescope.

They throw a life-sized cherry flavored lifesaver attached to a rope down to Charlyne, and she grabs hold. They pull her aboard. Picchu is foaming at the mouth and has completed her transformation into a vampire bat.

Picchu exclaims, "It smells like virgin up in here!" Then Charlyne Yi and Picchu both bite Machu. Machu turns into a yellow butterfly and perches herself on vampire bat Picchu's back. Charlyne Yi's hair falls out, and then she turns into Jean Luc Piccard and says, "Warts speed ahead!" The ship turns into a spaceship. It slowly moves toward space. Then the spaceship turns into a chocolate chip. Then the chocolate chip turns into pure love and spreads to all you readers.

Charlyne loves money ice cream money
ice cream money ice cream money
ice cream money ice cream money cream
ice money cream ice money cream ice
money ice cream money ice cream money ice cream money

2020 UPDATE FROM PICCHU

Picchu continued to live in bat form and is currently developing a Netflix special where she only makes coronavirus bat soup jokes for one hour and thirty-seven minutes.

Machu gradually turned into an Easter Island statue over time. She is floating somewhere in the Baltic Sea.

Charlyne got all seven Infinity Stones after punching Thanos in the armpit and is now contemplating obliterating all of humanity because you know... Trump...

(A Huntington Beach protest comes crashing through the wall and takes away this keyboard before I can finish typi...)

INTERVIEWS

DAVE CHAPPELLE

——

By Ryan McKee
Original Interview: November 2000

"Nothing with pork in it. It'd be some kind of stir-fry vegetables. Because it's got everything you need in it."

That's what Dave Chappelle answered when I asked him the final question of my big interview: "If your stand-up comedy act were a food, what would it be?"

What a dumb question. Why did I think that's something I should even say out loud? Still, Dave was kind enough to give me an answer instead of roasting me for it. In fact, his answer would've been longer if his cellphone hadn't died right then.

The following Q&A is the only piece in this book that we didn't originally publish in *Modest Proposal*. I conducted it while a staff writer at Arizona State University's weekly entertainment publication *State Press Magazine*. During this time, my editor Kevin Polowy would occasionally allow me to interview stand-up comedians and thus, the first seeds of starting a comedy magazine were planted in my brain.

I'm including the article because I tried to interview Dave again for every issue of *Modest Proposal* but never could make it happen. I wanted the chance to improve on my first attempt. However, not until June 2020 did I realize how much better I could've done with my first conversation.

I spoke with Dave four months after *Dave Chappelle: Killin' Them Softly* premiered. In the stand-up special, he speaks at length on police brutality and how white people do not comprehend how truly fearful the Black community is about even interacting with police.

Fast forward nearly twenty years. Comedy and the world are much changed. And yet in Dave's *8:46* special, following the death of George Floyd, his message is unchanged. He continues to deal with police brutality suffered by the Black community. At one point, Dave addresses Don Lemon's criticism of celebrities not speaking out sooner about George Floyd. He yells, "Has anyone ever listened to me do comedy?"

That line hit me the hardest.

The spirit of this anthology is to reflect on how comedy has evolved. I want this book to be a reminder of how much has changed and must continue to change. Watching *8:46* makes me hopeful that comedy can help inspire better change in the world.

"Has anyone ever listened to me do comedy?"

In 2000, I hadn't really *listened* to Dave Chappelle do comedy. Yes, I had repeatedly watched *Killin' Them Softly*. A friend had recorded it for me on VHS tape, since I didn't have HBO... or cable for that matter. Still, it didn't even occur to me that my interview with him might be an opportunity to ask Dave some honest questions about police brutality in an attempt to better educate myself and our readers.

Instead I opted to ask him questions about *Half Baked*, if he was popular in high school, why the movie *Screwed* bombed, and weed. I didn't avoid police brutality because it made me uncomfortable. It didn't even register in my twenty-one-year-old white guy brain as something with more weight or immediacy than Dave's jokes about weed. *Because I wasn't listening.*

Today, less than a month since Dave's *8:46* dropped on YouTube, it has thirty million views. It's infuriating that Dave has been unable to change his message. But that doesn't stop him from delivering it and delivering it and continuing to deliver it.

Perhaps the world is finally ready to *listen* in a way we weren't in 2000. I wasn't ready to understand his message back then.

And Dave, while I don't know what food I'd be, I'm certainly eating crow now.

———————

RYAN MCKEE: I read the idea for *Half Baked* came from a joke you were doing in your act?

DAVE CHAPPELLE: It started out as just a one-liner. There are actually delivery services like that—so I've heard (he laughs). I thought that these guys must see a lot of different people. It's a good way to look at the subculture of reefer. Then I saw *Trainspotting* and it was so dark. So, I said that if you applied that same principle to weed, it would be a comedy. That's how it came to be. It's one of those things that just happened.

Does everyone ask you to smoke weed with them?

Ever since *Half Baked* came out, someone has asked me that every day. Even now, it happens to me once a week.

You started doing stand-up comedy in high school. Is that right?

Yeah. I started going to comedy clubs when I was fourteen years old, after school, with my mom. And I never stopped.

Who are your main influences?

When I first started, Eddie Murphy was a big influence. *Raw* had just come out. Then in my later years, I got into Richard Pryor. I didn't get how funny he was until I was older. His jokes have a lot of depth. I was too little to get the full scope of it. I also like Woody Allen a lot. He's pretty nice with the stories.

If you had a choice between being the greatest comedian or the greatest actor, which would you choose?

If I could be the greatest at anything, and those were my only two choices, I'd much rather be a better comedian. I'd rather be Chris Rock than like Matt Damon. Comedy is the reason I'm here talking to you now. That was my start and I'll always do stand-up.

What do you think made you first stand out from other stand-up comics?

I think I got a lot of attention because I was a really young guy, and I was incredibly proficient at comedy. People always assumed I was older. Even now, people think I'm in my thirties because they've seen me around for so long. Also, I was pretty driven in my younger years.

You went to a high school for the fine arts and studied theatre. Do you hear your old teachers, and are they worried about the weed material you do?

Actually, I just got an alumni-achievement award from my school. The ins and outs of my work, they might have some disagreement with, but I think they're proud of me because while I was in school all I used to say is, "I wanna be a comedian." They saw me go to comedy clubs every day after school. So, when it paid off, they were happy for me.

What were you more like—a popular kid or a class clown in high school?

Ya, I guess I was popular. Not like Fonzie-popular, but I dated my fair share of girls. I definitely wasn't like the class clown. I'd sleep in class a lot because I'd be at clubs all night. So, I'd catch up on my sleep in class. I had a real "fuck it" attitude about school. I missed yearbook picture day my senior year. No class ring, no yearbook. I didn't want any of that.

I loved your movie *Screwed* with Norm Macdonald and Danny DeVito, but what happened with it?

It kind of tanked, man. Nobody really did press for it. None of the stars did press for it. The studio had held on to it for a long time. It was just one of those movies that had all the right combinations on paper and had all great people working on it, but it was just one of those things that in the end didn't mix well. But I got to know Norm Macdonald and to this day I maintain that he is one of the most hilarious people I have ever met. That guy is really fucking funny.

If your comedy was a food, what would it be?
Nothing with pork in it. It'd be some kind of stir-fry vegetables. Because it's got everything you need in it.

ZACH GALIFIANAKIS

By Ryan McKee

Original Interview: April 2003

Six years before *The Hangover* turned Zach Galifianakis into a comedy A-lister, the student activities board booked him to perform at ASU and then forgot to promote the show. Ron and I showed up to find around one hundred of Gammage Auditorium's three thousand seats filled. Zach, seemingly unfazed by the dreadful turnout, walked onstage and began playing a grand piano. I overheard a girl nearby say to her friend, "I thought this guy is a comedian." Then Zach spoke into the microphone for the first time.

"I was at TCBY the other day, and you might not know this, but TCBY stands for 'This Can't Be Yogurt.' So, I've always wanted to open a TCBY… and serve soup. So, when people come up to me at the counter and go, 'This can't be yogurt.' I'll say, 'I know. It's soup.'"

When Zach's publicist had confirmed our interview for *Modest Proposal*, I'd been advised to expect no more than thirty minutes with him after the show. But when Ron and I met him backstage, Zach asked if we could take him to a nearby bar for the interview. As we walked over to our neighborhood spot, Casey Moore's, he called Dave Attell and left the message, "No, that's not my joke, I don't know whose it is. Go ahead and use it. Call me back, asshole, I've got something to ask you." He slipped his phone back into his pocket, and I handed him a recent issue of our magazine. Right away, Zach spotted Todd Barry's name on the cover and started telling us a story. "Todd and I just did a club together. After the show, I got high and just watched Todd try to sell his CDs to people. I couldn't stop cracking up because Todd was so awkward about it."

Before the interview even started, it was my favorite interview. We'd been with him for less than five minutes and were already getting a look behind the curtain of our comedy heroes.

At the bar, Zach ordered a pint of Sierra Nevada and a vodka cranberry—at the same time—and then insisted on paying for our drinks, claiming the expense was no problem because he's "from a rich family." When Ron and I hesitated, he raised his voice and proclaimed, "Come on! Do it for America." We ordered drinks... for America.

Zach spoke to us for over an hour, insisting we order more drinks on his tab every time the waitress walked by. After paying the tab, he asked what we were doing next. Not expecting he'd want to go, we said that we'd probably head over to a keg party that ASU's student sketch comedy group, Farce

Side, was throwing. Zach let out an enthusiastic, "Let's go!" So, we did.

Ron and I received a hero's welcome for bringing Zach with us. My strongest memory of the night is Zach telling everyone that he had never smoked pot before. Then, he patiently listened as a gaggle of college students walked him step-by-step through how to use a bong. Finally, after what felt like fifteen minutes, he cautiously put the bong to his lips and ripped the longest hit I've ever seen. The party erupted into cheers. My memory is hazy after that, but when it was time for us to jump in a cab to go home, Zach opted to stay and keep partying.

I always mailed copies of the magazine to everyone we featured in interviews. Occasionally, I'd get a thank-you email in response, but usually heard nothing. Zach was the only person to ever mail back a hand-written note. At the time, he was in Vancouver shooting the short-lived supernatural crime series starring Eliza Dushku and Jason Priestley, *Tru Calling*, where he played a wise-cracking mortician.

It meant a lot to Ron and me, even though Zach thought Ron's name was "Rob." I still have the note to this day.

Ryan + Rob—

Thanks for sending me a copy of Modest Proposal — I quite enjoyed it.

I am currently in Vancouver vomitting out my lines. It is splendid here. I only work two days a week and spend the rest of my time looking for my wallet. There is a thing here called "pot" — I am thinking about trying it.

I trust all is well in Arizona. Good luck with the magazine. Thanks Again.

Sincerely,
Zach Galifianakis
professional something

RYAN MCKEE: Are you an alternative comedian?

ZACH GALIFIANAKIS: I don't understand that term. I mean, I do those rooms that are called alternative comedy. In the '80s, a formula started happening with the airline jokes, just a person with a microphone, doing very conventional material. But everything before that was alternative comedy. Like when Albert Brooks used to go on Johnny Carson and literally read the phone book. Or Steve Martin would do those great bits. I guess I am. I really don't know. I'm alternative (he says with raised eyebrows). I lead an alternative lifestyle. (he laughs)

Brian McKim of *Shecky Magazine* said that alternative comedians are the whiniest of comedians. True?
Well, I think a lot of alternative comics tend to complain about the industry a lot, but I don't think they're whiny. A lot of comics are whiny. I don't understand the point that he's trying to make. But, I guess, a lot of people in the alternative comedy world are snobs, with good reason. But comedy is like music. It appeals to some people. Some people like Creed. Those people are usually pretty stupid. But they probably also like Carrot Top. I would say that they're part of the same ilk.

You ripped on Creed a lot during your talk show [*Late World with Zach*]. Did you get any Creed hate mail?
I never got any Creed hate mail. We could do anything we wanted; nobody saw my show. And when I realized that, that's when I thought the show was getting good—when we started to just mock the whole Hollywood thing and the whole talk show thing. But nobody ever complained. Nobody watched it. My parents watched it. My mom complained a couple times.

You did a bit where you stood in line for your own show and nobody recognized you. Did that hurt your ego?
No, I wanted to play on that because nobody was watching VH1, and the people who were watching it were not the type of people I was trying to appeal to. So, with those two factors going against me, I wanted to make fun of the fact that nobody knows me.

You pissed off Lisa Loeb with an Asian joke on your show.
I was not purposely trying to be abrasive to anyone. I'm just not like that. I thought she would think it was funny. But she didn't. And she told me, "That's not funny." And I said to her,

"I know." I agreed with her and she didn't know what to do with that. But, anyway, Lisa Loeb.

What talk show hosts do you like?

I think Letterman is great. But, you see, I wanted the show to be like Charlie Rose. His show is just a black background, no audience, one on one. I begged them not to have an audience for my show. But they wanted to make it MTV-ish and all that crap. We started to do a few things differently, like we only had one person in the audience. We acted as if nobody wanted to see the show. But we still had this huge laugh track, over one person in the audience. That to me was my favorite. That was the only time I ever watched the show. We had a huge laugh track, a car horn, and just a six-year old girl laughing. We creeped people out. And the greatest thing, the band that showed up to do the show, I can't remember who it was, we told them there was no studio audience, just one person. And they were like, "We're not playing." We talked them into playing anyway, and it was just one guy staring at them. It was great.

I grabbed this quote off the internet: "The saddest thing about _Last Call_ and _Late World_ isn't Daly's and Galifianakis' studied indifference. It's the way these shows underestimate their audience. They think that if they offer a bunch of cool stuff it'll divert your attention away from the hosts, who look like they would rather be skateboarding."

That was from some Baltimore alternative paper [_Baltimore City Paper_] and was published after my first week. I called the guy who wrote that and begged him to come on the show and read his review. And he wouldn't do it. Even though we were going to fly him from Baltimore, he still wouldn't do it. So, I faked crying on the phone and told him I was going to shoot myself on the show that night, and I wanted him to watch it. (Zach has now pulled out a disposable paper cup, the kind dispensed at water coolers, and filled it up with Sierra Nevada Pale Ale) I'd like to make use of this.

I heard that if there's not a piano on stage, you use a cowbell.
Yeah, I did a show where instead of the piano, I banged the cowbell. But not for forty-five minutes.

(The waitress comes, and Zach insists that we order more drinks on his tab because he comes from a rich family. The waitress asks for the name on the card, and Zach acts like he forgets. He finally tells her and then picks up the recorder and says, "It's an American Express gold card," and smiles. "Put it all on the card, let's do it for America.")

If you had to have a soundtrack to your life, what song would be playing right now?
Right now, specifically, probably "Funky Cold Medina" or "Proud to Be an American."

I recently started growing facial hair and your beard is something I can aspire to.
You trim your beard. Don't you? Don't. Just let it go. What's great is when it gets big, nobody fucks with you. Homeless people don't ask you for change because they think you're crazy. It's one of the greatest defenses you can have. I was working in London, and facial hair there is just not that common. It just isn't. And my beard was down to here (he motions to his chest, right above his nipple line). Three different times, people tried to fight me, just because of my beard. I'm not kidding. One night, I'm in a bar by myself, and I'm writing. And these people are talking about

me, and I can hear them. And one of the girls says, "Leprechaun" because I'm short with a beard, and I was drinking by myself.

If alternative comics are always alternative to the mainstream, does that make it conformed anti-conformity?
That's a really hard question. When you're typing this up just make me go, "Uh, good question." Semi-colon.

Is there any movie you did that you would take back?
Corky Romano. Not because of the movie, but it was so embarrassing shooting it. Adam Sandler's producer was producing it. During my scene, he goes, "Cut." And says to me, "How many push-ups can you do?" I said, "I don't know, fifty." I was lying. And I swear to god, he goes, "Give me fifty push-ups. I need your energy up." I said that I try to do things subtly. He repeated himself and I said, "No, I'm not going to do that." And he said, "Well, then, what can you do to get your energy up?" So, I told him I'd go away and get my energy up. So, I hid on another set of a David Arquette movie that they were shooting next to *Corky Romano.* He and the director found me hiding. At that point, I was like, "I don't care if I ever work again. It's not worth this, being told to do fifty push-ups in front of the crew and everything. It's embarrassing. I'll go perform in coffee houses the rest of my life." So, he says, "Let's run in place." And he and the director start running in place. I didn't run in place. Then, he and the director start doing jumping jacks. I didn't know what to do, so I started. Three guys doing jumping jacks, and I'm doing them disdainfully. Have you ever tried doing jumping jacks angry? It's very hard.

How do you keep it real?
There's some irony there, right? I keep it real by, uh, you know whatever, talk to the hand. Been there, done that.

MARC MARON

By Ryan McKee
Art by Anna Hollingsworth
Original Interview: September 2005

Break-up songs are a genre unto themselves: tunes that compel you to listen over and over again after getting dumped. The best heartbreak earworms make you cry but also comfort you. A musician has somehow already recorded *exactly what you're feeling.* It's not just in your head. That's why you *have* to play the song on repeat until your roommates threaten to throw you out.

Great stand-up comedy accomplishes similar things. It makes you laugh and connects you to others. A comedian has somehow already written a joke about a thought or feeling you've never quite been able to express. It's not just in your head. Suddenly a whole room is laughing along with you, at a thing you hadn't realized others experience as well.

But you never hear about a stand-up comedy album acting as a break-up song. Once you know a joke, you don't listen to it over and over again like you do a catchy or cathartic song. Yet, that's exactly what happened to me with Marc Maron's first album, *Not Sold Out*, during my first major breakup.

I felt compelled to listen to the CD every day. Marc's material didn't grow old. It helped me realize my problems are neither unique nor insurmountable. It sounds like I'm describing a self-help book, but it's the opposite. Just like a break-up song doesn't explain the steps to fix your broken heart, Marc talked honestly about being a mess and found the humor in his total inability to fix his shit.

In Marc's act, I recognized my own problems that had led to my breakup: anxiety, depression, delusions of grandeur, substance abuse, a strong desire to be optimistic but consistently falling short.

His now-seminal podcast *WTF with Marc Maron* would later make him a household name... at least among households who regularly donate to public radio. He would sell out theaters, publish a national bestseller, and star in his own sitcom. In ten years, Maron would sit down in his garage to interview then-sitting President Barack Obama. But on this day in 2005, I was interviewing Marc Maron, and Marc Maron was still *my* guy.

———————

"Was that a good interview? It might not be as funny as you need, but I'm a fairly serious guy."

And with that, my long-awaited phone interview with Marc Maron had come to an end.

Early on in the life of this magazine, I got in the habit of ending my interviews with the question, "How do you keep it real?" I never thought much about it, just something I did because I thought it was funny.

Some take the question seriously, some make jokes, some laugh it off, and a few have even expressed hostility. I'm always interested how someone is going to react, but never as much as I was with Maron. Maybe it was because I respect him so much, or maybe because he seems an outsider in a world that harbors outsiders—the comedy world.

Before beginning as a comic in the late '80s, Maron was an "art department geek," experimenting with photography, silk-screening, poetry, and guitar. Coming from that background, he brings a sense of artistry to stand-up, a form too often wrought with cheap jokes.

"I always respected stand-up comics, so I never really thought about why I choose to do it," he said. "It was the perfect expression for me. I figured it would be a way to say whatever I wanted and solve some problems. I never deliberately looked at it as a business and designed my act. Then I would have come up with a more popular persona. Well, I'm still alive and marginally popular, I guess."

As times have changed from the years of the first George Bush and then become the same again with George W. Bush, so has Maron's material. On his last *Letterman* appearance, Maron commented on the difference between an American soldier serving in Iraq and a soldier who served in Vietnam. In the early '90s, he used the same joke on *An Evening at the Improv* to describe the first Gulf War. Over ten years apart, both audiences responded boisterously.

Is Maron just using the war as an excuse to dig up and Frankenstein dead jokes? No, he's showing us that with all our innovations, technology, and perceived social progress, we're actually right back where we were fifteen years ago.

"I've been through so many different voices over my career," he said. "As far as just being pure funny, I feel like I've never been as good as I am now. As far as my message, well, it's always been my intention to aggravate audiences—put it up their fucking asses until they begrudgingly like me. A lot of things I've been trying to say for years, though, are coming out now. I don't have to worry about trying to make the other side feel comfortable. At this level, I can deliver more to more people."

His audience has grown steadily over the years and while he used to joke that he personally knows all of his fans, a hosting position on Air America's *Morning Sedition* has enlarged his fanbase faster than Maron can shake hands or reply to emails.

"I don't know who's listening," he admitted. "I did the new Laugh Factory here in New York to good crowds, and I imagine a lot of them are Air America listeners. I'm not a preachy person. I don't pander to the audience. Now that I'm on the radio, people expect a certain thing. One night I did a filthy set where I just laid out all my nasty contentions. The new Laugh Factory is located right in the middle of where all the porn holes used to be. I must have been possessed by that, and I went off on this long weird masturbatory jag. And I look out and there are these older women just looking horrified, wondering where all the liberal politics are. The left cause is good, but I've got to show people me."

One can detect a number of influences in Maron's set. Early in his stand-up days he spent time with Sam Kinison at LA's Comedy Store. The darkness often associated with store comics and Kinison's rebellion both crept in and set up shop in Maron's head. However, he isn't over-the-top with it, like the bloated caricature Kinison could be. Also well-versed in politics and an apt social satirist, he begs comparisons to Bill Hicks. However, where Hicks would sometimes get preachy,

Maron takes things to conspiracy-theory levels and turns the joke back on his own tortured mind. Where Hicks had bravado, Maron has self-doubt. It doesn't come off as self-deprecating, though, just more honest and makes his dead-on social and political observations that much sharper. Like Woody Allen, he has turned his idiosyncrasies and insecurities into an art form. He uses all this with the alternative-comedy concept of the non-setup/punchline shtick.

"I have outlines before I go on stage with key words and triggers," he said. "The liability of working like that is you lose a lot of jokes. But really, I'll have these chunks that I've had since I started about sex, politics, culture, whatever it is, then it's just these revolving dialogues. I'll just toss that out on stage, see a strand, and jump on it until I see another line of thought. Then I'll try to add a new chunk. That's the great thing about the nature of improvisation: you're immediate, in the moment, spontaneous."

While seen as one of the pillars of alternative comedy in New York, having started the staple alternative comedy night *Eating It* at the Luna Lounge with Janeane Garofalo, he doesn't feel the whole movement ever really "panned out."

"Really, I've only viewed the alternative scene as a place to go work things out. All the comics that I know who are associated with 'alternative comedy' started out in the regular stand-up clubs. I don't really think you're really a comic until you can do the clubs."

Personally, I have a hard time understanding why Marc Maron isn't more well-known. Maybe it's just not in him or maybe the opening quote on his website sheds more light on it than I can: "Popcorn is a good analogy for show business. Every time you make popcorn, there are always those fluffy, white, happy popped pieces that are fun to eat and look at, and everybody likes them. But there are also always those burnt, hard kernels at the bottom that don't pop. You know why they don't pop? They don't pop because they have integrity."

Marc Maron has never done just that, popped. That, possibly, was why I was so interested in what his answer would be to the keeping it real question. Is he too real for mainstream?

"I don't really have any choice but to keep it real. I live in Queens, where right down the street I have the fish guy, the meat guy, a place where I buy vegetables. I'm into reading a lot. I'm fairly isolated, not a lot of friends. I keep it real by keeping close to people I trust, by breaking in my own pants, cooking my own food, and admitting my mistakes."

AMY SEDARIS

By Ron Babcock

Original Interview: April 2003

Amy Sedaris is not a household name. She's not even the most famous person in her family, an honor that falls to her brother, the writer David Sedaris. However, she is a legend in comedy circles and actually has been since long before I first interviewed her for *Modest Proposal*.

That is why I couldn't wrap my head around the fact she still waited tables at a restaurant... oh and sold cheeseballs and cupcakes out of her apartment as a side hustle, which was when this phone interview went down.

During this same time, I had just started working as a waiter at Pizzeria Uno in Tempe, Arizona. That meant I got to quit my job at the drive-thru liquor store, where the true alcoholic miscreants shopped for booze. Once, I refused to sell a taxi driver beer, and when he asked why, I said, "Because you're drinking one right now sir." So, while the pizza restaurant was a definite step up, I dreamed about being light years ahead in my career... to exactly the point Amy Sedaris was.

Her cult classic Comedy Central show *Strangers with Candy*, which she starred in and co-created with Stephen Colbert and Paul Dinello, continued to find audiences with the DVD releases. (Kids, imagine Netflix on metal disks.) She also started getting more mainstream work with roles in *Elf*, *School of Rock*, and *Maid in Manhattan*. Sure, the last movie is hot garbage, but hot garbage pays cold hard cash. As a waiter, I'd be lucky to go home with free breadsticks and enough money for beer. Why was she still serving?

We weren't able to contact Amy in time for an update to this interview, so I can't be sure if she's still waiting tables on the side. On one hand, it'd really surprise me, since she's been working so much on various projects: her show *At Home with Amy Sedaris* on TruTV, as the voice of Princess Carolyn on *BoJack Horseman*, and roles in everything from *Broad City* and *The Unbreakable Kimmy Schmidt* to *The Mandalorian* and *The Lion King*.

One the other hand, it totally wouldn't surprise me. Amy seems like the type of person that no amount of success will change... plus, counting your tips after a long shift is a great feeling.

———————

RON BABCOCK: Why are you still working as a server?
AMY SEDARIS: I like making cash. Last night I made $312 from 6 o'clock until 12 o'clock. But I didn't get to sit down once, and I like that. I'm not going to feel achy after an acting job.

You actually like that?
I don't have to do it, so I like doing it. I like busy work. I like
the timing. It's an opportunity to wait on your audience. Last
night was great, but if I had to do it five nights a week, I don't
know what I would do. It's so hard.

**You know what I hate? When people ask for extra lemons
because they're too cheap to buy lemonade.**
I hate it when people order tea because you have to do the
whole setup for tea, and I hate it when they sit down and
they say, "What's good?" when you're really busy. But at the
same time, I love it because it keeps you grounded. It's always
important to have a job like that, no matter what. If you hang
out with a lot of actors and people in the theater, you'd go
out of your mind. You'd go out of your mind!

**In an interview, you said, "I like to give advice." So, here's
a problem...**
Oh, exciting.

**There's this guy at work who keeps stealing my tables when
it's obviously my turn. I'm scared to tell him to stop because
he's 6'5" and looks like he just escaped prison. What do I do?**
Why don't you say, "Hey look, you intimidate me because of
your look and your size, but the truth is, you're taking my
tables, and I don't know what else to do. I don't want to be
a little sissy and run to the manager, but I just want you to
know." Unless you think it's stupid to admit to someone that
you're intimidated by them.

No, I think that might take him off his guard.
It's always good to be honest. It scares people.

Have you ever said the following to anyone, "Do you know who I am? Do you? I'm Amy Sedaris goddammit."
Eww, no. I'd never say that, not in a million years.

That's all right, you don't have to admit it.
God, can you imagine? I just don't think of myself in that way at all, at all.

But you're a celebrity. You have to have an ego.
I guess when I'm cooking, it might come about.

Ever get in a fight?
I used to be a bully in my neighborhood and beat people up. We'd have contests; who could beat somebody up? I would.

Funny to think you were a bully. Now you give the aura of a 4-H Leader.
I was a girl scout until I was in twelfth grade. I was definitely in my own little world.

How are you so productive?
Yeah, I guess I am. I sell cupcakes and cheese balls out of my apartment. I deliver to a couple of bakeries in my neighborhood. To me, I'm always lazy and to other people, it sounds like I am productive. To me, it's mindless work. It's not like I'm doing anything hard. It's just stuff I like doing. I like having a job you can bitch about; you know what I mean? "Damn, butter went up to five dollars a pound," or "I got to get that order in by Tuesday." It's fun having a job just to complain about.

You've created so much great comedy with Stephen Colbert and Paul Dinello since meeting them at The Second City in Chicago. What makes you work so well as a team?
We all get along. We've worked together for fifteen years, and we can be honest with each other. If we don't laugh at something, we know it doesn't go on paper.

What's your role?
I'm good at coming up with the idea. Paul's really good at making it serious, and Stephen's really good at wording it in a certain way. When two of the three of us work on a project, it's pretty obvious that the three of us didn't.

What was *Strangers with Candy* like?
A total sense of freedom. It's the best thing in the world. There were no grownups there to slap our hands. I'd always give the script a high test. We'd write it, straighten everything, but then I'd be like, "Okay, let me take it home, let me smoke some pot, and I'll read it and give you notes." Half the time we were writing it the same time we were doing it. We were so behind in our writing. If you do a network show, oh my god, you have nothing. It's so much rehearsal, it takes the fun out of it. "God, do it again? What do you mean, do it again?" I wish everything could be like, "You got one shot, that's it."

Do you miss doing *Strangers*?
I don't want to miss anything about anything. I'm doing pretty much everything I want to do right now.

How many characters do you have in your repertoire?
I don't know, but I know I've been dragging the same ones around since I was a kid.

That's cool. It makes them more in-depth.
Yeah, I guess. I need something to hide behind. I like playing unattractive people who find themselves really, really attractive. That way I can be more physical. One of my favorite quotes is "It's easier to apologize than ask permission." I trust my instincts and instead of asking a director if I can do it, I'll just do it. If it doesn't work, I can say sorry. It's easier to do that than to ask because you're always going to know. You're always going to know.

(Editor's Note: Once again, notice the repetition, again.)

One of my favorite quotes is "Ambition makes up for a lack of natural talent."
What makes up for a lack of natural talent? Bitchin?

No, ambition.
I'm not a very ambitious person. That's one of my weaknesses. I don't mind ambition in other people, but sometimes it's enough for me just to have the idea. I don't need to see it through. I'll walk around and exhaust a possibility, and then I'm done with it because what I imagined in my head is always better than what came out of it.

Do you watch a lot of comedy?
I don't like to watch comedies. I can't stand it. I like to do it. I don't like to see it.

How come?
I'd rather see something serious and be like, "Okay, what's funny about that?" Whenever I see something funny, you have to drag me, kicking and screaming. I always walk away

thinking "Okay, that was funny, whatever." But if you tell me it's depressing, I'll be the first one in line.

What about the stuff you're in?
I never watch shows that I've done. *Sex in the City, Monk,* that David Spade show, the movies, I don't watch them. *Strangers with Candy* I would because I had to be in editing sometimes.

Aren't you curious?
No, because all I do is remember what I was doing. I don't want to see it because then I'll just be so critical.

About *Maid in Manhattan*...
I had to see that because I had to go the premiere. I had to see it.

You were great.
That's very nice.

The movie, um...
I know.

I think you have some apologizing to do.
I know.

Did Jennifer Lopez realize how bad it was?
I don't know what people think when they're in bad movies.

Did you watch the whole movie?
Yeah, we were getting drunk.

What were you drinking?
Mostly beer.

So, what are you going to now, like right now?

Well, I have a rabbit. Her name's Dusty. So, when I get off, I'm going to give Dusty some attention, and then I have my laundry that I folded on my couch, I'm going to put that away. I was eating while I was talking to you. I'm going to do those dishes and put them in the sink. I'm going to wash my face and brush my teeth and go to bed and read until I fall asleep.

Can you give us any words of advice for our career?

Just do it and things will come. That's the only advice I have for people and read. Keep reading. Whatever interests you, read as much as you can.

MARIA BAMFORD

———

By Eric Koester
Original Interview: March 2004

Maria was a younger comic who built a name for herself as the "chick with funny voices" (actual review) and had a popular stand-up special with Comedy Central. When I finally secured an interview with her, my plan was to leverage her participation to secure an entire series dedicated to female comics.

It turned into a series of one—Maria. Our conversation was different than I expected. She wasn't the funny, sharp cracking woman from on stage but had a calm peace about her. We spoke about her dogs and when it turned to performing, I vividly remember our conversation about performing as a woman at that time. Maria was performing in that pre-MeToo era, and as a young, attractive comic you could tell she felt conflicted about being objectified on stage. We spoke about performing to a largely male audience at comedy clubs where she spoke of the regularity of a drunk patron approaching her after assuming she'd want to sleep with them. The story was told in a funny way but reflecting back it's clear that comedy at the time was still very much a boys' club and it wasn't easy to make it.

Since that interview, Maria's comedy and entertainment career has truly exploded being named the 2014 comic of the year and launching and starring in a Netflix series *Lady Dynamite*. With the rise of many incredible female comics today, I do look back on Maria's work in the early 2000s as setting the stage for much of what we're seeing today.

ERIC KOESTER: Your voice is obviously very unique and important in your show. Once you got into comedy, did you get an insurance policy on your voice?
MARIA BAMFORD: It'd be okay if I lost my voice. I'd do prop comedy. I'd bring out puppets and stuff, but I wouldn't make any noises. That would be really... actually, I might want to look into it.

You've been described as "weirdly cheery." Why?
Well, I'm from the Midwest, so you're all smiley, but you stuff all your emotions inside and act "happy" to others. But then things come out—despite your best efforts. My voice is also high, so I think people confuse that with cheeriness. I'm really a bit more morose—I don't know.

Has your sarcasm ever gotten you into trouble?
Yeah, I mean, I get people in the audience that get all mad cause, "Uh, I never learned to read, so I don't know what comedy club I'm supposed to be at, so I'll express myself by acting obnoxious and loud during your show..."

So, yes, I always got in trouble when I was younger for doing things that were very passive aggressive. I went to the Science Olympics and afterward got brought into the principal's office because I was "a ringleader of trouble." Let's just say I totally didn't do anything. Such bull if you ask me.

You did a show on Comedy Central where you were doing *Cribs* for comics.
Yeah, trying to show comedians really aren't rolling in the "bling bling." Some comics are, but there's no guarantee you'll be on as giant a scale as… say Carrot Top. Frankly, I'm very jealous, and so I have to hate him. That's what I do. I lash out. I lash out from my little cave of misery. I guess it is good to be in touch with my feelings.

Is that your pug on your website?
Oh, man. That always makes me sad when I'm traveling because I have to leave her at home. Right now, she's at what I like to call, the "Spa." She's having a meditation massage session wrap right now.

Have you ever flown with your dog?
Yeah, I always keep her in that case 'cause people are either wildly excited like "Oh my GOD, YOU HAVE AN ANIMAL!" Or they are pissed, "That dirty beast… get that dirty beast out of here." I get the angriest because they don't let you get frequent flyer miles for your animal. It's totally profit-oriented too because they put a limit on dogs, so the flight won't become like Calcutta or something. Which might be fun, but it's not a game… it's business travel.

At what point did you feel like you've made it?

I really felt like I'd made it about three years ago. I'd done my Comedy Central special, so it was such a wonderfully creative experience. And they did such a good job with the whole special, so I totally felt like I'd made it. Especially since it is such a long process and fame or success is so fleeting, so I know I have so much to grow in, but I appreciate where I've gotten to.

I read that you have a boyfriend. Does that put a damper on your road life?

Yeah. It's a weird situation on the road because you are lonely, and you are put on this weird pedestal where people are like, "You're great and fantastic," plus you are only there for a week. I don't think that's bad or good or anything, but obviously it doesn't make for a long-term relationship. So, I'm hoping to be home a bit more now.

Some people really like the road for partying, but I'm just not much of a drinker. I have like two drinks, and then I just get pissed because I can't say what I want to say. I just get kinda googily. Then I just get really mad and angry and sit in the corner and read *Ziggy* cartoons on the calendar. I tried partying a lot when I was in college, and people had to always carry me home... but I had so much to say!

You've got some very loyal fans.

I know. They are super nice. I've had a few people come out who are just naturally obsessive- compulsive and have chosen me. In my Comedy Central special, I have so much material in there about being single, and that is unfortunate. And it's like four years ago, I'm like four years younger, and I had like big blond hair or whatever. So, I put that image out there.

What image is that?

I guess it just puts out a different image from who I really am—at least from the emails I get. I guess I put out an image that I didn't realize. I was like, "Oh, I'm a single lady, and I don't know why I'm still single, and I'm so pretty." So stupid. So, I get the occasional emails from gentlemen from the dugout... in Alaska... who want to take a little lady like me out on the town. They just want a sweet little lady. But I understand it somewhat, 'cause I think Jon Stewart is totally foxy, but I wouldn't ever tell him that over the email.

You talk about your mother in your show. How do you two get along?

It's funny; I want to be like my mother. I could use the extra pounds. She is such a good cook. I got some cookbooks, and I was just like, "This is not happening." I made some coleslaw once, and that's about it.

If your life were a movie, what would be the background music for this point in your life?

"Stayin' Alive" by The Beegees.

How does Maria Bamford keep it real?

I keep it real by always wearing pajamas. That way, even if I'm super-famous, people see that I'm "just like them" when I wear pajamas. On the other hand, if I never become famous, I can always wear pajamas. See how I do what I do? That's how I do it.

JIM GAFFIGAN

By Ron Babcock
Art by Anna Hollingsworth
Original Interview: 2006

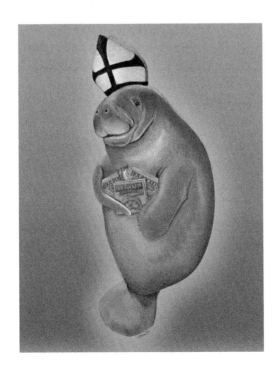

Whenever comedians come out with an album, they hope to sell enough copies on the first day to get the #1 spot on iTunes, so they can say "#1 ALBUM ON ITUNES." You may snag the spotlight for a moment, but you will inevitably be overtaken by The Pale Force known as Jim Gaffigan.

I've always identified with Jim although that's not hard when you're also the youngest in a large family of pale Catholics. It's also not hard for the rest of the world. Jim loves to talk about food and laziness, two things we Americans know about. Although it's hard to call someone with his touring schedule and catalogue of albums lazy.

Since our interview in 2006, Jim has cranked out specials including *Mr. Universe, Obsessed, Cinco,* and *Quality Time,* all of which have received Grammy nominations. He's appeared in dozens of TV shows and films and also created *The Jim Gaffigan Show* on TV Land. He also wrote two books, *Dad Is Fat* (2013) and *Food: A Love Story* (2014). Oh, and he had five kids with his wife and collaborator, Jeannie Gaffigan.

I've met him a few times over the years. Once at the Tempe Improv, he very politely asked if he could get a six-pack of Heineken to go and I said, "Sure." Then years later at the Upright Citizens Brigade Theatre in New York City, when we performed on the same show. Strangely, he again asked me for a six-pack of Heineken to go. Kidding, he just shook my hand and said hi. Still, I regret not handing him a six-pack of Heineken right then and there because who wouldn't like that?

RON BABCOCK: If you were a poster child while growing up, what cause would it be for?
JIM GAFFIGAN: I suppose sunscreen or doing nothing.

When you worked in an office, were you the "funny guy," or did you have to do battle with another "funny guy" to obtain the title?
I suppose I was considered the funny guy, but more I was considered the guy following a crazy dream. There were a lot of moments like, "How's that stand-up thing going?" I spent most of my time waiting to get laid off, so I could get the unemployment insurance.

The following Q&A's were taken from the FAQ on Hotpockets.com. I was hoping you could provide alternative answers from a consumer perspective: How many flavors of HOT POCKETS® brand stuffed sandwiches flavors are there? Answer: There 22 delicious HOT POCKETS® brand stuffed sandwiches. Try a new one today!
The irony is that they all seem to have that same hot pocket flavor. I want my own hot pocket. It would be filled with sunscreen.

Can the crisping sleeve be reused? Answer: We do not recommend that the sleeve be reused because it was not designed as a permanent container.
I like to use them for sweat bands when I play tennis with Tom Selleck.

What causes ice crystals to form on top of the product? Answer: Ice crystals occur naturally on frozen product. Excessive ice crystals (a snowy appearance) may result from fluctuations in storage temperature.
I always thought that was sugar.

Is it safe to use a HOT POCKETS® brand stuffed sandwich item once it is thawed? Answer: We do not recommend using any HOT POCKETS® brand stuffed sandwich, LEANPOCKETS® brand stuffed sandwich or CROISSANT POCKETS® brand stuffed sandwich if it is thawed.

I find it easier to eat hot pockets when they are not frozen.

Are you jealous of comics who tell stories rather than quick jokes like you?

I wish I could tell stories on stage. I feel my quick style is a result of developing and working NYC where you get short sets and need to really get the audience. I think watching Attell really influenced my quick joke, joke, joke style. Attell is a master.

I'm noticing a lot of young comics are using an "inner voice" to comment on their jokes while they perform. Do you feel like they are hacking you?

Well, I'm not thrilled by it, but what can I do?

What's the gig that made you want to quit it all?

I try to block these out of my memory. There have been plenty. When I first started, I did a show in Harlem where I was booed approaching the stage and someone tried to trip me.

Would you recommend a comedy class to a beginner today?

If you lack discipline and guts like I did, I don't think it's the worst idea. I just would recognize that you can't learn stand-up in a classroom and that a lot of those classes are just a way for someone to make money. I think a lot of creative classes (acting and stand-up, etc.) are a racket.

Was it a huge blow when your sitcom *Welcome to New York* got canceled?

I remember there was a sense of relief. I loved the process, and I thought it was a good show. However, I had no input on the show or even in my character, which was frustrating. The writers never saw me perform stand-up live. When I would suggest jokes there was a lot of, "What do you know about writing comedy?"

At what point did you switch from being a Midwesterner to being a full-fledged New Yorker?

I didn't realize I was a Midwesterner until I got to NYC really. I suppose I still am, but I feel like a New Yorker. I guess the switch was when I started looking at tourists on the subway and thinking, *"Check those people out."* Then of course I realized, *"Oh that's what I look like."*

Has your comedy changed since you got a family?

I'm really resisting the "I got a baby" or "I got a wife" comedy. I have some jokes on that, but I try to be really selective.

You have two kids, so we know you've had sex twice. What's it like?

Fun. It's like cake, but you're more tired afterward.

You talk about food a lot, so I know this will be difficult. What is your favorite food?

That is a tough one. I guess hot dogs or cheese. I've literally woken up dreaming about cheese.

Do you really like Sierra Mist? In case your answer is yes, the follow-up question is—are you serious?

Yes. Hey Sierra Mist got me an apartment!

You have two profiles on Myspace—a personal profile (3,859 friends and counting) and a profile a fan setup (156 friends). What's it like to be friends with a less popular version of yourself?
I'm flattered that anyone would set up a profile for me. A guy told me he uses my name when he signs on to porn sites, which is funny but frightening.

What's the coolest thing a fan ever sent or did for you?
Wow, so many cool things. I love when people bring Hot Pocket boxes for me to sign. I've signed a couple of Bibles, which was fun but weird. I have a thing on my website about being a ballet dancer and a couple years ago a guy showed up at a college show with a Jim Gaffigan Ballet School T-shirt. It was so funny I made it into a T-shirt. I also think it's cool when people tell me they adopted a manatee because of my joke.

What is the holy grail of achievement for a stand-up comic today—an hour-long Comedy Central presents? HBO special?
I think this is changing. Being from Indiana, doing *Letterman* was a huge goal for me. I think the prestige of an HBO special was enormous, but the success of Comedy Central has changed things a lot. If I had a choice between an hour special on Comedy Central or a half-hour on HBO, I still would have chosen Comedy Central. Way more people see Comedy Central.

Compared to five years ago, is stand-up in a better or worse place?
Way better. However, I do feel like we're not at a point where audiences in clubs would embarrass the next Steven Wright.

How do you keep it real?
By not bathing.

PATTON OSWALT

———

By Ryan McKee

Original Interview: 2004

Friendships between stand-up comedians can be the fucking best. When you're doing shows together night after night, it's you versus everyone else—comics versus the audience.

Friendships between stand-up comedians can also be fucking confusing. There are the obvious problems, like professional jealousy and spending too much time in bars. But it's also hard to know if you are friends, or if it just feels that way because you spend more time with them than your actual friends.

Ron Babcock and I are actual friends who also do comedy together. Years ago, as the duo act "Ron and Ryan," we landed our first booking at the Tempe Improv. Patton Oswalt was in town, and we got to open six shows for him. The shows went well—even better than I'd imagined—but the best part was just getting to hang out with Patton and his friend/feature act Dave Anthony after the shows. One night while we were at the bar across the parking lot from the venue, Patton said,

"Fuck it, let's go back to my hotel room and drink everything in the mini-fridge!"

So that's what we did. Patton complimented our act, and he seemed super excited about *Modest Proposal*. And when Ron and I mentioned the open mic show we ran at a local bar on Sundays, he and Dave decided to drop in after the final show at Tempe Improv. Word got out—*because we told everyone*—and the open mic was absolutely packed for the first and only time. Ron and I walked in like total badasses because we brought our new friend Patton Oswalt to perform—for free—at a small bar.

After that weekend, Patton asked us to help him produce a big comedy benefit show in Phoenix to register college-aged voters before the 2004 Presidential election. The show featured David Cross, Brian Posehn, Nick Swardson, Dave Anthony, The Naked Trucker and T-Bones Show, our buddy Patton, and Ron and Ryan! We helped him book the twenty-five-hundred-seat Celebrity Theater, and then we promoted the hell out of it! The show was a sold-out success.

When Ron and I moved to Los Angeles in 2005, we assumed we'd get to occasionally hang with Patton and do comedy shows together. Well… not so fast. We didn't understand the difference between a friend and a "road friend." A road friend is a comedian who lives in another city and you hang out when you're in that city. However, if a road friend moves to Los Angeles, that changes the dynamic.

Patton didn't have time to hang out with every comic he met on the road. To his credit, he helped get us booked on a popular LA comedy show. To our *discredit*, we bombed and were never invited to perform there again. Then, after a few weeks, Patton kinda stopped returning our emails.

I was disappointed, but I understood. Patton was blowing up. During our initial years in LA, he went from alternative comedy darling and "weird neighbor" on *The King of Queens*, to mainstream success with *The Comedians of Comedy*, his album *Werewolves and Lollipops* and voicing the lead rat in *Ratatouille*.

A few years passed. I moved to New York City. After eighteen months there, nothing seemed to go my way. I couldn't get booked on good comedy shows. I couldn't find a full-time job. Comics who I'd thought were my friends stopped returning my messages... because I had been their "LA friend," but now that I was in their backyard...

My actual friend Kevin Polowy was the editor at Moviefone.com and did his best to assign me freelance articles as often as possible. One of those assignments was interviewing Patton Oswalt over the phone about a movie he starred in called *Big Fan*.

His publicist connected our phonelines and introduced me to Patton as "Moviefone." Fine by me. I didn't want to identify myself. I didn't want to have that awkward moment: "Oh, hey man... been awhile. How's it going?" We were only talking because I needed the $75 for writing the article, and he was contractually obligated by the studio to do press for the movie.

It sounds stupid as I sit here writing it... and if you agree... hold on, it's about to get stupider. I decided before the interview not to identify myself, but I also thought we'd fall into the familiar patter we had five years prior. Because of that, I didn't really prepare many questions to ask.

The familiar patter didn't happen. And as any of my UCB Theatre improv teachers will attest, I'm not great at thinking on my feet. I mumbled my way around something Patton had just talked about on *The Adam Carolla Podcast*. He grew frustrated and said, "I'm not going to repeat something I just said in another interview. You can just listen to it there." I doubled down and asked him to expand upon what he said on the podcast. For the life of me, I can't remember the topic now. Patton went from frustrated to pissed and then expanded on why I was a shitty interviewer.

We sat there in an awkward silence for what felt like months. I remember thinking, *Why isn't he hanging up on me? Will he get in trouble with the studio?* Finally, I asked another question that I don't recall now. He sighed and gave me a one-word answer. And that's when I put both of us out of our misery, "Okay, thanks for your time, Patton." "Yep," he said and hung up.

I haven't been able to watch any of his stand-up specials since. It's a shame because he's a brilliant comic, and I know I'm missing out. I don't hate him. It's just whenever I see him, I feel ashamed and small. I know it's not rational. And I know this is a very weird introduction for a silly interview from sixteen years ago.

I did reach out to both Patton's publicist and manager recently; I even tweeted at Patton directly to get an update for this interview. Never got a response. I almost decided not to include this piece in the book, just to avoid feeling that way again. Then I figured, what the hell. Writing is therapeutic. Maybe this'll help me get over my irrational feelings, and I can do what everyone should be doing, enjoying Patton Oswalt's comedy.

RYAN McKEE: Who would win in a fight between Batman versus Spawn?
PATTON OSWALT: I hate these fantasy fight thingies. I want to see a fistfight between Kathy Bates and Mickey Rourke.

What would your superpower be?
The ability to turn consumed Cheetos into six-pack abs.

When you write a comic book, do you write the story first and then the artists come in, or do you work on it together?
I've only done three stories so far, and I always write out the script first, and then the artist goes to work on it. Luckily, I've had four really amazing artists so far, so they've always improved on my pacing and layouts.

What age group is your comic book *JLA: Welcome to the Working Week* aimed at?
I wanted it to be for people in their mid-twenties, but they made the protagonist look like he was thirteen.

Have you thought about writing something aimed at an older group?
I'm developing an idea for a monthly comic that I think could be aimed at people who read comics growing up but

would like to follow more adult themes still within a masked hero universe.

Why'd you pick the 40 Watt Club in Athens to record your first CD?
So I'd have a cushion of coolness, so that I'd have some people who are really into what I do, but still have that big block of audience members I still have to win over.

That comes from pride and thrill, and I think I'm finally past it. I'm done winning people over. I'd like to build a really solid fan base, so I don't need to waste fifteen to twenty minutes of my set walking people toward the subjects I want to tackle but rather start in the stuff that matters to me and go deeper from there. I think it's all part of a bigger process that all comedians go through. This is where I am now.

You're putting together a tour of rock clubs you said because you want to build that strong following.
Comedy clubs are fine for what they do, but they can be very restrictive. They rely on appealing to the largest number of people possible. They rely on offending no one. Most comedy clubs are not interested in cultivating an intelligent audience that's discerning about what comedy they see. And you can't argue comedy with anyone, anyway. Comedy and eroticism are beyond argument and qualification—if something makes people laugh or gives 'em a boner, the argument is over, which can be very frustrating.

I remember working at the now-defunct Slapstix in Baltimore. It's a Wednesday through Sunday week—me and Blaine Capatch. So, on Saturday night, before the show, the club owner calls us into his office, and he's got two stacks of comment cards. One is a thick, high stack, the other a slim pile of six. And he holds up the six cards, and he's saying, "These are some of the most negative comment cards we've ever gotten." And I say, "What's the other pile say?" And he explodes at me, saying they can't afford to lose ANY customers, for ANY reason whatsoever.

Here's a guy who's got comedians provoking these extreme reactions. If people hated us that much, it must follow that people also loved us just as strongly. And THOSE people—the ones who loved us—will definitely return and bring friends, and he could build on that. But all he could think of was six comment cards—which probably represented twenty-four people—and he could see the drinks and nachos they wouldn't be selling to people who probably only go to comedy clubs twice a year, anyway.

That's why the boom ended in the '80s because clubs appealed to the slowest, dumbest, meanest, most uncreative. And I don't want to sound mean, but that group tends to not make as much money as other people, tends to not pay for name liquors, high-end food items, or spend an evening out watching live entertainment as a habit. So you've got clubs booking hypnotists, jugglers, magicians, and prop acts, and bringing in audiences who can only afford to go out twice a year, and get themselves drunk in the parking lot on cheap beer, so they can come in, buy two soft drinks, and put no money back into the club. They've also chased away the more sophisticated customers, and they wonder why they've got sold-out shows, but no repeat customers and no money.

So instead of knocking my head against the wall, trying to bring something more expansive or different to a setting that not only doesn't want it, but also doesn't need it, I and a lot of other comedians are creating our own thing in different spaces. I think it will be an explosive trend in the next ten years.

Last year in Pittsburgh, after some anti-Bush material in your act, your crowd began chanting, "Bush Rocks." Instead of attempting to calm them down, you said, "It's not like Bush is Hitler... Hitler was elected." What the hell happened that night?

I don't know. It was a 9:30 show on a Saturday night. Young people, too. The show beforehand was older, more suburban people. They laughed their asses off at the exact same routine. Looking back, I think it had a lot to do with the fact that the war was really getting started, that people were scared and confused and, worst of all, I think I looked like I was having a lot of fun. I don't get shrill and lecture-y when I do political stuff. I think it's funny, and it's the part of my set where I'm really enjoying myself. Also, the more they booed and screamed at me, the happier I got, which I don't think helped.

When I was sitting in the manager's office—locked inside—I could look out over the bar. And some guy was down there, saying, "Send that guy down here. I'll wipe that fucking smile off his face." Something like that. That also upset me; because the times when people have had problems with my jokes, I'm always sitting at the bar after the show. I talk to people face-to-face, and discuss it, and hear them out.

That got me in trouble in DC when I last played there because I was standing up on the sidewalk with a bunch of Marines. They'd all just gotten back from Afghanistan and were kind of in my face, but I was listening to them, and talking, and after about ten minutes, we found things we really agreed on. Especially the fact that these combat soldiers were being used as police, which got my dad seriously injured in Vietnam.

So, the whole time we're talking there's this Ann Coulter-looking lady standing ten feet away, glaring at me. And the better the Marines and I got along, the angrier she got. So, the Marines and I say goodnight. They're walking away, and she gets up in my face. Now her husband is standing next to her, and she says, "Little bit of advice, when you've got military people in the room, you don't bad mouth the president. You got it, asshole?" Her husband looks at her and says, "You're not in the military. Shut the fuck up." She flashes him the bitch-light and walks off. He turns to me and says, "I'm so sick of her shit." I think I ruined a marriage.

As a comedian, do you need to stay up on pop culture references more than the average thirteen-year *Tiger Beat* reader?
Pop culture references are fine, but they only take you so far. I'm trying to deal with bigger actualities, but that's hard to do, so I'll throw in a Cookie Crisp reference instead.

You majored in English. Got anything to say about *Beowulf*?
I never read that. I loved John Gardner's *Grendel*.

In your most obsessive months, how many hours a week did you get on stage?
I did 312 shows in one year. I just saturated myself until I got good.

Bob Odenkirk talked about how alternative comedy was very marginalized about ten years ago, and now it's considered totally legitimate for performers and writers to be working in that area. Do you agree or disagree?

I disagree because anyone calling themselves "alternative" has an agenda and is not just enjoying it for the free art form that it is. If alternative comedy was so marginalized back in 1994, how did Janeane, David, Bob, Dana Gould, Greg Proops, Margaret Cho, and so many others get so much work?

Are you pleased with the LA comedy scene now?

It's fantastic. There are so many amazing comedians coming up right now—and the ratio of good comics to bad comics is so much better than when I was starting. I was blown away by how good the comedians were in Tempe when I did that open mic. Really solid writers. There's actually an "alt. comedy" backlash going on, where young comedians are not reading from a notebook, and not doing all that navel-gazing bullshit like we did. They're becoming solid, punchy, joke- writers. It's really exciting.

How does Patton Oswalt keep it real?

By entering a magic land at the back of an old wardrobe in my house, where the ground is made of marshmallows, the sky is a never-ending hug, and cancer makes you grow head-horns that squirt lemonade!

CHELSEA PERETTI

By Ron Babcock

Original Interview: 2003

I originally interviewed Chelsea Peretti over the phone during her second year into doing comedy. I was very intimidated by her. A few years later, I ran into her in person at the San Francisco Punch Line and continued to be intimidated by her. One of the hallmarks of almost everyone we interviewed in *Modest Proposal* is that they were just fearless (or at least they were good at hiding their fear). I'm not sure what it says about me that I find fearless people intimidating, but one thing for sure is fearless people get shit done.

While Ryan and I were still cobbling together a decent ten minutes of stand-up in our second year, Chelsea had already reached a level of notoriety in New York with her brother Jonah Peretti (who later co-founded Buzzfeed) by creating the RejectionLine.com, a phone number you could hand out to unwanted suitors. When they called it, they were informed by an automated message that they have been rejected and could then press a number to be comforted by a rejection specialist or listen to a sad poem.

This interview covered Chelsea's follow-up social satire, Black-PeopleLoveUs.com (still up btw!), a site about two white people, Sally and Johnny, and their patronizing attempt to connect with their Black friends.

Since we interviewed Chelsea, she has graduated from creating websites to being a cast member on *Brooklyn Nine-Nine*, writing and appearing on *Parks and Recreation* and *Kroll Show*, voicing characters on *The Simpsons, Big Mouth, Adventure Time* and a bunch of others. She has a Netflix special entitled *One of the Greats* and also recently released a new music EP called *Foam and Flotsam*. It's delightful.

RON BABCOCK: Why BlackPeopleLoveUs.com? Why not HispanicPeopleLoveUs.com or JewsThinkWereCool.com?
CHELSEA PERETTI: Well, because I think it's something that I've noticed most acutely between Black and white people, largely due to my own social environment. As a Jew, I haven't experienced it as much, maybe because I'm not Orthodox or maybe because I don't hang out with tons of Jews and then occasionally hang out with WASPs. Just because in America so often things are boiled down to a Black-white issue. That was just an attempt to also skewer that tendency. It points to a bigger problem of people just being condescending in their attempts to relate to people they think are different than themselves, so we just simplified it.

When you were recruiting people to help, what was your pitch?
I emailed and said I'm doing this satire of interracial friendships where white people use patronizing attempts to relate to "Black" friends.

How many hits do you get a month?
I haven't even looked at the stats recently. Last, I think, I can't remember how many thousands. Either three or eight thousand visits a day still.

Did you ever think it would blow up to be something that big?
I guess I thought it was a possibility. You never know what's going to wind up being successful. But just because of the Rejection Line Project, I knew that it was possible, and it could get a following.

With a name like BlackPeopleLoveUs.com, it's quite an attention getter. Do you think people go there to laugh, to learn, or just to be offended?
I think everyone goes to it for different reasons, and also what you go to it for might not be what you leave with. I think some people go just to have a cheap laugh and not really think about what's going on, but just be like, "Ha ha, these are funny pictures of Black and white people." Other people are like, "Um, this is clever and political," and other people are like, "This is just stupid." There's really been such a wide-ranging reaction that I'm sure people enjoy it for very different reasons.

Do you ever want to just scream and throttle the necks of those who just don't get it?
At first, because the first rounds of responses I got were all mostly people who knew about it from someone who knew

me. As it started to widen out and there were people who really didn't get it, I was just like, "Oh my god." Because people would so often send in an email where they spelled out, "You're treating your Black friends as if they're different." They would spell out exactly what was being satirized. They would be like taking it as face value and saying how it was really racist. That was always frustrating to me that people didn't have the analytical tools or that kind of humor or that kind of sensibility to understand what was going on. After a while you just kind of get used to it. So many people are praising it excessively or shitting on it excessively that it all becomes noise. At this point, I think I'm more affected by the people who have no real opinion or critique of it.

Has it resulted in any more comedy writing jobs?
Yeah, I'm sure it hasn't hurt. I'm completing my second year in comedy, so I'm just getting to that point where I'm not just a hobbyist. I'm actually really into it. It's hard to say whether it's the work I put in on stage or it's the website, but I think it's a combination.

Any new sites in the works?
I'm working on something right now. It's not quite ready to be up yet, but that will probably be linked to the BlackPeopleLoveUs.com site. And I'm working on my personal page, ChelseaPeretti.com.

What are some of your other favorite websites?
I am obsessed with Google, but that is probably not the most exciting. I used to be really into Am I Hot or Not? A bunch of comics have cool pages like EugeneMirman.com or Todd-Barry.com. I just mainly Google people I think are funny, and I look at all the sites that relate to them.

When the *New York Times* called you for an interview, did you look in the mirror and say, "I am God. No one can touch me. I'm famous."

Is my room bugged or what? (She then let out this nerdy laugh that was like "Nah-ah-ah-ah." Then she coughed. Like, really coughed. It was scary. I thought she was going to die. Then she was okay, and I wasn't scared anymore.) I was happy about it. I didn't think I was necessarily God. Not yet.

When we called for an interview, did you look in the mirror and say, "What happened to my godlike status?"

No. I like *Modest Proposal*. I think it's cool you guys are doing a comedy magazine. I think there should be more out there. It's weird to me that there's not.

How are you going to top this?

You know, it's like I'm working on so many different things. You start thinking that everything you do is going to be huge. You just have to keep plugging away. Everyone, even when you watch *The Comedian*, Seinfeld's thing, even people who totally become a success are always trying to worry about the next thing. The next thing is going to be my whole entire life and career.

Finally, what are you going to do now, like right now?

That's a good question. I was going to start a book that's called *Cavedweller* by Dorothy Allison. *Bastard Out of Carolina* was such an uplifting novel that I figured I'd read another one. Then I will probably work out, go for a run, and do some writing. And then I'm going to go to a comedy show tonight.

ROBERT SCHIMMEL

By Eric Koester
Original Interview: April 2003

I wouldn't say I knew Bob Schimmel well by any stretch. We only had one long phone interview and a brief conversation outside a DC comedy club while he was pushing a stroller with this wife and young son.

But hearing of his death in 2010 hit me harder than I would have expected. I felt sad. His death seemed so unfair.

When I'd spoken to Bob in 2003, he'd just begun his comeback after a rough period that including losing his son to cancer, a heart attack, and his own battle with cancer. By 2003 he was performing again and had released a book where he spoke about the comedy in tragedy.

Given where he was and the public face he'd put on about tragedy, I began the interview by asking if he ever felt like he might be a modern-day Job from the Bible.

I expected a flip, punchy reply, but the discussion got very personal, spiritual, and real as we dove into how faith and family had carried him through these rough periods. I was struck by his resolve. He felt he'd been given a second shot to make an impact through comedy. We discussed a variety of things over our hour together, but I walked away with a very different feeling about a guy most often compared to Lenny Bruce. He was kind, he was real, and he viewed this "second act," as he described it, as a next opportunity.

Health had continued to be a struggle for Schimmel with several run-ins with medical challenges in subsequent years. When I heard of his passing in early fall 2010, I assumed it had to be cancer or something related. But it was a car accident; his daughter was driving, and his son was also in the car. Both would survive, but Bob would not.

The fast-talking, curse-word-blaring comedian was taken much too soon. But I won't remember him for that. I'll remember him as a man who hadn't let tragedy stop him; instead, he'd let it empower him to do more in his too-short life. RIP Bob.

Eric Koester: Do you ever feel like you're this generation's Job from the Bible?
Robert Schimmel: Absolutely. And I like it. I think faith is about exactly that. Having faith when you should be angry and questioning instead. I don't blame God for anything that happened, and I think I'm more spiritual than religious. What happened happened. What I do with the rest of my life says who I am.

Have you ever apologized for anything you said on stage?
No. You've got nothing to apologize for in a comedy club. It's comedy and if you have to apologize, something's not right.

Do you ever talk about politics in your act?
Yeah, if you want to divide the audience real fast. Why don't you ask the girl from the Dixie Chicks if you should talk about politics in your act? She sure changed her story really quick. Boy, the almighty dollar is so powerful. When the label says, "Okay, that's it," and radio stations started kicking them off, then it's "what I meant was..." No. If she had stuck to her guns, they would have been back on the air quicker than they were. The other two were probably going, "What the fuck are you thinking? We worked all this time and we're the number one country thing and then you... Why don't you just go fuckin' blow Saddam Hussein on television?" These fuckin' people.

And Martin Sheen and Susan Sarandon and all these people painting this picture like Saddam Hussein is a victim. If you like it that much over there, I'll buy your fuckin' ticket and go move over there. I'm serious. You can't cry about it, because when the chick from the Dixie Chicks cried about it, it reminded me of Dice crying on *Arsenio Hall* that time. Well, anybody should cry if they're on *Arsenio*. But you don't do that. If she had said, "Hey, that's what I believe and fuck you," I could see people coming around and saying, "That's her opinion, and obviously, with the threat of not being on the air and everything else, she's still sticking by it, and that you have to respect." The minute they go, "Okay, you're never on the radio again." "Well, oh, I love this country." You can't do that.

Do you think they'll ever find Saddam or Osama?
It's amazing with all the technology and everything else they can do. I mean, they can have a fucking bomb dropped from a plane and it could come through your keyhole in your hotel. And they can't find these people. If they wanted to find Saddam Hussein and Osama bin Laden, they should have left it up to the student loan people. They find you wherever you are. You can change your name, your social security number, the whole thing, and they'll still get you.

Where do you get most of your material from?
There is so much to laugh at in everyday life. I was looking at *USA Today* the other day, and they are voting in the Texas Senate whether sodomy should be against the law. And I'm thinking, is it against the law? And that people have to vote on it. I mean, are they going to be in a room and is that a secret ballot vote? Or are you like, "All those in favor, say aye." Then it's like if you aren't raising your hand, you are telling everyone in the room that you're into anal sex. I think that shit's hysterical.

You don't seem to be much of a fan of people using celebrity status to give a political view?
No. I think my favorite is Sean Penn visiting people. Man, that's the first time it dawned on me what an impact it had that Madonna left him. He showed up at the hospital in Afghanistan with a fucking thirty-five-millimeter camera film crew going, "Hi, are you feeling better?" I'm like, "Who are you?" "Oh, I used to be Madonna's husband." I mean, that's the only thing he could tell them. They wouldn't know any of the shit that he did. "Oh yeah, I was in a movie called *U Turn*." What? "Maybe you saw me in *Shanghai Surprise*?" I think that shit's

funny. You don't have to look far to find humor in life—even in the worst things in life.

When you were diagnosed with cancer several years back, were you able to find any humor in that experience?
Yeah, of course. I was sitting at the Mayo Clinic in Phoenix. My doctor came out and he said, "Listen, you're going to start chemo in two days, and if you're open minded, you should consider marijuana because it will help with the nausea and your appetite." And my mom and dad are sitting there devastated, and I'm sitting there thinking that is a dream come true. A doctor telling my mom and dad I have to smoke pot. Where was this guy twenty years ago? I used to get kicked out of the house for it, and now my parents are picking up rolling papers for me down at the 7-Eleven going, "Is this the kind you use?"

The advances of modern medicine.
I know. I had open sores in my mouth from chemo, and they said you have to avoid oral to anal contact. When you can't swallow water, why would you think about licking somebody's asshole? But they feel obligated to tell you. I love it because that means someone did it, and that's why the doctor has to tell you. Now because one person wasn't responsible, everyone has to get the "Don't lick somebody's asshole" lecture.

Have you contemplated writing a book about your experience?
Everybody's asking me to. You know, wherever I go, on the road, I ask my fans to donate comedy CDs and books on tape and music CDs and Nintendo games and drop them off at the venue where I'm performing. And then I donate them to cancer centers in the community where the venue is, so they

help other people in their own community. But it's a sticky thing writing a book. I mean, I've had cancer, my son died of cancer, and I do want to help other people. I try to every single day because if I can make a difference in people's lives, at least what I went through wasn't for nothing.

I heard on *Stern* that you are now married to your daughter's best friend. Is that true?
Yes. I got remarried in April. I'm having a baby in June. They told us we could never have children because of the chemotherapy. They said, "Save your money on birth control." Yeah, why would I waste it on that when I really need to save up for a crib?

You mentioned Andrew Dice Clay before. What do you think about him?
I like him, and he happens to be a really great guy, but he made a mistake. He should have never backtracked. Because, then, when he came back, he did another HBO special that was even more way out than anything should have ever been because he wanted to prove to his fans that he was still him. But he had already sold out when he was on *Arsenio,* and when he did the sitcom. Because that's how Hollywood is. They're fucked up. Unfortunately for him, people don't see the difference between Andrew Dice Clay and Andrew Silverstein, who's the real guy. He's a real person offstage, he's not like that twenty-four hours a day.

Who would you rather sleep with, Martha Stewart or Hillary Clinton?
Wow. I don't know. That's really tough. I've had fantasies about Martha Stewart. A comic buddy of mine, Jon Ueberroth, told me he was talking to his friends about that. If you could be

with any celebrity for a one-nighter, who would it be? He said Martha Stewart. And they said, "Martha Stewart? You'd pick her over anybody else?" And he said, "I don't know how good she'd be in bed, but you know the next morning the breakfast would be fucking awesome." So that's probably it.

BOB ODENKIRK

By Brodie Foster Hubbard
Original Interview: 2004

As a weird young man and comedy nerd, I held Bob Odenkirk up as one of my showbiz heroes long before Saul Goodman was dreading his cinnamon bun flavored fate on *Breaking Bad*. At the time of this interview, Bob had already earned legend status as an Emmy Award winning veteran writer at *Saturday Night Live*, *Get A Life*, *The Ben Stiller Show*, *Tenacious D*, and *Mr. Show with Bob and David*.

Even as the sun was setting on *Oz*, *The Sopranos*, *Six Feet Under*, and the rest of HBO's first wave of original programming, Bob predicted the emergence of prestige cable television in this interview. However, if he had any inkling that he'd be a major character in one of the most prestigious drama series in prestige cable television, which would then lead to four (at the time of this printing) Emmy nods for Outstanding Lead Actor in a Drama Series, Bob didn't give me any indication.

In fact, when this conversation took place, it seemed like Bob was heading more behind the camera rather than in front of it. He had directed his first feature film, *Melvin Goes to Dinner*, the previous year and mentioned his desire to develop more projects. One of those projects became Tim and Eric's first series for Adult Swim, *Tom Goes to the Mayor* (weird coincidence with those titles) and another became Bob's directorial movie debut for a major studio with *Let's Go to Prison* (again, these titles, are going places).

Sure, we could expect him to pop up occasionally in small comedic roles, like Dr. Phil Gunty in *Arrested Development* and Joey's nemesis in an episode of the *Friends* spin-off, *Joey*. But serious roles in serious prestige cable television series seemed unlikely for a man in his forties—with a wife and two children and two decades of highly regarded work in comedy—even more unlikely than a low-stakes con man nicknamed Slippin' Jimmy McGill becoming Albuquerque's craftiest lawyer Saul Goodman.

After Bob's brilliant dramatic performances in *Breaking Bad*, *Fargo*, *The Post*, *Little Women*, *Undone*, and his mainstream breakout as the star of *Better Call Saul*, it's almost tough to picture him playing the absurd sketch comedy characters that first introduced him to me and legions of comedy nerds.

BRODIE FOSTER HUBBARD: Do you grasp how large the following is for *Mr. Show*?
BOB ODENKIRK: I don't know if I do. I live about ten minutes from my office, I have two kids, and I have about eight projects that I'm working on. I basically just get up, go to work,

go home every night, and play with my kids, so I don't really know. I know we've grown exponentially since we've gone off the air. I'm proud that it has a life.

We just got a check because we self-published the *Mr. Show* book; no one else would publish it. It's a pretty big check. I guess that means a lot of them are being sold.

I want to ask about *Run Ronnie Run* since it's out on DVD...
David Cross and I got cut out of the editing process on that. We were able to affect it more than not. We sent in our notes; we were able to see cuts. So, it's much better than it was and the version that came out on DVD is better than the version they were going to release to the theaters. I think the director finally got a sense of how bad it was after the studio said, "We're not releasing it." The version you're seeing on DVD is the best possible version. It still drags, and as far as David and I are concerned, it's nowhere near the movie it could be.

The film process being so difficult, is cable TV or film going to be a better medium for groundbreaking comedy?
I think it changes every three or four years. Cable TV is a great venue to do something interesting. I actually think there's a crazy potential that network TV could become something valuable and worthwhile. They're just getting so trumped by cable.

You have to work in the best possible place. If your idea belongs on cable TV, that's where you should take it, and you shouldn't try to force it into network TV. I think independent movies are actually very challenging right now because it was this huge scene and it was great for a few years. Now, it's become very corporate. The bottom's dropping out of it and, in a way, that's going to open it up to real alternative films again in a few years. I have this weird feeling it's sort of evolving in a great way. It's falling apart and that's very good.

In that vein, what about the alternative comedy scene?
The alternative scene, for a couple years now, has been taken seriously. I don't think it's exploded, but it's still affecting people. We're still doing alternative nights here in LA. M Bar is great, Largo still does shows, and there are shows all over town. It's more legitimate than it was when I was doing it at first with Janeane Garofalo and David Cross, and all those guys about ten years ago. It was marginalized and now it's considered totally legitimate for performers and writers to be working in that area. When I go to M Bar, which is totally alternative, there are all kinds of agents there, looking for people who are doing good stuff. Like Fred Armisen making it to *SNL*. Fred came out of Largo and the alternative scene here.

How have your sensibilities changed being married and having two kids?
I would say marriage hasn't changed my sensibility. I'm probably a little less apt, because I have kids, to do a joke about someone with a mental handicap or even about Hitler or something. Just because certain things become more serious when you have kids. You just can't take them as a joke anymore, because you have this strange connection to the world that you didn't have before.

Tell me about the characters you've created for others over the years, like Matt Foley, motivational speaker.
Farley was made to do that character. As much as I wrote it, he brought it to life. The other night, I was watching TV, and there

was an ad for *The Best of Chris Farley.* There's Matt Foley, and it's just: "Goddamnit, I wrote that. I was in a fucking shitty, shitty apartment in Chicago feeling like shit, and I just wrote that out on some lined paper and there it is on TV, twelve years later, and people are buying it, and I'm getting no money for it." But so what? There's my friend and he's dead and he killed himself. Fuck.

What is this world? It is so weird to be on this side of that because when you're starting out, and it seems like you're starting out for so long, you look up to the people who have made their mark. It's not what you think, being there. I guess the key to that is I wish I enjoyed it more getting there. But you know I probably wouldn't have worked as hard if I enjoyed it more.

What projects do you have on the horizon that you're looking forward to?
I'm trying to get a movie going about the Disco Demolition, which was this event that happened in Chicago years ago*. It was where this DJ had a promotional event where he was going to blow up disco albums. Basically, it turned into a riot, and it really did change the tone in the country against disco music. It's really just a silly event that, for a short moment, seemed to be kind of dangerous and possibly a tragedy, but it just kind of went away. It was this crazy confluence of teenagers and opinions, just a crazy night. [60]

And David and I wrote a sketch movie that we're still finishing. I'm very proud of it, and I can't wait to shoot it, and

---

60 *While this movie still hasn't been produced as of 2020, Odenkirk did tell the Disco Demolition story in the fourth season finale of* Drunk History *on Comedy Central.*

I hope we get to. I'm also writing a screenplay of a book called *The Fuck-Up* (written by Arthur Nersesian). It's a book I really like.[61]

How do you, Bob Odenkirk, keep it real?
(long pause) I smoke pot once a year.

---

61 *According to reports, Odenkirk owned the rights to The Fuck Up until 2011. At one point, Jesse Eisenberg, Juliette Lewis, and Michael Shannon were attached as the leads. Unfortunately, for unknown reasons, funding fell through and his rights to the book ran out.*

NICK SWARDSON

———

By Eric Koester

Original Interview: April 2003

I'll never forget how I got Nick Swardson to agree to an interview. He was a big enough comedy star in 2002 that he'd already done two Comedy Central specials and was the co-writer for *Malibu's Most Wanted*, a widely released (but critically panned) comedy film. As I plotted how I could get to him to speak to a no-name comedy writer, I did something crazy (in 2002): I typed his name into Yahoo! That's right... *Yahoo!*

And the first result was his website. It was NickSwardson.net. Why .net? Did someone else buy the .com? I guess we'll never know. I'd been stalking comedians to try and get interviews, and this was the very first time one of them had their own website. His site was definitely terrible; he probably put it up himself using a Geocities template, and he actually let anyone post comments to it. (I guess it was before trolling was a thing.) It was shocking to see a big deal comedian with their own website then. As I scrolled around, it was even more shocking that it had an email address in the contact page. I figured it probably went to a manager, but I could start there. I typed up a couple of lines, exaggerated my credibility a bit and shot him a note from my own yahoo email. And sure enough a day later I got a reply. But it wasn't from a manager or a publicist, but it was directly from Nick. And even weirder was he gave me his number and said to call him anytime to talk.

It felt almost too easy. But I replied and told him I'd call him the next afternoon.

"It's Eric Koester from *Modest Proposal*... we emailed yesterday about..."

"Oh yea... yea... just woke up. This is good... sure... what is this about?"

The next forty minutes we talked about nothing and everything. It was as freewheeling a conversation as you could find, and I kept asking about growing up in Minnesota (which he clearly, from his answers, didn't care to talk about). But it also felt like talking to a buddy from high school who just happened to be one of the biggest up-and-coming comedy stars on the planet.

Since then, Nick has become a true comedy "sidekick" with more than thirty movie credits, dozens of television appearances, countless writing credits, and a regular spot in Adam Sandler's *Happy Madison*-produced films and movies.

And it turns out he wised up, and you can't just find his personal email on his website anymore.

ERIC KOESTER: If you weren't doing comedy, what do you think you'd be doing?
NICK SWARDSON: I would probably be the President of the United States.

Don't you have to be thirty-five years old?
I would get a fake ID. I think all you have to do is show your license at the door of the White House. A guy kinda looks at it and says, "Yeah, you're good."

When you go home for Christmas, does your mom still make you sweep the driveway?
No. No, I'm established enough now. I just tell my mom, "I'm on TV. You're gonna have to do that, Mom."

If you go out to a bar, does that work? Can you just tell a girl, "I have a special on Comedy Central?"
I can. Some girls will just think you're so fucking dumb that they won't believe you. But it's still kinda funny. They're not like "Oh," and then blow you. It's not that instantaneous. A show on Comedy Central doesn't pay off that much—even Attell doesn't get laid like that.

For your movie, *Malibu's Most Wanted*, how did you get in touch with your inner hip-hop?
The funny thing is Jamie Kennedy and I were laughing that we were both really like that at one point in our lives. I remember when my pants were down to my fucking ass—below my ass, I had a fucking silver chain, I had a fucking Starter jacket with my hat to the side. Literally, I went for the gold on that one. I was really into hip-hop. I mean, I'm still big fan, but it was scary how into hip-hop I was.

You have a writing credit in this movie?
Yeah, I wrote the original script off Jamie's idea. We've been trying to get it made for a couple of years, but once Jamie got his show on the WB, they were asking if he had any movies he wanted to do, so he threw them my script. And now, it's one of those things I figure I might as well keep doing. It works. This wasn't something I planned on doing, but now my managers and agents are like, "You gotta fuckin' write another movie, immediately." So, I've been working on another film, and I like it a lot. It's fun. And slowly I'd like to write more of my own stuff and become like Owen Wilson and Wes Anderson. And Adam Sandler and people like that.

Who would you like to work with on future projects?
I already talked to Jack Black and some other guys about doing this next movie. Jack's a buddy of mine, and we've always wanted to do something. I'd love to do something with Ben Stiller, too. Those two guys, I think, would be a lot of fun.

What do your old friends think when you go back and visit?
It's weird. I dunno. It depends upon which friends. To my friends from high school, it's still me, but my friends from comedy and acting and stuff, it's weird; it's a little different. I make sure they know who they're messing with. I go, "Anybody that makes fun of me, you may never get on TV again."

How was the transition from Minnesota boy out to LA guy?
That wasn't that hard. The biggest transition was from Minnesota to New York. That was really fuckin' weird. That's like two extremes. I mean, in LA, you drive to places and shit. But, New York, everything smells like piss, nobody has cars. You're on top of everyone.

Have you become a Lakers fan?

No, I actually hate the LA teams more than anything in the world. I mean, I hate the Lakers more than any other team in any other sport. All my friends have great Lakers tickets and we would go, and I'd be miserable, and they'd be mad at me.

When Minnesota won the college hockey championship this year, there was a riot on campus. If you were in Minnesota, would you have rioted?

Yeah, I would have rioted. But I maybe would have tried to start my own riot—rioting against the riots. Seriously, is there anything more pathetic than a Minnesota hockey riot? All these twenty-year-old white kids screaming, "Go, yeah," until midnight and then saying, "Aw, we gotta get up tomorrow."

I was looking on your website, and some girl named Amber thought you were so funny that she would remove your dingleberries. Does that kinda fame go to your head?

That statement is definitely going to change my outlook on life. Somebody actually said that? Wow... I mean, I guess I should probably take her up on that. Wow. I really get a lot of stuff like that. I almost did this actually. Some girl was like, "Will you go to my prom with me?" And there was a beat where I thought, "I should just fucking do that and take this chick to the prom." Then I realized that joke would get old after about ten minutes.

Have you dated anyone famous?

I dated Sarah Silverman. But since I've been in LA I haven't really dated much. It's really hard to meet people who are cool when you travel a lot. All the comics I know are either married or hard-core single. It's hard to find a middle ground.

Do you have some problem with corn?
I don't even know how that even came about. I really fucking hate corn. Just not a fan.

Have Korn ever called you and been pissed about it?
No, because I always make sure to spell mine with a "C." I look out for Jonathan Davis.

Now, for a very serious question: Is it soda or pop?
Wow, that's a very good question because I had to actually deal with that head on. Because I called it "pop" my whole life and then moving to New York and LA, I had to switch to soda. Total pop action though.

Do you put sprinkles or jimmies on your cupcake?
I had a cupcake problem, so I don't even eat them anymore. I would have to say sprinkles though. Jimmies? Aren't those condoms? I'm gonna take a pass at putting a condom on my cupcake.

Is it a water fountain or is it a bubbler?
See, I personally call it a magic water box. I guess that's just how I grew up.

If you had to choose a reality television show to go on, which would you pick?
Probably *Moesha*. [laughs] I can't do those reality shows like *Survivor*. I'm such a pussy, I can't eat a bug. *Fear Factor* is like the most horrifying thing I've ever seen in my life. Yeah, I'm not putting my fucking head in a fucking tub of blood for fucking anybody. But it's fucking TV. People are whores for it. Look at me, I have a fucking TV in my ass right now.

Is there a character of yours that you really want to see played out in a movie or television show?

There is one that I did on *Mohr Sports*. Jay Mohr asked me to come on his show and do this character called Rollerboy. It was me in the tight little shorts and tight shirt. It was just the gayest character you could possibly imagine, and I always had roller skates on. And I would skate on his show and play his younger brother. It was so fucking funny. We had talked about doing Rollerboy as a movie—just making it on our own.

Can you make sure not to have LL Cool J and Chris Klein in it?

Yeah, I would really love never to see Chris Klein again—to not see any of those *American Pie* kids again.

How does Nick Swardson keep it real?

I guess for me, I just put on my roller skates, grab a Zima, and hit the beach.

JIM BREUER

By Chrystyna Golloher
Updated Intro by Ryan McKee
Art by Chrystyna Golloher
Original Interview: April 2003

Chrystyna and I started dating our sophomore year in college, and after we graduated, rented a small house together in Tempe's historic Maple-Ash neighborhood. We felt like a true adult couple, holding hands as we strolled on treelined streets to dinners at our favorite local restaurants. She was an elementary teacher, and I wrote for a weekly alternative newspaper.

It was a romantic time, just Chrystyna and me... and Ron... and *Modest Proposal Magazine*. Ron moved in with us to help me create the magazine, and that meant Chrystyna also had to live that comedy life.

We made her read every article, asking her what she found funny, and then argued with her if she didn't like a joke. She patiently watched us rehearse our stand-up sets over and over and then did her best to give us feedback on the three words we changed from the last time she watched it. Whenever we needed a woman for a sketch or a visual joke in the magazine or for a bit in our live shows, she was always game, no matter how embarrassing. Stand-up comedy specials, episodes of *Mr. Show, Upright Citizens Brigade, Kids in the Hall,* and *Insomniac with Dave Attell,* and movies like *Rushmore, Big Lebowski, Office Space, King Pin, Half Baked,* and *Outside Providence* dominated our television at all hours.

After a year-long crash course in all things comedy, she wanted to write her first interview and picked Jim Breuer. We all loved his work as Goat Boy and other memorable characters on *Saturday Night Live,* as well as his standout performance in *Half Baked,* but Chrystyna also really connected with his stand-up. The year prior, Jim released a one-hour special for Comedy Central called *Hardcore* and the comedy album

Smoke 'n' Breu. In both, he jokes about his marriage. Not the played-out "Take my wife … please" stuff, but he talks honestly about the difficulties that come with committed relationships, even when both partners love each other. I think she really related to it because of the struggles I brought to our relationship.

Seventeen years later, Jim and his wife Dee are still together. They've been married for twenty-seven years. Chrystyna and I broke up about a year or so after this interview published. But we're still friends. And she still likes Jim Breuer's comedy.

CHRYSTYNA GOLLOHER: I'm going to be honest with you, this is the first interview I have ever done.
JIM BREUER: Really, get out of here!

So, bear with me please.
So, uh, how did you propel into journalism.

My roommates are in charge of the magazine.
Awww...that's the way to go!

I'm actually a teacher.
You're a teacher… or like a teacher?

I am a teacher.
What grade?

Sixth grade.
Woooooaahh!

I know. It's tough.

You have a lot of patience.

I don't actually.

(Crazy laughter coming from Jim)

I have a couple of students who drive me nuts.

Now I know as a parent why those kids are like that. They're just bored. They're just like fuck this... I want to play.

So that was your problem as a child?

Oh, without a doubt, I wanted to play kick ball instead of learning what is 2 + 7. What does that have to do with anything?

Then give me some advice.

Umm... relate to them. Get on their level. Learn to relate to them rather than having them do what you want. You know what I mean? Every kid is different. I'm starting to notice that. I can't treat my older one like the other one. They are completely opposite. So, to get them to put on clothes, one I gotta trick 'em. "Don't put those pants on... I said... hey! Don't put those pants on!" And then of course she'll put 'em on. Or I could stand there for an hour explaining to them, "We have to go here, the reason we have to go here..." It's not gonna happen. The other one, no problem.

Okay, I'll try and work on that. So, you've been pretty honest about being the fat kid.

Yeah! You know what else I was gonna say... do you mind me interrupting?

No, not a problem.

I noticed that even sixth graders, a lot of them don't know how to express their feelings. Sometimes you can take it personally, but it's really some whole other shit going on in their life. You know what I mean?

They are very hormonal and emotional.

Like, "I only have three hairs on my pee pee. Why do I have these hairs over here? Should I go on a date? Should I go on a date or play football?"

Right, totally! So, anyway… you were the fat kid?

Oh, yeah. I was eighty-two pounds in kindergarten. Broke a hundred in second grade. Had to see a nurse once a week.

Well, this is what I noticed recently. There isn't just one fat kid in each grade, there are six or seven in each class.

Actually, there were three of us.

Oh, there were?

The other two were fatter, thank god. One kid was always ten or twelve pounds bigger. And then there was Sally Ann Castello… she uh, was obviously a girl but she was fatter too.

If you had to choose the best fat kid from a movie, who would you choose?

The fat kid from *The Bad News Bears*. Classic, all time, he was the funniest fat kid ever.

So, as a comedian, you're the funniest guy in the room, and after the show everyone wants to hang out with you. True?

Pretty much. With me, everyone wants to get me stoned.

Do you drink much?
No, I literally will have a glass of red wine. I just don't like the way it makes me feel anymore. I hate hangovers. I hate feeling bloated. I hate waking up in weird places.

How old were you when you stopped?
Ummm… probably about thirty-one.

So, I have a few years left in me?
Some people have a lifetime left in them.

I love it when you talk about your wife. Is she okay with that?
Well, sure. That's life and that's real. I'm not gonna hide what is real. I really think that is part of society's problem. We all pretend we're living in Disney World, and we're not. You know I think that is why there are so many divorces because everyone pretends it's hunky dory, and we have the perfect life, and it's like, no you're not. You scream at each other; your daughter hates you. There's a lot of shit going on. Your sister's an alcoholic. You're fuckin' nuts. And when you acknowledge that, okay, I'm not crazy, this is all of us, and then you begin to change or talk about it. It makes you feel better. Years ago, therapy was called a friend.

Now we all have shrinks, right?
Yeah! Find a friend. Don't be afraid to have problems. Shit, that's what life's about—makes you stronger.

I have a question for you. If you could choose one woman in history, dead or alive, to have dated, who would you pick and when?
Awww, that's a good question. Wow. Let's come back to that one.

When did you start calling yourself a comedian?

1989. In 1988, I started saving my money because I knew I was going to go full blown into stand-up. I didn't care what anyone else said; this is what I was going to do. Tried college, tried what everyone else said. I had it, and this is what I was going to do. In '89 is when I started and in a couple months, maybe three months of open mic and all that, I got paid for my first show. I only had to do like ten minutes and opened for two other people. I just had to make sure to say, "Don't forget, there's a buffet. Remember to tip your waitresses. Next week, Charlie O'Grady is here. He's the hypnotist." But, yeah, I got paid twenty-five dollars, and I was so excited.

When did you know you had made it?

I still don't think I've made it. I have way too much to do. I'm exhausted thinking about it. It's really weird. People keep asking me, "What are you doing?" I live my life at my pace. I wanted to do stand-up to get on TV. Poof, okay did *Saturday Night Live*. I wanted to make the funniest fucking pot movie of the '90s. Poof, we did that. I won't say it was the funniest fucker, but I gave it a shot. Then I wanted to do a one hour special. Poof, I just did that. Then I wanted to start mixing music with comedy, getting a little heavier with the music. That's my next project. And then it will be back to writing the funniest movie that has come out in years. That's where I'm at right now. So, made it. That's such a weird word. I guess when it really started was in '91 in Harlem on a TV show called the *Uptown Comedy Club*. That's when I would say it started for me, when I started really saying "Wow, I can do this."

So, what about that one woman in history?

Hold on, hold on… I had somebody. She came to me and then she went away. Okay, *Charlie's Angels*… Kate Smith, was that her name? No, there was Jacqueline Smith and Kate... the short browned haired one. I just remember watching that show, and I had no idea what making out was, but I know I just wanted to do it with her. I just wanted to sit on her lap and make out for hours. Stop, have some coffee, then make out for hours. I didn't want to do it. I just wanted to fuck face hard.

DOUG STANHOPE

—

By Ryan McKee

Original Interview: November 2002

In 2020, Doug Stanhope is comedy's patron saint of fuck-ups, road dogs, broken toys, substance-abusers, and unbookable performers. He owns a compound in Bisbee, Arizona, (google it) that is equal parts acid funhouse, sports bar, comedy club, flophouse, and podcast studio. While his former *Man Show* co-host Joe Rogan has more followers, Stanhope's hardcore fans exhibit Branch Davidian-esque loyalty.

In 2002, Doug Stanhope couldn't get booked as the headliner at Tempe Improv. Despite working as a comedian for over a decade at that point (living in his car for three of those years), his act earned as many adversaries as fans. Many of those adversaries were club owners. Longtime Tempe Improv booker Dan Mer once told me he couldn't book Stanhope again due to the sheer number of negative comment cards left behind by customers after his performances.

I discovered Doug by pure chance. As I mention in the David Cross introduction, I knew very little about great comedy before deciding to start a magazine devoted to it. During an Ask Jeeves binge, I found a list of up-and-coming comedians (probably *Variety*'s 10 Comics to Watch). I don't remember anything about the list other than Doug Stanhope and Dane Cook were both on there.

At that point, most stand-up comics didn't have a web presence, let alone their own website. Doug, on the other hand, had a full website with debaucherous journal entries, including one about his threesome with two Costa Rican prostitutes. There was even a photo of the naked women with "Doug Stanhope" stickers covering their nipples. Another page had photos of celebrities (including Nicole Kidman, Brooke Shields, Joey Buttafuoco, Weird Al Yankovic, Roseanne Barr, Ray Romano, and Carrot Top) all holding the same photo of an unhappy-looking man. They were grouped under "The Victor Collection"—but with no real explanation.

I found his website so intriguing that I had to interview him. Plus, he listed contact info, too, which made it super easy.

RYAN MCKEE: Are those real Costa Rican prostitutes in that photo?
DOUG STANHOPE: Those are actual Costa Rican prostitutes, branded with the Doug Stanhope stamp.

What is The Victor Collection?
He's a pen pal I have in Florida. I wrote him as a goof out of a personal ad I had seen in a newspaper. The ad said

death row inmate, 6'3," 185 pounds, and will respond to all correspondence. So, I just wrote him a good letter, saying, "I saw your ad in the *LA Times*, and I was intrigued with the fact that you included your height and weight." So, he wrote me back and sent his picture and I took his picture to all the Oscar parties that year and the American Comedy Awards, just took pictures of famous people holding his picture.

How'd your vasectomy go?
I didn't do it. I got a stay of execution. I decided to put it off because you're supposed to wait two days after you get it, and I had to be in Shreveport the next day. You're supposed to sit around with an ice pack on your bag for two days.

I listened to your comedyspeak.com interview...
Could you tell the incredible disdain for the guy who runs the site in my voice?

You seemed annoyed, but I wasn't sure if it was toward the interviewer or...
No, it was for him. He's just a complete idiot. He's not even allowed to go into that club I was playing because he was stalking Mitch Hedberg so badly.

That's disturbing.
Yeah.

The interviewer asked you if you like women. Do you get that question a lot? Do people think your act is misogynistic?
No, I don't get that very often. Stupid people think I'm a misogynist.

You also said that you're never going to get married...
I would never get legally married.

The photos on your website are of a wedding. Is that a goof marriage?
No, it's a real marriage, just not a legal. A legal marriage is ridiculous. There's absolutely no point, absolutely no reason for it other than to empower lawyers. There are no benefits to it other than tax benefits, and if that's your reason for getting married, fucking incorporate.

In your act, you say love is a bad drug like alcohol because you say stuff you don't really mean. Is being horny also a bad drug?
Being horny, that's love, same thing. Duration is the only difference. Well, it's not exactly the same thing, but one can be confused for the other very easily.

After being a comedian for twelve years, what are your frustrations with comedy today?
No different than my frustrations with... I don't even want to say America, but, you know, the fact that everything is so dumbed down. Same problem as with television, the shit that the masses are watching at eight o'clock at night.

Has your main audience aged with you, or do you still get mainly twenty-somethings?
Mostly twenties, yeah. 'Cause most people who go to a comedy club have no idea who they're there to see. A bar crowd tapers off as you get away from twenty-one. My core audience, those who actually understand what I do, are more around thirty.

People can stay at home now and watch comics on television. Does that have anything to do with lower attendance at the clubs?

When they're bringing TV comics into clubs, why would you go out if you're going to see the exact same thing on TV? You can blame TV as much as you can blame the clubs. If there's a lot of stand-up on TV, that might bring people out to the clubs if you give them more. If you give them something they can't see on TV, they'll keep coming back. But when there's a thousand Jerry Seinfelds or Paul Reisers, then it doesn't benefit the live experience.

Are there too many comedians out there?

No. There are too many bad ones, but they're fun to watch too. The mediocre kills me. I love really bad train-wreck comics.

In an interview you said that Crocodile Hunter jokes are the biggest hack jokes today. What else is the sure sign of a hack?

There's a million of them. One is "I look like if so and so and so and so had a baby." That's my favorite opening. Then if someone is relying on racial stereotypes. You see guys saying, "I'm half Irish and half German, so I get drunk and want to take something over."

Before I asked my next question, which was smarter than all the previous questions, Stanhope's phone cut out. At first, I was worried that the hitchhiker he picked up had stabbed him in the throat. However, after a couple hours of me staring at my phone, wondering if I should call the police, he called back, apologized, and said he was all right.

PAUL F. TOMPKINS

———

By Brodie Foster Hubbard
Original Interview: June 2005

One of the things I really loved about my experience as a journalist for *Modest Proposal Magazine* was that I was allowed to deviate from the typical promotional piece for an actor or director's new work. Instead, I got to interview my favorite people in comedy about projects that failed at the box office or were canceled by TV networks, and they talked with me about those failures AFTER they happened.

Certainly, as a body of work, Paul F. Tompkins's career can only be seen as a resounding success. As an actor, he's appeared in *Mr. Show, Tenacious D, Magnolia, Anchorman, There Will Be Blood, The Informant! Bojack Horseman,* and *Tangled: The Series*. He's deeply loved by comedy fans for his three decades of stand-up comedy as well as often popping up in podcasts, political pundit shows, and documentaries. PFT is a performer but also a voice, an institution, a very legit dude.

But at the time of this interview, Tompkins took the time to discuss the challenges of working in television and, specifically, his experience on a short-lived sketch comedy program with star Kelsey Grammer.

I have a distinct memory of sitting on the floor on the second story of my South Scottsdale condo, with then *Mod Prop* webmaster Rhonda Aburomi listening in on this call, the micro-cassette recorder running and my flip phone on speakerphone setting. I haven't spoken with either Paul or Rhonda in fifteen years, but I still admire their work and wish them both well.

BRODIE FOSTER HUBBARD: *Kelsey Grammer Presents: The Sketch Show* **shot six episodes, but Fox only aired half of those. What happened?**
PAUL F. TOMPKINS: Well, for those who say, "people will watch anything"… as it turns out, they will not. I feel like it could have been a good show—the format of it, the quick hit-and-run sketches because a lot of sketch comedy has a tendency to go on too long. It was a good time slot, but the network did not promote the show until about a week before, and then after that, they ran only a few ads, and that quickly stopped. They just didn't care about it.

Overall, it was a really frustrating experience. It was so slapdash… it just felt like nobody really gave a fuck about it. If this is your show, if this is going to be on television with your name on it, you should really kind of give a fuck.

It's adapted from a successful British show. Why didn't it work here?
It just needed better jokes. The scripts were adapted straight from the original British series. What nobody seemed to see... there's a much bigger difference in the sensibility between British humor and American humor. All our crappy comedy aside, I think we are, as a nation, less forgiving of the corniness that ran throughout the show.

How was the experience of shooting in London?
I loved everyone on the cast. We all certainly bonded from that experience. Most of us had come from comedy and sketch, and it was a frustrating experience because we didn't feel like we were listened to a lot of the time and treated like we didn't know what we were doing. We were directed to mimic the original performances of the British cast of the original show. It's more than just insulting; you don't do that to an actor at all. You have to let people put their own personality on it.

Much different than working on *Mr. Show*?
I was completely spoiled on television by working for *Mr. Show*.

Do you think lazy audiences or unimaginative network executives are responsible for bad television?
Part of me thinks it's television's fault because they're constantly second-guessing the public and saying, "Here's what you like to watch," and it's a lot of stuff that's just not that good. On the other hand, there's plenty of shit that's on the air that people are watching in the millions.

What comedy shows do you like on TV right now?

Arrested Development, that's a really great and unique show. But like many things that are challenging in any way, it's not promoted well. I don't know. Networks are much quicker to axe things nowadays as opposed to when shows like *Cheers* took a few seasons to find an audience. The *Cheers* set is in the fucking Smithsonian now. That will never happen again.

But I get it, reality TV is just cheaper to produce, and people love it. It all comes down to money. When they say, "Why should we put this show on the air?" You can't really say, "Because it's noble to do so?"

For aspiring stand-up comics out there, how did you get so good?

I try to be aware of when I could have done something better and not necessarily just listen to everybody telling me, "That was good." I like to be extremely hard on myself and assume everyone's lying to me. You have to know you're doing what you think is funny, not trying to predict what an audience is going to laugh at.

NEIL HAMBURGER

———

By Ryan McKee

Original Interview: 2004

As a society, we're obsessed with solving mysteries now. Everything from true crime to decade-old deleted tweets that reveal a celebrity might kinda be an asshole. The internet has empowered amateur investigators, podcasters, and Reddit sleuths to research and overanalyze everything. Questions *must* be answered, even if the questions themselves are fun just as they are.

Discovering Neil Hamburger in the '90s and early 2000s meant you got to enjoy him in four stages.

1. Is this guy real? Is he really this bad? He can't be real.

2. The internet says he's real. I guess it's so bad, it's funny?

3. Wait, this random indie rock message board says it's some guy named Gregg Turkington. Who the fuck is Gregg Turkington?

4. I'm telling you, dude, he's totally real. He's hilarious.

As Neil Hamburger fans, we had an unspoken agreement to believe in anti-comedy's Santa Claus. Despite logic, it was more fun to believe the indie record label Drag City actually discovered the world's saddest road comic and began releasing his albums. No one went digging to find indisputable proof Neil was actually Amarillo Records' owner and experimental rock musician Gregg Turkington. If you believed, it meant you got to be in on the joke.

I scheduled a phone interview with Neil Hamburger through Drag City's press department. When I called the number given to me, no one answered except Gregg Turkington's voicemail. Minutes later, Neil Hamburger called me back. I didn't mention the voicemail. It's still the most fun I've had doing an interview.

The next time Neil came to Arizona to perform at the small rock club/dive bar Hollywood Alley, I convinced as many friends to go as possible, all the time swearing Neil is a real person. Most of the people in the bar were fans, but there were also normal bar patrons there. Watching them react to Neil's bad jokes, his constant clearing of the throat, and the four glasses of water he was holding at once, made the night all the more enjoyable.

We got to be in on the joke. All you had to do was ignore reason.

RYAN MCKEE: You're on the road all year round. How are you able to keep so physically fit?
NEIL HAMBURGER: I owe that all to these cans of fruit cocktail. I pick up a case on the first and fifteenth of each month at

some of these close-out markets. The exercise from carrying the box from the shop to the car and then, of course, eating the fruit cocktail helps keep your caloric intake down and provides the fiber and different vitamins that you need to maintain mental clarity.

Since you're on the road so much, maybe you can give our readers some tips. What are some good things to have on a road trip?

It's always good if you have a car, first of all. I've done some of these on foot when the car wasn't working, and it wasn't as fun. A trash bag is good to have because sometimes the car becomes so full with broken potato chips, chocolate bar wrappers, peanut shells, napkins, and discarded Taco Bell burritos because sometimes you take one bite and realize you can't eat the thing, and what happens is the floor on the driver's side becomes so cluttered that the burritos and napkins will get stuck under the brake and you can't safely stop.

How do you deal with road rage?

Tape your middle finger to the palm of your hand and that way you can't flip these guys off because you don't have the finger.

How do you avoid being taken advantage of by traveling salesmen or scams?

Oh, I don't avoid that at all. It happens all the time to me. It's just good that when you have as little money as I do, you have less to lose.

How do you avoid heartburn from road food?

I kind of have a continuous case, but that's why I'm trying to stick more to the fruit cocktail. Those peeled grapes and sugary syrup, the acid content isn't as bad if you were to eat at Arby's or whatnot. Have you ever been to the Dollar Tree, that chain of stores where everything is one dollar? Now, if you go into your regular supermarket and buy some Tums, you'll be paying $1.29. If you go to the Dollar Tree, you can get a package of children's chalkboard chalk. The chalk is essentially the same thing as calcium. You break the chalk into smaller pieces and carry them around in your wallet. Then you're ready for anything in terms of heartburn, indigestion, or upset stomach.

Have people thrown things at you while you're on stage?
Never. Everyone is a perfect gentleman at my shows. The applause is always standing ovations. Every show has been sold-out for the past fifteen years. No, of course, I get things thrown at me! Sometimes it looks like I'm standing in the middle of a dust devil with all the hubcaps, and rocks, and tomatoes, cans of tomato paste, shoes, and shoelaces, foot fungus in little plastic capsules. I do have things thrown at me, but it's something we're trying to slow down. We tried putting up a little sign, but somebody stole the sign.

Do you have any advice for new comedians who are getting things thrown at them?
Well, I hope people are throwing things at the new comedians because they're of no help to me. They take my bookings, they take my jokes, and they take my pitchers of water. Go ahead and throw anything you want at these new comedians. If you want to shoot them, that's fine. Run them over, anything. But, please, come out and catch my show.

You've been called the Anti-Emo Phillips. Would you like to comment on that?

I don't know what they're talking about. But it's good that they're thinking of me when they're writing these reviews and articles. As for the specifics of what they're saying, a lot of times it makes no sense.

You've also been compared to Andy Kaufman. Were you a fan?

I haven't had a chance to see him yet, but if he comes to my town, I'll definitely check him out.

After the messy breakup with your ex-wife, what kind of woman does Neil Hamburger need?

Probably a booking agent or some kind of management that can get this career of mine in full gear. Somebody with clout. Either that or Barbara Streisand, who could do some duets with me and help the career along.

You're a wordsmith, if you will. What are some of your favorite words in the English language?

Words like: Dollar, Success, Achievement, Award, Grammy, Million-Seller, Return-Engagement, Encore, Bonus, Accolades, Kudos, Extremely Funny, and Thank You.

Did *Laugh Out Lord* help you to cash in on the religious audience?

That was the idea, but no, there was no cashing in at all.

Have you performed at any churches, mosques, or temples?

Decommissioned churches that have been turned into pizza parlors.

I'm from Phoenix. When did you start performing at Phoenix Greyhound Park?

Let's face it, when you bet on the dogs, you only win about ninety percent of the time. The other ten percent you probably picked the wrong dog. In order to then keep their spirits up, I believe the dog track thought the best thing to do was have a young, fresh comedian capable of eliciting laughter from the most stone-cold cynic.

When this sort of comedian wasn't available, they got me instead. It's hot there in Phoenix and the crowds are hot people. We always have a sweltering good time. It's great to be in that state and experience the hot Friday nights and hot women, hot pizzas, and hot tomato soup.

How does Neil Hamburger keep it real?

Well, I don't really. I would like to, but it's sort of out of the question with the lifestyle I lead and the hours I keep. It's just not possible.

CHRIS HARDWICK
& MIKE PHIRMAN

By Ryan McKee & Ron Babcock
Art by Bryan Hollingsworth
Original Interview: 2006

At the Café 101 in Los Angeles, Ron and I sat waiting to interview Chris Hardwick and Mike Phirman, the music comedy duo known as Hard 'n Phirm. We showed up much earlier than our scheduled time, excited for our conversation.

When we'd met them at SF Sketchfest the year before, I had given them copies of *Modest Proposal*, and I remember Chris, in particular, being very complimentary. I think he even said Patton Oswalt had mentioned the zine to him. Or maybe that last part's a memory fantasy.

Once the UCB Theatre LA opened, we'd run into Mike and Chris often. They were always friendly. And when we asked if they'd like to be interviewed for the magazine, they seemed genuinely excited. We didn't even have to bug them to do it.

At the time of the interview, Mike arrived promptly. Chris showed up a little later, not much later, but late enough that Mike had time to warn us about Chris's health nut order. "He's gonna order something really healthy and tell them to hold everything with flavor," Mike said.

I don't remember what he ordered, but I do remember enjoying the time spent. Chris even picked up the tab.

Ron labored over graphics for the article. This was before graphics software was easy, and he really wanted a funky font for the title. He spent an embarrassing amount of time on it and was proud of what he'd come up with. So, when the issue was published, Ron was eager to deliver their copies in person. As soon as Chris opened the magazine, however, his face fell. The title was spelled wrong. Correction, their group name in the title in the funky font was spelled wrong. *Har 'n Phirm*. It was the very first thing Chris noticed. Ron felt horrible. He felt so bad about it that he wrote the missing 'D' with a Sharpie in the remaining fifteen hundred copies.

Chris and Mike have gone on to pursue solo careers, and I'm not entirely sure where they left off with Hard 'n Phirm. It is one of the interviews I was really hoping to update, but we weren't able to connect with them.

Below is the original interview conducted in that LA café. Maybe they will see that we have spelled their name correctly and reach out.

RYAN MCKEE: You formed Hard 'n Phirm while at UCLA, right?
HARD: I guess you would call it comedy. Put it this way, we would've been big on the college circuit. We were just doing parodies and playing silly versions of songs. Everything was very recognizable and accessible to the lowest common denominator.

RON BABCOCK: Like singing "Diarrheaville" instead of "Margaritaville?"
HARD: Not even that much thought into it. It was more like singing "Rainbow Connection" in dueling Kermit voices.

PHIRM: You remember that TLC song, "Scrubs"? We did one called "Grubs" that was all about farm bugs—those little worms that eat shit.

HARD: We also used to do an a cappella version of Blind Melon's "No Rain."

PHIRM: No jokes, just that.

RYAN: Chris you once said, "We cheat. We use music." What did you mean by that?
Phirm: You said that?

HARD: Well, I feel like even if the song doesn't grab the audience, there's an element to it that's still engaging because you're not just some guy talking.

PHIRM: But if you've got music, you aren't guaranteed funny.

HARD: At the time I was just feeling that music can be a kind of prop. It can be a hook you can fall back on rather than just writing a well-crafted joke that you don't need a video or music to rely on. Still, we're finding that it is hard to write a song that you like, is listenable, and is also funny.

RYAN: On the road, why perform at comedy clubs rather than music venues?
HARD: We don't really have any connections as far as music clubs, and the music club route is more arduous. You're essentially out there driving from gig to gig in a van. A comedy club will fly you out and put you up somewhere. But in LA we've done a lot of music clubs like Spaceland, the Viper Room, and other places. And each time we went thinking that people would be like, "Fuck you!" and throw bottles, but every time it went great because we're always surrounded by really serious bands. The music venues tend to be more fun.

RYAN: Was Radiohead cool about "Rodeohead?"
PHIRM: We heard their manager played it for them, or at least two of them, and they enjoyed it. It's not like there's anything in it that says, "fuck Radiohead." It took us like a year to make, so the attention to detail hopefully translates into people realizing we were serious.

HARD: The program on Mike's computer during the process was fucking up for months, and we couldn't figure out why. But literally it was one box that needed to be checked that wasn't and that fixed the whole problem. You know, software companies need to do a better job at tech support. They make it so difficult because they don't want people to pirate their software, but in the end, they make it so difficult to deal with them that you want to pirate their software out of spite because their service is so shitty. A lot of times it's just like, "Yeah, dude, I can't help you." So in the end I'm saying pirate software! They should be more skilled than your roommate or neighbor going, "I don't know, dude."

RON: How important is it for you to do a Comedy Central special?
PHIRM: There seems to be two ways you can get huge. One: you tour, and you literally build a following. You just take the country one place at a time.

HARD: That takes forever!

PHIRM: It works. Or two: get on TV and boom, overnight success... in theory.

RON: When you get that TV recognition, what do you want to do?

HARD: When you have TV recognition, you get to pick the cities you want to play at. Pockets around the US have really cool clubs like Minneapolis, Tempe, Austin, San Francisco, and it just saves you the trouble of sifting through the shit. But a pure comic would say, "Fuck you, you have to go on the road and pay your dues."

PHIRM: Yeah, but you don't have to see it as a means to an end. You could see it as, "Hey, I've got two hundred shows this year. That means I'll be in front of a crowd two hundred times and doing my thing." As opposed to doing twenty select dates.

RYAN: As Hard 'n Phirm gets more successful, will you both do solo stuff?

HARD: We both still love doing stand-up, and I think we've been eeking it in when we can, but the Hard 'n Phirm stuff seems a more unique package than, "Oh, here's another white guy being sarcastic about something."

PHIRM: I don't really enjoy going on stage solo with just a guitar. I do it sometimes, but that's pretty hacky. I mean there are people who do it well, not me, but Henry Phillips does.

HARD: And it's also fun because we've been best friends for thirteen years, and it's fun to travel together and be on the road together. Maybe this is cowardly, but it also feels safer because you never go down alone: "Hey, we're dying together. There's one other poor son-of-a-bitch that has to suck it up just like me."

RON: **Mike, what were some of the names of your high school bands?**

PHIRM: Uh, the only one I was really in was called Paul Meyer because I had a friend named Paul Meyer.

RYAN: **How have your CDs been selling?**

HARD: We've been selling a couple a day on CDBaby.com because of the "Pi" video. And if we do a *Kimmel*, we'll sell a chunk. When we first got our CDs pressed, we went to Austin to perform with Paul F. Tompkins. We thought, "Well, there's gonna be six shows and like eighteen hundred people." So, we brought 120 CDs. Then we ended up selling like fifteen, so we had all these boxes of CDs. That was such a walk of shame on the plane ride home.

RON: **How do you guys keep it real?**

PHIRM: Take out your own trash.

HARD: I felt like it's kept real for us when we do shows and drunks come up and say, "How come you're singing songs about dinosaurs?" If we ever got tremendously successful, I don't think we'd keep it real anymore. I think we're trying to get where people just agree with everything we do or say. And we can just shit money. But I guess we really have to keep it real at this point. We're humbled by our own level of success.

HUMOR AND ESSAYS

DREAMCRUSHER

—

By Mary Mack
Originally published: 2006

During my comedy set last night in Iowa, a train went barreling by just outside behind the stage. It was very loud and distracting to both the audience and me. The rumbling threw off my timing mostly because I kept wondering how fast I would have to run to be able to keep up and jump into one of those boxcars and be delivered safely to another area of the country. That's a lot of calculating and way too much multitasking for me to do while on the stage.

To my dismay, I had to ditch the idea of jumping on board because I remembered something about trains my mom told me when I was younger. I used to dream about being a train stowaway, and I'd talk about it quite a bit. Then, my mom told me about a mass murderer who was getting around the country in the same fashion. And that was the end of that dream... twice.

2020 UPDATE

I really should have set up the original story by mentioning my obsession with train hopping in my twenties. I *wanted* to do it so badly, even traveling between cities like that. Interviewing strangers who *looked* as though they had done it proved valuable. I got a lot of advice for illegally riding the rails.

Before I accomplished my goal, it came up in conversation with my mom one day and she mentioned the serial murderer who traveled in that fashion as well. After that, upon seeing an open train car I'd get excited, but then immediately get sad. I was too scared to do it because of the murders. But that's the thing about your mom telling you stuff like that: Not only does it depress or scare you at the moment she tells you, but every time you see whatever it is you were excited about, you *do* get excited but then remember her story and get sad again. It's like there's a little shithead angel on your shoulder spoiling a good time for the rest of your life.

I think I always used to jot something down quick after one-nighters, so I wouldn't forget them. This was just one of those quick jots, but it's bringing back some good memories of the unique places and people I've been introduced to through comedy. There used to be so many one-nighters on any given day of the week in the Midwest, and seventeen years ago when I started, it was actually feasible for me to drive six hours on a Monday to make $100 hosting or middling. Not the case for most comics nowadays with the cost of living being what it is.

Mary Mack is a comedian and actress whose credits include Last Comic Standing, Conan, *and* Grand Ole Opry. *She voices* Jesse *in Hulu's* Solar Opposites.

THE FIRST TIME I DIDN'T HAVE SEX

———

By Ryan McKee

Originally published: 2005

You hurt the ones you love. That's a given. What about the people you don't love, but you really like because they let you feel them up in the woods by your house even though you're an awkward thirteen-year old boy? Are you supposed to hurt them too?

Silvia moved to my hometown, Payson, Arizona, two months into the seventh-grade year. Immediately, she was shunned for being new at our small redneck junior high. Since I too had been shunned that year for liking the New Kids on the Block and proving it with a T-shirt, Silvia and I had a lot in common, including living in the same neighborhood.

Simply by not shooting her dirty looks or spitting on her, I caught her attention. Our first conversation went like this:

"Hey, you're new here," I said, trying to sound like I had just noticed. This was after a month of riding the same bus.

"Yeah, I'm Silvia," she said and shoved her hand over the bus seat that separated us to shake my hand. I shook it and held on a little too long.

"I'm Ryan." Fearing that I was running out of things to say, I blurted out, "The New Kids on the Block totally suck, huh?"

She shrugged, "I don't know."

I was drowning.

"Where you from?" I asked

"Chino Valley."

"That's a cool place."

"You've been there?"

"No," I said. "It's in Arizona, right?"

"Yeah, it's an okay place. Better than here."

"Yeah."

"How do you know; you haven't been there."

"Well, yeah, but here sucks."

"Yeah," she said. "How come you don't have any friends on the bus?"

"Because I think everyone's stupid." That was the toughest sounding lie I could think of.

"Oh."

"But you seem cool."

That seemed to make her happy and she smiled. She had a little crossbite and two pigtails held by neon elastic. Though still fighting the evil grips of puberty, Silvia managed to pull off a sultry Fly Girl-style, made famous at the time by the *In Living Color* dancers. I felt as cool as Keenan-Ivory Wayans just talking to her.

"Do you wanna go out with me?" I asked.

"Sure," she said and then turned and looked out the bus window until we got to school.

She must have forgotten to say good-bye and walked off the bus into school. I didn't care. I had my first junior-high girlfriend.

December brought the holiday break, and Silvia and I were still together as far as I knew. It had been a week since school let out, and we hadn't spoken.

My aunt lived in LA and "understood" the scene, so she had given me a badass Nirvana T-shirt for Christmas. Cocky in my badass Nirvana T-shirt, I called Silvia. She sounded happy to hear from me. We made plans to meet by the woods near our neighborhood.

It had been a white Christmas, but the snow was melting. I threw on a flannel shirt, no jacket, and didn't button it up. The yellow letters spelling "Nirvana" had to show. I ran outside before my mom could tell me to put on more clothing. Freezing but excited, I jogged with my arms clutching my body and jumped around like a slam-dancer at the meeting spot to keep warm.

She took another fifteen minutes getting there. When I saw her come into view, I tried to act like I wasn't cold.

"Aren't you freezing?" she asked, wearing a black Raiders parka.

"Nahh, it's not cold," I said and then clenched my teeth so they wouldn't chatter.

"I got this for Christmas," she said grabbing at the Starter jacket. It looked like straight out of an Ice Cube video.

"It's nice," I said and put my arm around her, moving toward the woods where we had French-kissed a couple of times before.

We couldn't sit on the log we usually sat on to French-kiss because it was wet with melting snow. So, we stood and stuck our tongues in each other's mouth.

I'm not sure if it was the confidence my badass Nirvana T-shirt gave me or my survival instincts telling me to get warm at any cost, but I stopped kissing Silvia long enough to unzip her parka and begin feeling her breasts.

I just went for it. I had never before. I hadn't planned to, I just did. And she didn't stop me. She didn't even skip a beat. We just went back to Frenching while I grabbed at her very firm right tit.

After a while, I got braver and put my hand under her sweatshirt, under her undershirt, and tried to wedge it up in her bra.

She giggled, stopped kissing me long enough to unsnap her bra, and let me continue. She even let me lift the three layers of clothes to look at them.

Paler than the rest of her coffee-skin, they seemed to give off an angelic glow. They reminded me of grapefruits you buy at the store, take them home, and say, "Wow, these are some great grapefruits!" Amazingly well-shaped, her breasts caused me to believe for a while that the only imperfectly shaped breasts in the world were in *National Geographic*, due to my experience with seeing breasts limited to Silvia, *Playboy*, and *Nat G*.

A day later Silvia called me and said she wouldn't be coming back for second semester. Her dad was making better money now, so she didn't have to live with her aunt in Payson anymore and would be moving back to Chino Valley.

I felt depressed the rest of Christmas vacation.

Back at school, maybe it was the false confidence from my badass Nirvana T-shirt or maybe it was because she wouldn't be around to deny it, but at lunch I blurted out: "Hey, I did it with Silvia over Christmas break."

My friends rightly doubted me and almost in choral harmony said, "Phssf, did what?"

I took a long breath. I wasn't sure exactly. "It, ya know, it," I said, hoping they'd believe me and just drop it.

Seventh grade might seem a young age to lose your virginity, and it is; however, at the time, there were multiple stories circulating about kids our age having sex. I believed every one and just figured everyone would believe mine.

What I didn't account for was the fact that I wasn't cool. Not even near cool. I sat at the lunch table where kids would read Stephen King novels and D & D strategy books while stuffing tuna sandwiches in their mouths. I was the only one of my friends who even had regular contact with girls and most people were surprised by that.

Proof of my conquer was needed. I had heard girls bled after their first time and that guys sometimes got it on them. Stealing a razor blade from my dad's medicine cabinet, I made a few small incisions on the inside of my calf and held a pair of my boxers to the cut. When I got the crotch pretty well covered in red, I stood up. Light-headed from either the loss of blood or my genius plan, I stumbled a little.

The first friend I saw the next day, I pulled into a corner of the school. "Look," I said opening my pants.

"What the hell?"

"No, dude, see, she bled on my boxers when we did it. Do you believe me now?"

He looked skeptical. I explained in a frenzy that girls bled their first time. He nodded unsurely and went to go consult others. At one point, I had seven or eight guys huddled around me in the corner staring at my crotch. If our very Christian principal had walked around the corner at that point, he would have gone screaming through the halls.

Like my father popping the hood when the car doesn't start, none of these onlookers had any idea what they were looking at. So, the consensus was to consult an expert.

Shannon Darnile was in eighth grade and rumored to have slept with seven high school guys and Joe Watson, who was still in junior high but had a mustache. She was infamous. She smoked cigarettes, laughed loudly, wore Wranglers so tight that her ass ate them, and hair-sprayed her bangs higher than anyone. She was wise beyond any of us, and we all feared her immensely.

However, in the name of science and truth, my friends were willing to brave her wrath. They dragged and peer-pressured me over to where she always sat with her similarly intimidating friends.

One of my braver friends stepped forward and explained the situation to Shannon while all her crew looked on disdainfully. She seemed to understand why we had come to her and agreed to give us her expert opinion.

Nervously I unbuttoned my pants. She looked at the stain on my quivering crotch like she was reading a crystal ball. Finally, after what seemed like an extremely long time, she announced, "This boy has been laid!"

My memory wants to tell me that everyone cheered, and my friends boosted me up on their shoulders and carried me away like I had just won the big game.

However, what really happened was my idiotic friend screamed, "All right!" Then he tried to boost me up on his shoulder by himself. I was too chubby and toppled down. Embarrassed, I got up and cheered like I'd meant to do it. A special education student was nearby and cheered as well, which he always did whenever he heard someone cheer. I do not believe he understood what he was cheering for.

The cool smoker kids stared at us, wondering what we were still doing standing there after their leader had already told us what we wanted. Not meeting each other's eyes, we walked away in different directions.

So, to Silvia, if you're reading this, I'm sorry I defiled your name in Payson. It seemed like a good idea at the time but did not make me any cooler. My badass Nirvana T-shirt, however, did a little bit.

UNEDITED CD REVIEWS BY CHILDREN

———

By Chrystyna Golloher
Originally published: January 2003

This idea really made me excited, and I thought my sixth graders would dig it. Because music is cool, right? But middle schoolers have a knack for finding any idea not cool enough for their precious time. They enjoyed this as much as they appreciated my well-planned lessons that perfectly aligned with several Arizona language arts state standards... which is to say, not much.

I had some hope that they might dig Ms. Golloher's music. After all, I was only eleven years older than my students. But to them, I might as well have been sixty-five years old. My taste couldn't compete when I was contending with 50 Cent, R. Kelly, and Nickelback.

I recall being a little concerned about quoting children for a comedy zine without receiving permission from anyone.

However, not concerned enough to actually *request* said permission. I'm pretty sure I even kept their first names but changed the grade levels. In the event I was ever questioned, I had plausible denial: "I don't know anyone named Lesley in fifth grade. I know of a Lesley, but she's definitely in sixth grade."

Luckily, no one ever figured it out. And I'm not sure why I even considered they might. It's not like anyone could've posted it on Facebook or Twitter.

So, here are sixth-graders reviews (even though they say different grades) of Arlo's "Little American" and The Format's "The First," completely unedited to include every glaring spelling and grammatical error.

ARLO, "LITTLE AMERICAN"

Ryan, 6th grade: "The CD is by Arlo and it is rock I think but I really like it. The Little American is about a kid who lives far away from someone. I think I would recommend it to myself because I am a little American boy."

Lisa Marie, 5th grade: "This music is punk rock. It will be good for pro skaters like Tony Hawk! Some may like punk rock and some may hate punk rock. Hey, it's your decision!!!!"

Tony, 5th grade: "Good in the beginning and pretty much the whole song, but it could use a better name. It has a nice beat, and good melody, too. But it has kind of bad leeriks and bad singing. Good music, drummer, and good guitarist. It sounds kind of like country, too (bad thing)."

Gabrielle, 6th grade: "The words are ok bu tthey got to work on there beat and get that got-damn gator out. Sounds like something Tony and Ryan would like!!!!!! Ryan would mach this song cause he is wired jest like this song!

Jorge, 5th grade: "I hate it. But it's better than the Format."

THE FORMAT, "THE FIRST"

Lesley, 5th grade: "The guy singing is talking about this girl he likes but she doesn't like him and he is trying to get her to like him but she doesn't. He is very depressed becuse he rilly likes this girl. I would recomend this song to my 20 year old sister because of her ex-boyfriend."

Austin, 6th grade: "They are copying the voice of the lead singer from Sugar Ray. They should get rid of the tamberine plus the drummer sucks because it is a drum machine. They could be better if they did faster songs and plus the beat kinda like that one Michael Jackson song."

Netha, 5th grade: "I think it is okay, it need a little like Backstreet Boys a little. I really like it ok to me. I ame not say that it need to be like Backstreet Boys. It is cool, clap your hands and stomp your feet. The Format is cool! It is not like hip hop, hip hop is faster.

Kasey, 6th grade: If you can't dance to it or understand the words then don't waste your money. A garage band I saw of 14 year olds sounded better than this.

WHY ARE FILM STUDENTS ANNOYING?

———

By Chris Keener

Originally Published: January 2003

1. Because we refer to twenty-five-minute, underexposed, handheld, VHS documentaries of horse fodder as "pieces."

2. Because we are under the illusion that "maybe if it's in black and white, people won't find my naked body hideous, but rather, well-composed."

3. Because we think we're the only ones who really understood *Memento*.

4. Because we swear we knew the ending of *The Sixth Sense* before it came.

5. Because we represent sixty-two percent of undergraduate enrollment, nationwide, and resultantly:

6. Augment America's unemployment rate tenfold.

7. Because, if by some freak chance, a snowball rolls through hell and anoints one of us a director, we steal all the money from more philanthropic humans.

8. Because we think that taping up soiled sheets on the side of a brick house to diffuse a light in a gale is somehow prerequisite to being a director.

9. Because we look down on people who haven't seen a particular movie, because:

10. We are bitter about wasting our carefree sexual peaks watching Wes Craven marathons in big dark rooms with sticky floors.

MOST ANNOYING THINGS ABOUT
DATING A FILM STUDENT

By Kristen Hof
Originally Published: January 2003

1. Tells me the entire acting history of every cast member of every movie.

2. Points out every editing flaw, rewinding to make sure I see it.

3. Quizzes me on movie trivia and dialogue randomly and unnecessarily.

UPDATE 2020

I did indeed end up marrying that film student. All those annoying habits still exist, except now I'm guilty of them half the time too. My favorite asshole response to the verbal IMDB list of each new actor on-screen's history is "Yup, actors acting." I love when I can stump him on something or find an editing error he missed. I know. I'm a dork. Nothing new.

WHAT I REALLY LEARNED IN SCHOOL

By Chrystyna Golloher: Arizona State University
Originally Published: March 2003

Updates: May 2020

WHAT I REALLY LEARNED IN PUBLIC SCHOOL
By Chrystyna Golloher:
Arizona State University

FRESHMAN YEAR

- Going to class is important. Grades are important. College is important.

- Frat parties suck. They only let girls in. My boyfriend who writes deep poetry cannot get in.

- Beer is good. Some of the best brands: Natural Ice, Ice House, Bud Ice.

- I can figure out my major later. I'm still young, and I have three more years to go.

- Mmm... tequila is fun! But remember, liquor before beer... very important.

- I can look forward to Fridays and Saturdays, so I can forget about the week's troubles.

- I discovered a fun way to enjoy my evenings—drinking games! I'm spending quality time with my friends, and it's also the quickest way to get drunk.

- Should get eight hours of sleep, but four will do.

SOPHOMORE YEAR

It does not matter how late you schedule your first class; you will sleep through it.

- Keg parties are awesome![62] Always have an escape route in case the cops show up.

---

62 *We lived for keg parties. However, when the door guy had the audacity to charge a cover of $5 instead of $3, you better believe we complained and threatened to leave! Five bucks is a lot to ask for unlimited beer. But eventually we'd just pay the money and go in... 'cause we didn't have anywhere else to go anyway.*

- "Oh my God! I can't stand cheap beer! I only drink Bud Light or Coors Light."

- "Hmm? Major? Oh, yeah. I'm thinking Psychology... or Communications."

- One shot of tequila is okay before each beer.

- There are actually four days of the week when you can party: Thursday, Friday, Saturday, Sunday.

- Playing drinking games with hard liquor will get you fucked up, but you can only wake up naked and confused so many times.

- If you have an exam and a party coming up around the same time, go to the party and then stay up the next night cramming. Coffee will help.

Junior Year

- Maybe I don't have to go to *every* class.

- I tried to relax on the drinking for a while... but then turned twenty-one. It's almost as if the town planners purposely lined ASU with bars.

- "I can't believe people who only drink domestic beer! Please get some taste! I'll take a Labatt's Blue please."

- "Oh, shit! I need a major! They won't let me register for classes without one."

- I learn to obey the tequila.

- Happy hour only happens Monday through Friday. Take advantage of it.

- I can do a PowerPoint presentation on drinking games and get an A.[63]

Senior Year

- "Must go to classes… must go to classes… must go to classes…"

- I can tell you all the Happy Hour specials in and around the area.

- Drinking wine is much more sophisticated than drinking beer. And you can get a box for $10.

- Playing drinking games with wine is fun, until you wake up feeling like an elephant sat on your head.

- Can't drink tequila anymore. Bad experience in Mexico.

---

63 *True story. I had an assignment to create a PowerPoint presentation on any topic of my choosing. I chose drinking games. And I did get an A.*

- What's one more semester? It's my parents' money anyway. Drink up.[64]

WHAT I REALLY LEARNED IN PRIVATE SCHOOL
By Andrea Golloher:
Washington University in St. Louis

Freshman Year

- Latin: The most useless language ever. I am fairly certain Professor Pepe has accepted this fact and does not look at homework before grading it.[65]

- Cultural Anthropology: One can identify different sects of Amish by the length of the ribbon on the women's bonnets. The rest of the class was useless.

- Bon Appetit is ranked number one out of all college catering services. Center Court offers a wide variety of foods for just one flex off your meal plan. All you can eat weeknights, with brunch on the weekends. What more could you want?

- The chancellor has a bowling alley in the basement of his house. The chancellor also looks like a leprechaun.

---

64 *After all these years, just reading through this list gave me a contact buzz, and I'm pretty sure I'll have a hangover in the morning.*

65 *As a professor myself now, this is the only way I remain sane when facing a mountain of grading.*

- Public schools in Missouri get cable and internet access for free. We have to pay for it, never mind the fact that we pay twice as much for room and board.

- Walk In, Lay Down, also known as WILD, the bi-yearly concert/party held in the quad usually ranks around a three on the Richter scale.

Sophomore Year

- Human Anthropology: Lorises are all over the fucking place. Lemurs are only found in Madagascar. Bonobo chimps have sex like we shake hands and nod hello.

- Ancient History: Professor Pepe still doesn't read the papers, but now I look really smart for taking a class called "Ancient History."

- After a year and a half of eating dinner every day at Center Court, and brunch on weekends, over half the sophomores at Washington University are suffering from acid reflux, ulcers, or acute stomach diseases.

- When eating out in a large group, it is acceptable etiquette to start eating after three people are served, unless you're sitting with a king or queen, in which case you should wait until his or her majesty takes the first bite. This I learned from the chancellor, although I still do not know why I was invited to eat lunch with the chancellor or if he considered himself the king of the campus.

- It is easy to steal cable in the old dorms. Stay away from public computers though; the construction workers use them to look at porn.

- Black pants are no longer just worn because they are fashionable and go with everything. They are now known as CFM pants, or "come fuck me" pants, and are usually spotted on roving hordes of sorority girls looking for M.R.S. degrees.[66]

JUNIOR YEAR

- The American School: Professor Tatalovich, "Lo," don't read no papers as long as they be long. Am beginning to lose writing skills from lack of critical feedback?

- A girl can live a long time on a diet of Strawberry Shooter Smoothies and bagels with cream cheese from the campus bakery although she should be wary of those "vitamin supplements" they offer. They suspiciously resemble Sweet Tarts.

- The chancellor is suspected to have patented the chemical that causes the Glow Stick to glow after being cracked. This explains why Glow Sticks are present at every university function.

- In the new dorms, it is impossible to steal cable, and the windows face the poorly designed new parking garage that we've paid for but cannot use (a "$1,000 donation" will get you a FREE parking spot). Car alarms sound through the night.

---

66 *Way to slut-shame, young Andrea. Embarrassing to read now.*

- Study Abroad in Australia: Stomach problems cease, drinking increases, and cry miserably all the way home. It is cheaper to fly to Australia and attend school there than it is to go to Washington University.[67]

Senior Year

- Personal Finance: The one useful class at Wash U. Professor Gordiner taught us that we can hide our money from the IRS by donating it to the school... only it made more sense when he said it.

- Avoid campus food at all costs; there are roaches everywhere.[68]

- A girl can live well as long as she has Ragu in the fridge. However, the new dorms, aka "small group housing," which seem to house more frats than "small groups" as we were told was the original concept of the beautiful buildings, offer gourmet meals carefully constructed by a nutritionist to ensure the good health of our future leaders.

- The chancellor doesn't remember me from lunch sophomore year. I am just one in six thousand students to him. I'm crushed.

---

67 *Should I have just transferred? What would my life be like now if I emigrated?*

68 *Having attended four universities on my way to a PhD, I'm surprised I've lived this long. Campus food is not for the weak of stomach.*

- After years of hiding the fact that we've been stealing cable, we find out that Washington University was stealing all the premium channels we enjoyed. Good-bye HBO.

- $120,000 later, no graduate of 2002 is making as much per year as it cost to go to Washington University per year.

WHAT I REALLY LEARNED IN MILITARY SCHOOL
By Joey Sullivan: Air Force Academy

- How to iron my bed.

Actually, I just got good at sleeping on top of a made-bed with another blanket so that I wouldn't mess it up. I did that for six years. I've since stopped making the bed altogether.

- Acronyms can be fun.

I now use them on my kids as a way to control them. News flash, it isn't working. My kids are beasts.

- Drinking and chasing girls is neat, but Friday night could be better spent shining your boots.

I wrote this in direct rebellion to Ryan's "ASU life" where I imagined he was "sex, drugs, and rockin' rolling" it all the time.

- Saltpeter in your food = no more Mr. Happy time.

I don't even know how to respond to this one. I'm pretty sure there was never saltpeter in our food.

- Don't go, period.

Eh, you know, it wasn't that bad. I went because I wanted to. What the hell was wrong with me? Could have been rockin' and a rollin' with Ryan.

- Having an American flag sticking out of one's ass during Light's Out roll call is neither funny nor a good show of American pride. You will do push-ups until you puke.

That actually happened. I'm not proud of it, but it happened.

- Saluting is not fun. We hate it. Please quit saluting us, and tell your children to stop. It's not cute.

Little kids saluting is adorable. I was a jerk. Salute away please. Except that old drunk guy who makes a big deal about it at the stoplight by Whole Foods. Just let me get my kombucha, bro.

- Pity us. Teach your daughters to date us. Have your seen our haircuts? Wait, hold on, I hear someone coming... "Ten hut!" "No sir, I was not making fun of this place... yes, sir, I love push-ups... 1... 2... 3... kill me... I mean 4...

I have daughters now and I don't want them dating guys like I was back then. I want them to grow up independent and strong and able to discern a good guy from a horny cadet guy. I'm not sure how to do this. Should I be a strong example of how a male role model should be? Should I warn them of douchey dudes? Should I let them make their own decisions and only provide them with love and encouragement? Right now, I'm just using the acronym thing to control them, so we'll see if I change my plan anytime soon.

WHAT I REALLY LEARNED IN CATHOLIC SCHOOL
By Shall Remain Anonymous
Due to Current Profession

- You aren't supposed to understand how a virgin gave birth to God because faith is supposed to be blind... and deaf, and mute. It's basically an overall head-scratcher.

- Jesus traveled on a donkey, repeat, traveled on a donkey—not rode on an ass.

- Being taught Sex Education class by a priest is the most uncomfortable thing known to man.

- Second most uncomfortable is hearing Fr. Jim say, "The man inserts his penis into the vagina."

- Communion wafers are not potato chips. Communion wafers are not meant for salsa.

- A rosary is not jewelry.

- You are not, and never will be, starving. Saying you are will get you a lecture on and slide show of starving Ethiopians. You won't, however, get food.

- Mass is much like a football game—stand up, sit down, chant, raise your arms, etc.—but without the fun.

- Girls and staircases results in mass droppings of pens, books, pretty much anything in our hands.

- Jesus was way cool.

WHAT I REALLY LEARNED IN HOME SCHOOL

By Anonymous Nerd

- Yellow school buses are for future vagrants and homeless people, so don't go near them.

- "Schools" are really sweatshops where bad children have to work, so don't go near them.

- Crossing guards protect the sweatshop. If they see you, they will shoot you, so don't go near them.

- Don't bother not going near bullies. They will find you. They will hurt you. There is no escape. The outside world is cruel.

- Snow days and sick days can only be found in a magical kingdom far, far away called college.

WHAT I REALLY LEARNED DROPPING OUT OF SCHOOL

By That Guy With a Hollowed-Out Spirit

Working at Taco Bell can be done even after smoking three bowls of kind bud.

You go from being the creepy guy in class to being the creepy guy hanging out in the parking lot.

Only freshman girls, whose fathers didn't give them enough attention, think older dropouts are cool.

It's not just the high school principal trying to keep you down, but the whole damn world.

It's everybody else's fault.

There's not a lot of good daytime television.

After you beat *Super Mario Brothers* fifty times, it kind of becomes a sucky game.

I'll tell you what I didn't learn—how to insert bullet points into text.

FUCKING A, A REAL-LIFE *OFFICE SPACE*

———

By Ryan McKee

Originally Published January 2003

Updated footnotes by Max Burger: September 2018 .

I met Maxwell Burger because he and my girlfriend at the time (Chrystyna Golloher) had gone to high school together. He had recently moved back to Arizona from Northern California to "figure shit out," which included taking a stand-up comedy class taught by local comedy veteran Tony Vicich. I kind of became obsessed with Max (in only a mildly creepy way) because he was the first "normal person" I knew pursuing stand-up.

During this same period, I compulsively re-watched *Office Space*. Sure, it's a masterfully crafted comedy, but it also scared me shitless. It felt like writer/director/oracle Mike Judge had created it specifically for me as a cautionary tale.

I would become the film's lead character Peter Gibbons—directionless, apathetic, depressed, and chained to a cubicle—unless I cracked the secret code allowing me into the entertainment business.

Max had already experienced the cubicle of consternation and escaped. That's why I shoehorned the *Office Space* thing and his story together into this article.

Stand-up comedy stardom never materialized for Max, nor me for that matter. However, neither of us became Peter Gibbons either.

———————

Max Burger had a plan. A good plan. And things went according to plan.

He graduated valedictorian of his high school class, graduated in three and a half years from college[69], earned a business degree in purchasing, and started working for a Silicon Valley company that manufactures refrigerator-sized machines that clean the silicon wafers used in manufacturing microchips.

"First day I walked in, they welcomed me by saying, 'Here's a computer, here's a phone, get to work,'" Max said. "At that time, the market was good. Everyone was believing in the system: work hard, get orders... but then *boom*."

———————

69 *Real smart. Leave the party early to sit in a cube all day.*

The *boom* is the bottom dropping out.[70] The economy slumped, the company began laying people off, and Max started doing the job of two people. They insisted he work longer and longer hours and come in on the weekends.

Max began staring blankly at his desk for long periods of time. An hour of every day went into hiding in the bathroom.

"I was running around so much. I'd have seventy emails a day. I'd have to be on the floor with assembly workers and then be in the clean room. I remember wearing a gown and hairnet and thinking, '*What the fuck?*'"

Max volunteered[71] to be laid off fourteen months after starting the job. He figured better him than some poor bastard who really needed the job.

After spending the majority of his severance package on trips to Mardi Gras and Vegas, Max did what all former valedictorians do. He moved back in with his parents and started collecting unemployment checks.

With hiding in the bathroom and wearing a hairnet off his schedule, Max decided to use his free time to enroll in the Tempe Improv's Comedy College, a six-week course designed to instruct people on how to become a stand-up comedian.

---

70 *After getting my real estate license, the housing market also went boom. Is it me?*

71 *Ha! More like voluntold. It's called getting shit-canned*

"They teach facial expressions and accents," Max said. "You have to change characters and be happy, sad, drunk. They teach you how to write jokes, how a joke works. It seems basic, but it really taught me how to write a good setup and a good punch line. How to write less setup and more punchline."

The first six-week session, the students learn the basics and don't get up on stage much. Then, in the advanced class, you get up once a week in front of the class. After six more weeks, the class puts on a showcase for the public.

I went to Max's showcase. I was skeptical. A stand-up comedy class taught by a stand-up comedian who doesn't earn enough money doing stand-up comedy, so he has to teach a class.

And many of the students were bad. However, Max killed. His first public performance and you would've never known it. Maybe he had it in him all along, but the Comedy College brought it out.

Unemployment checks bled dry; Max is now working for himself. He took a crash course in selling real estate.[72] He hopes working for himself will allow him the time to pursue his stand-up career. Imagine if you'd bought your house from Chris Rock before he got big. Fucking A, man, fucking A.

---

72 *I only learn things from short, crammed courses apparently.*

CLASSIFIEDS

———

By Ron Babcock
Originally Published: February 2003

Reading early attempts at your own comedy writing is a cringe fest (see "Breast Surgeon" entry). But then you come across a joke that actually foretells the future (see "Donate Your Plasma").

In the early 2000s, Phoenix was covered with neon signs that encouraged people to "Donate Plasma for $$$" in big, black, block lettering. I always felt sorry for people so in need of money that they would have to donate their plasma. "People donate blood for free," I thought. "So, if they're paying for plasma, it must hurt like hell."

Cut to a few issues later, Ryan and I are both donating our plasma for $30 a pop so we can pay to print the magazine. We learned two things from the experience. One, you could get really drunk off only two Coronas after donating plasma, so in a strange way it actually saved us money. Two, don't eat Burger King before you donate because it makes your blood "fatty" and will keep clogging the machine. Ryan was done in fifteen minutes, but ol' fatty blood took forty-five.

SICK LEPERS WANTED

St. Mark's Bible School is looking for a live, but close to death, leper to show our students what happens when God smites them. Must be blanketed by sores and sorrow. Desperate sighs are preferred but not necessary.

PHARMACEUTICAL SALESMAN

Looking for ambitious entrepreneur to push product in urban ghettos. Must be willing to take a bullet. To apply, wait in a dark alley for Eddy.

ANARCHIST MOVEMENT PRESIDENT

Candidates needed to plan, organize, and lead an anarchy movement. Must destroy all government and currency. Payment will be given upon completion. No need to apply, just come in and take over.

BREAST SURGEON

Hands on experience required. Much room for development.

WORK AT HOME

Make $5,000/week stuffing envelopes! Promised bonus of $500/month. To apply, lose your grip on reality.

CUSTOMER SERVICE REP

No experience necessary, but we will not train you. We will throw you to the wolves and laugh at you gregariously. To apply, just come in crying because that's what you will be doing.

COMEDIAN

Looking for a neurotic, overanalytical candidate to self-deprecate themselves in hopes of making an audience feel better about their lives. To apply, publish an indie comedy magazine.

RECORD STORE MANAGER

Are you a musician who almost made it but didn't? Do you spend your days listlessly dreaming, muttering how you would have made it if the stupid van didn't break down? If so, please don't apply. We have nine of those already.

UNEMPLOYMENT

Looking for a secure, sound, and happy businessman to get fired, so I can take his place. Benefits include me not putting a dagger in your back if you don't get fired.

APPLE SALESMAN

Young, strong men needed to rough customers up and ask, "How do you like them apples?" Benefits include beating them up if they indeed do not like "them apples."

DONATE YOUR PLASMA

Go to the brink of existence and back again for $30. Donate your plasma to needy victims and in the process, become a victim (but not as needy as the other ones). No need to apply. Any "body" will do. Get it? Anybody, anybody? C'mon, that's funny.

DEAD HORSE BEATER

Candidate who doesn't know when to quit needed to beat dead horses into the ground. Immaturity and the ability to never shut up a plus. To apply, copy down the last joke you heard until we call you.

WOMEN SEEKING MEN

MEOW KITTEN

Me SWF, twenty-five, named Kat, but call me Kitten. I lick myself and purr. I also have a tail. And I eat mice. So, don't screw with me, or I'll claw your eyes and bury them in cat litter. Let's play cat and mouse.

LOOKING FOR ADVENTURE?

Never have stories to tell your buddies at the bar? Call me. I'm completely UNPREDICTABLE. I'll accuse you of atrocities in public, steal your stuff, and burn your car. Oh, the places we'll go and the stories you'll tell. Me SWF, 5'9," blue eyes, with massive scars. You are able and willing.

DADDY?

Why won't you come home? Mommy and I miss you. Please come back. SWF, 2'5," 6.

DON'T VOTE FOR NIC WEGENER

By Nic Wegener

Originally Published: February 2003

The following is the acceptance speech given by Nicholas Wegener upon receiving the Apathy Party's nomination for President. The speech was given at the Apathy Party's first ever convention, held at Arizona State University before five people.

I would like to thank all those attending. I would like to thank all those not attending even more. As you can see, more people are not here than here, which means we've done our job. This is a great honor. Many of you know me. Many of you don't know me. Many of you don't care. Kudos.

I have in the past performed comedy. However, today I come to you not to be funny but serious. And even more than being serious, I come to you out of laziness. Yes, that's correct, laziness. I believe I am the choice of the people. I will be the next President of the United States.

I know what most of you may be asking yourself, "How do I get away with scratching my ass in public when I feel the need but don't want everyone to see me do it?" Well, that's a hard question. It's a question for which I don't have an answer. Many of you may also be asking yourself, "Hey Nic, get real, how are you going to be President?" That question, while hard, is answerable.

I am a maverick. I am a maverick in that I listen to the people. And, the people have spoken. The people have spoken by not speaking. And what they are saying (without saying) is that they don't like to vote. And honestly, who does? I don't. And, I won't. And, neither should you. I continue...

If elected, my first action as the new leader of the free world will be to abolish voting. Some may say stupid stuff like, "That's not even a respectable platform." Well, let me remind you that these are the same people who once thought the world to be flat (it is not). So many politicians spend their time talking about stupid things like taxes and abortion and hungry people. Politicians have been talking about these things for years. If they were so smart, they would have solved this stuff in the '70s or '80s or '90s. Also, people don't care about taxes and abortion and hungry people. If they did, they would watch taxes, abortion, and hungry people on TV, but they don't. So, let's not talk about any of that stuff and instead make voting illegal.

"Okay, Nic, I'm all aboard, now how do I get you elected?" Well, when your friends decide to vote and try to get you to vote, don't. Each vote that is not cast this election I consider a vote for me. In a way, when you decide not to vote, you are voting. You are voting for me. And, I am going to end voting. So, when you vote by voting not to vote, you are voting for me to vote to make voting illegal. Frankly, I think you see the point.

Now, you're thinking, "Nic, I'm with you, America's with you, but Washington doesn't work like this." It does work like this. You see, the President is not elected by votes. Instead, they are elected by the Electoral College. So, I just have to call up these guys and explain the agreement I have made with America on behalf of the Apathy Party. Some of the members of the Electoral College are not members of the Apathy Party. They prefer the Big Two. These people might take some convincing. I encourage you all to write these people. I don't know their names, but trust me, they are very real.

My analysts are very positive when it comes to the chance of people not voting, therefore voting for me. In fact, they say there is a good chance I would become the first candidate to ever win every state. Some states I could take by as much as seventy percent. I was really worried that people who didn't know that not voting was really voting for me would get mad when they found out. "Au contraire," say my analysts. My analysts say they may get mad at first, but they are actually the most likely to support no more voting.

So, to support me in my quest for liberty and other stuff, all you must do is nothing. Instead of voting, spend time with your family, plant a tree, repair a road, or increase trade with a foreign country (stuff that will actually do some good, unlike voting). Please tell your friends to do the same. I would like to expand my speech to areas not involving not voting, but I have not thought of anything else, and I have a couch at home calling my name. Thank you for your time, especially those of you who did not give your time by not showing up, and God Bless.

A dog is thrown at Nic, which he pets. A baby is thrown at Nic, which he catches. And kisses.

NEED A SCENE?
FOLLOW ME

——

By Nic Wegener

Originally Published: April 2003

I've been on the scene for years. You know the phrase, "see and be seen?" I'm usually doing both. I'm seeing while being seen at the scene. Many times, I see someone burst onto the scene, and they fade out right away. Not me. Being on the scene is nothing new to me. I've been doing it my whole life.

It all started in preschool. My teacher set out a bunch of juice boxes on a table in the back of the class without saying anything. I was the second one there. Johnny Milton beat me there by about a minute and my fate was set. I still remember him looking over at me, "These things are great, huh?" "Yeah," I replied, "should we tell everyone else?" "No, if they're cool, they'll come." And they did come. Johnny got the credit for the juice-box bonanza, but I was from that day forward known as someone who knew what was cool. And, Johnny and I were the only ones with the new, sweet 1983 Osh Kosh B'Gosh baggy overalls. So, we pulled bitches as well.

In the early '90s, I moved to Seattle to play in a band. We only performed together four times, but once we opened for a little band by the name of SugarCube. While this may not ring a bell for a lot of people, many members of SugarCube went on to form the one and only NutraSweet—the same band that opened for Nirvana, twice. So, we hung out with Kurt Cobain many times at his trashy-ass apartment (really hip at the time). All this can be proven in Issue 47 of *Guitar God Magazine* (March 1992). It's a great pic of Kurt looking sad with a bottle of Full Sail Ale. I'm the one behind him laughing, also with a bottle of Full Sail Ale. Cool enough for Kurt, cool enough for me. I'll never forget the last (and first) words he ever told me: "Can you get me one too while you're up?" Those words move me more to this day than the lyrics of "Rape Me."

An important thing when you're on the scene is to know when it's dried up. I left Seattle in 1997 to move to Los Angeles, and I lived in a studio on Crenshaw and Martin Luther King Boulevards. I had met a man named Suge Knight on the plane ride there. We talked for hours. We had so many common interests. He liked music. I liked music. He liked money. I liked money. He liked negotiating through hostile means and intense pressure. I liked the Queen/David Bowie track "Under Pressure" (years later my knowledge of this song would help Suge while dealing with former client Vanilla Ice).

I knew this was the place for me. He would introduce me to his client Mr. Tupac Shakur. Pac and I were instant friends.

Since my mother once had to give up sugar in her diet (diabetes), I could relate to his mother's heroin/crack addiction and pending imprisonment. I can still smell the hops from our forties as we laughed while watching LuLu and JayJay play double-dutch. I miss him every day and pour a forty his way when I can. This can all be proven in the crime photos of me driving the car from which the shots that killed the Notorious B.I.G. were fired (cannot technically be proven, though, big ups to Mr. Shapiro).

Again, though, a breeze was blowing, and it turned out to be the winds of change. These winds carried me to a new realization. I did not know who I was. I needed to add depth to my life. These winds smelt of marijuana. I found this depth at the pointy end of a hand-rolled spliff. I had been smoking the reef for quite a while. However, that was all Indo. The first time I inhaled the sweetness of homegrown, I did so with a breath of community. I remember smoking and drinking and woke up three years later in Madison, Wisconsin, on the floor of Trey Anastasio's Quality Inn suite—Room 208. That's the only thing I remember from that time. However, it can all be proven in the liner notes of the popular 2000 release *Farmhouse*. "Finally, we dedicate this album to Nic. Who after clearing the Tower of Power exclaimed, 'Where are we?' Where are we indeed, Nic?" I'd had enough. With only a frisbee and four T-shirts (where did all my stuff go?) I headed back to LA.

That's where I find myself today. Los Angeles is a different place since I last left it. I knew I couldn't go back to my old life (or even the neighborhood of my old apartment, according to my plea bargain). Word on the street was that Suge and the gang weren't what they once were anyway. Like always, I didn't have to look far to find the scene. A friend of mine from my Seattle days was now working at *Maxim* magazine, and I attended a party they were throwing. Simply by attending that party, I was invited by someone to another and another and so on...

I've gone corporate and that's fine with me. You see, now hanging with the corporations is where it's at. Just last week I partied with Avril Lavigne. It was okay. But the coolest shit was when I got to meet Ken Berry, head of Capitol Records. We had a long discussion. Next year, Avril won't be able to get a ticket. But I'll still be there. Keep an eye out for me. Next month alone, I'll be in *US Weekly* standing behind Justin Timberlake in line at the Coffee Bean. You can catch me holding Colin Farrell's jacket at the premier of *Terminator 3*, and I'll be singing backup on the new P!nk album. (Turns out if you know the guys at the top, you don't even have to be able to sing!) It's amazing how far a juice box can get you.

RESTAURANT REVIEWS

By Nic Wegener
Originally Published: March 2004

If you're not like me and you don't like good Chinese food, then do I have the place for you! The Chinese Food Place Near My Apartment has exactly what you're looking for and loads of it!

I knew I was in for a special treat when my complicated order was ready in mere seconds. What's that, you say? You're running low on fried rice, and it may take a moment longer? Oh wait, it won't because you're cramming cold noodles on top? Terrific! That's exactly what I don't look for in Chinese food! I thought they must have run out of taste on this particular day. And boy were my fantasies confirmed when I tasted the fried (says who?) rice! Maybe they only use that prized spice, flavor, on weekends.

For my main course, I ordered the Shrimp in Lobster Sauce. If you thought the food looked great in *Shawshank Redemption*, you'll love it. As I ate my second and final bite of this splendid dish, I set out to remove the putrid taste from my mouth. My eyes scanned back and forth from the egg roll to the paper sack my food was shoved in. Not learning my lesson, I bit into the egg roll. HOW THE FUCK DO YOU FUCK UP AN EGG ROLL? HOW THE FUCK DO YOU FUCK UP AN EGG ROLL! That is what I screamed out in joy. Of course, if you like the interior of your egg roll to have the consistency of split pea soup and the taste of a prairie dog's ass, you may have very well exhaled. HOW THE FUCK HAVE THEY PERFECTED THE EGG ROLL!

All in all, my trip ended beautifully. I exited the restaurant relieved to know that the next time my friend starts a conversation with the statement, "Well, you know, not all ethnic restaurants are good…" I no longer have to stand by idly. Oh no, those days are over! Now, I say, "What's that? You're not like me and you don't like Chinese food. Do I have the place for you."

It also works when people say, "I hate myself and don't want to eat things that are good. Where should I go?" Or, "I used to eat rotted food out of the trash receptacles in Chinatown. Do you know where I can replicate that experience?" To all, I answer one way. "Why, the Chinese Food Place Near My Apartment, of course…"

LOOKING BACK AT MY *MODEST PROPOSAL* PIECES

———

By Nic Wegener

September 2018

After reading back through the issues of *Modest Proposal*, I say only one makes me sound like a total dickwad. One's just fine. One is basically what every Yelp review is now, so maybe I'm a trailblazer, or maybe it proves how truly lowbrow I write. And one is so flawless and evergreen it places me among the great writers of our times.

And that's why my story is so tragic. I could have been one of the greatest writers of all time. Whether in books, or papers, or zines, or pamphlets, or signs, or menus, or instruction booklets, or labels, or graffiti, or receipts, or on the sides of trucks or planes, or comics; I was destined to go to the top of some kind of writing thing. What's even more impressive about all this is (and I don't tell a lot of people this) I don't have a very big word pool in my mind or know a ton of punctuations. You just gotta understand that where I come from people read a lot more than they write. Like a lot a lot.

I still remember the day I got the first *Modest Proposal* issue in my hands and showed my friends my article. It was a day that changed my life forever. Cause my friends weren't happy for me. They were confused (or at least that's what they'd have me believe). They said they didn't know that people still even made 'zines. That seemed to have peaked in the late '90s and with this internet thing coming, who would want that?

Let me tell you, hearing that spun me out. I guess I had just been building the moment up in my head differently, and when my friends acted like this, I questioned everything. You have to understand, where I come from, nothing is more important than what other people think of you. And that's hard. 'Cause you have to please—your family, your friends, people you meet on the street, bosses, co-workers, strangers, the people that you give your food orders to, the bus driver, the other people on the bus, the other people in your building, even your enemies. But if I didn't have all that pressure, I wouldn't be the guy I am today. I wouldn't be able to constantly doubt what I do. But that's what happened that day. I doubted the future of zines. So, I stopped writing. I mean stop-stop. I stopped writing everything. And instead I got a job testing diabetes needles on the tips of my fingers. It's not writing but it's good work, and I like it. (The irony is that today, I couldn't even type *Mod Prop* articles if I wanted to. With all the diabetes-needle testing my fingertips hurt when I type on a keyboard or play piano or tap people on the shoulder or even press elevator buttons.) All because I doubted the future of the zine industry.

Well, we know how that turned out. The internet flamed out like Crystal Pepsi, and all the world's billionaires live up in Zine Valley. These days even little kids read zines. No one even looks up these days, walking around with their nose wedged against the crease of the latest zine. But I don't regret it. I've still got feeling in over ninety-two percent of my hands, and I also have the knowledge that for one brief article, I was the greatest living writer, dead or alive, in the entire universe. And for that, I thank you, guys. I dedicate this article to the fans.

KEEP IT REAL, REAL FAKE

———

By Ron Babcock

Originally Published: April 2003

If you don't recall NBC's short-lived reality dating show *Meet My Folks*, you're not alone. There's nothing memorable about the series, which must be why they cast this guy Josh. I hung out with him for over an hour, wrote an article about him, and now can't remember anything about him except he wore Oakley sunglasses and a chain wallet. Why do people with chain wallets never have anything worth stealing?

I only booked the interview because Josh and I had a mutual friend, and reality TV seemed like a funny topic to write about. That year, the genre felt like it jumped the shark with *Joe Millionaire*, a show featuring twenty women competing for the heart of a handsome construction worker posing as a handsome millionaire.

By today's standards, it seems quaint. Reality TV has since jumped much bigger and sharkier sharks. Remember the plastic surgery reality show called *The Swan*? Or how about *Kid Nation*, which taped in New Mexico to get around child labor laws?

Joe Millionaire made waves because the show lied to the female contestants about Joe's true identity. The general public still trusted reality TV shows at this point. If I'm being honest, when he first said it was fake, a part of me clutched the pearls around my neck and went, "But, but… it's called *reality* TV!"

The interview with Josh went just okay. I didn't know how I would make it interesting until I went to Borders to finish reading the book *Wigfield: The Can-Do Town That Just May Not* by Amy Sedaris, Paul Dinello and Stephen Colbert. I couldn't afford the book, so I just read it a few chapters at a time in the store like an educated hobo.

The satirical book featured interviews with Wigfield residents by "journalist" Russell Hokes, who always made himself the centerpiece of the narrative. It spoofed gonzo journalism, but I had never even heard of gonzo journalism then, so I thought the entire narrative device was brand-new and brilliant.

That's how I'll make this reality TV interview interesting! I thought. In an old journal entry, I wrote, "I am borrowing the reporter device from the book *Wigfield* for my reality TV show piece." Borrowed, homage, tribute—they are all just words for the same thing. Stealing. Good thing that book wasn't on the end of a chain wallet.

A boatload of psychology is cruising on the lake of Reality TV that America is swimming, nay, drowning in. But while cynics and critics argue over the detrimental effects it has on contestants, in addition to pondering the ethics of thrusting someone's head into a vat of scorpions, we forgot to ask, is it even real?

"Reality TV is not real. There's no such thing as Reality TV. There is such a thing as structured TV," says Josh, a twenty-three-year-old waiter who recently appeared on NBC's *Meet My Folks* as one of the suitors. "They type-casted my personality as a bad boy."

I looked at his Abercrombie and Fitch pants and saw a chain connecting his wallet to his belt. They were right, total bad boy.

"They want the conflict. They want the struggle, the whatever image they are looking for…"

He stopped and gave a look, the look a Vietnam Vet gives when he hears the local news chopper. I yelled at him, "Josh, Josh…" But his eyes echoed no response. He was gone, gone because they distorted his words, manipulated his emotions…

"What are you writing? Are you even listening to me?" Josh yells.

"Yeah, totally. I'm just taking notes," I said. He was scared and crying on the inside. Salty tears soaked his organs.

"Then why are you talking out loud?"

"Sorry, Josh. Please, continue."

"I was talking about the pain and suffering of people. That's what they play on."

"Yeah. They're bastards like that."

More people watch Reality TV than watch the news, read a newspaper, and listen to the radio, combined. That's not actually true, but I'm sure there's some heart-stopping statistic like that out there. Why don't we just agree that Fox executives eat drugs out of buckets, and everything has gotten out of hand.

Josh says, "People like it because they say, 'Wow, this guy's just like me. I can get on there.'"

And he's right. People can and do get on Reality TV, and Josh is living proof. His example renews my faith that Reality TV isn't a lie at all. It's just not the truth.

"But, Ron, it is a lie."

"Stop reading over my shoulder."

"I'm not reading. You're talking into a tape recorder."

"Josh, do you always eavesdrop on personal conversations?"

"Listen, all I'm saying is there was a very, very big sitcom feel to my *Meet My Folks*. It wasn't even the parents' house. It was some soap actor's house. They sent his family on vacation and we used it. They moved out his furniture, moved in their own furniture and put up their own pictures. The girl wasn't looking for a mate. She had a boyfriend. She's a swimsuit model for Body Glove and there to promote her modeling career."

I couldn't believe it. Next, he was going to tell me they had to do retakes.

"Absolutely. The show was three days of shooting. And a lot of times it was retakes and takes and retakes and takes."

Was it all a fake? It seems a little crazy that the same people who brought us *Joe Millionaire* would withhold the truth. I knew I had to ask Josh the serious questions.

"Was she hot?"

"Hell yeah."

"Cool?"

"Way cool."

"Good kisser?"

"Very good kisser."

"Did any other guys kiss her?"

"Everyone except for the winner Pete. I was the first one though. I was pretty pissed actually because they cut out my shining moment when I actually made out with the girl."

Aha! It's obvious now that Josh is spreading vicious falsehoods about Reality TV to seek revenge for an editing decision.

"It can only play out for so long, just like NSYNC was around for three years. People can only take so much."

Oooo, Mr. I Kissed A Model on TV knows everything.

"Why are you still talking into the tape recorder? I can hear you. The only reason I did it was for exposure and to get a reel. I've already had people call me for other things, like *Extreme Dating*. I told them to shove it up their ass."

Remember, Josh, just keep reaching for the moon. If you miss, you might end up falling on a star. And let's hope that star is the producer of a real Reality TV show, like *Survivor* or *The Real World*.

"It was what it was, and I'll never make it bigger than what it is, and I'll go on from here. It was just a fun experience."

Whoa, mind turning down the ego, Josh, because I can't hear you. The real you. Not the Reality TV bad boy they made you into it. Where's the Josh I know?

"If nothing better, it's going to help me get laid."

That's my Josh. And, with all this newfound knowledge of reality TV, girls will be able to say, "I heard that show isn't even real."

SEX, DRUGS, AND CHURCH OF LDS

———

By Jen Wood

Art by Kristen Hof

Originally Published: April 2003

Updated footnotes by Jen Wood: 2020

"Mormons love their alcohol."

This, from a nineteen-year-old self-described "street pharmacist" and ex-Mormon who says the biggest misconception people have about the people of his former religion is "Since they have a lot of kids, the girls are horny. This is not true."[73]

As was the case with everyone interviewed for this story, the street pharmacist ("Mark") wanted to remain an anonymous source. Even church members who stick by the religion—like a twenty-year-old girl who attends college in Pennsylvania and doesn't have any complaints about Mormonism (although she might complain about us calling it that)—didn't want their names to be used.[74]

Why? Because one of the suggested headlines for this article was "Mormons Gone Crazy" and sources familiar with the Church of Latter-day Saints don't want people to know they also are familiar with drugs, alcohol, and premarital sex—all things that practicing Mormons are quite against.[75]

"Not like I give a shit, but my grandma just might come across your paper for some weird reason and read my shit. Like I said, not likely, but it would kill her if she did," wrote a

---

73 *Oh no.*

74 *Boy, there's a lot of punctuation happening in that sentence, isn't there? Let it be known I'm still a huge fan of the dash!*

75 *Don't forget hot beverages!*

fifth-generation Mormon ("Sara") who hasn't been to church in five years.[76]

While it is impossible to know how many Mormons have gone crazy, are going crazy, or are about to go crazy, most know of at least a few members who have gone against church teachings. Not that people haven't been known to betray religion before (need we mention Judas?), but when Mormons rebel—as any non-LDS who has witnessed a Mormon mutiny will tell you—they don't mess around.

"Of the Mormons I know who are 'inactive,' most of them are having sex, drinking, smoking, and maybe even pot. Most aren't 'horrible' ex-Mormons but wanted to go against the grain a little. I think this is common for those who leave the church. Many who leave will participate in these things, but few leave and don't do at least one of the major 'bad' things—sex, drinking, or smoking. Otherwise, they'd just stay in the church," explains Sara, that last point warranting at least twenty-seven red flags.

Mark, whose hobbies include music, photography, doing drugs, and drinking,[77] believes the strict rules placed on young Mormons, both by the church and by their own parents, is cause for rebellion. "But I also believe many act out due to the fact that their eyes are opened to religion at such a young age that when new things come into the picture, they explore them."

---

76 *Little did "Sara" know, but* Modest Proposal's *only target market was Mormon women in the sixty to ninety age bracket.*

77 *Only a nineteen-year-old would list drugs and drinking as hobbies.*

Neither Mark nor Sara have plans to return to the Church of Latter-day Saints. And not just because he has found success in street pharmacy, and she in premarital sex with her longtime boyfriend.

Mark not only hates how LDS act like "they are always right no matter the case." He doesn't appreciate some members' hypocrisy. "I find it funny how male Mormons party hard until their missions, and then the week of their mission, put on an angel face for their entire mission. Then, upon their return, they transform back into the assholes they were before and drink just as they did before departure."

Sara, on the other hand, just doesn't agree with the church's central beliefs: "Mormons believe that only Mormons can reach the highest degree of heaven, through temple marriage in the Mormon church. I don't believe that God is so exclusive. I don't even know if I believe in God or Heaven anymore, but if I did, it wouldn't just be for Mormons."

Because the Church of Latter-day Saints is really, really against drugs, alcohol, and premarital sex (things some refer to as "fun"), members who do engage in those evils are often riddled with guilt. Sara put on her Sunday Best for years, pretending to go to church for three hours, before admitting to her parents she was no longer practicing the faith.

But just because a young Mormon makes a few mistakes here and there doesn't necessarily mean he has to say good-bye to the prospect of a two-year mission, followed by marriage at an early age. Take, for example, the twenty-year-old LDS who has no complaints against her religion ("Martha").

Martha was relating her passion for movies when she changed gears and wrote, "Switching to the dictionary of Jen, I have spent many a weekend out on the exciting streets of Scranton, drinking with my friends."

I was a little offended by the first part,[78] but her example brings up an interesting point. Some Mormons out there have gone crazy and are still practicing members of the church.

Whether they will be able to resist drugs, alcohol, and sex in the future is up for interpretation. As Martha put it: "I had freedom. I have my agency. I exercised it. Do I regret things

---

78 *Still am.*

that I did now? A lot of it, yes. But I wouldn't change the past for anything. I learned a lot because of those experiences. I learned that I do believe the teachings of my church concerning drugs and alcohol. I've learned that parents aren't stupid and know when their daughter is experimenting with college life. I've learned that they've done it too, and so has everyone else, and it's not a tragedy as long as you eventually find your footing. Oh, and I've learned that while I can hold down up to eight shots of rum and play four games of beer pong, for some reason the citrus nature of Smirnoff Ice makes me puke."[79]

---

79 *The ending is very sweet! I like to think we all found our footing. :)*

BRUSH WITH GENIUS AND THE '80S SCENE

─────

By Carol Pinta
Originally Published: April 2003

Updated footnotes by Carol: 2020

Madonna. Leg warmers. Neon. Guys named Chad. The eighties did its part to help further the lunatic agenda of modern America. However, raised in suburban America by an Ozzie and Harriet-type who cut the cable the day MTV launched,[80] about as much of the '80s as I was ever able to participate in was the side ponytail.

Until one defiantly brilliant Christmas morning, I received a stocking-stuffer that would end up being my first stop on the blazing railway to the ultimate '80s experience. The Rubik's

─────

80   *True story. My dad did NOT think his daughters dancing like Madonna was going to end well.*

Cube was a colorful bit of illogical fun that could provide hours of entertainment with no real measurable conclusion. Sort of like the other popular pastimes of the days: *Goonies*, Iran-Contra, Cyndi Lauper, cocaine. What started as an innocent Christmas gift ultimately ended as the diagnostic tool in the raging debate of this author's own mental (dis)abilities.[81]

My dad, a PhD and patented scientist, was expecting that upon his ten-year-old's "solving" of this '80s challenge, he would be gleefully willing to accept that the heir to his mental throne was his very own daughter. Daddy's Little Girl set to work. And five minutes later when it became clear that this was a novel waste of time,[82] I calmly took the cube to my room where I was free to work out this problem in private. I shut the door and began peeling each colored square out of its chaotic confusion and began reapplying the squares in an orderly and genius manner. When I was done, to the outside eye, it looked as though indeed, I was brilliant. I had solved the great mystery of the Rubik's Cube. It was 10:30 on Christmas morning. I could relax in my newly acquired "genius" status, in front of *The Lost Boys*.[83]

---

81 *I am still outrageously wordy in my writing. I don't know how many words you actually need to say, "I got a Rubik's cube for Christmas once..."*

82 *I am legit famous for my lack of an attention span. It's gotten worse as I've aged. Thankfully most of my friends and siblings have children now, so we all still can hang out without it being too noticeable.*

83 *Again, with the verbosity... seems like it would've just been funnier to say, "I peeled all the stickers off and reapplied them to make it look like I solved it..."*

My parents got the greatest and shortest-lived Christmas treat in the knowledge that their little terror would indeed grow up to become one of the smartest women on the planet.[84] And then at about 12:30 or so, I looked in horror at the Rubik's Cube, which had been inspiring about as much enthusiasm from onlookers as Christ himself must have drummed up, only to see that the stickers had begun peeling up at the corners—completely revealing my innate mental abilities. I was forced to admit to the entire family what I had done. I still maintain it was a great fucking idea, much like Don Johnson still insists shoes with no socks was a great fucking idea.

I have used this story a lot in my professional life. I have a collection of them in my office. In that context, it's a story about integrity, putting in the right work now for the right long-term outcome. It's totally not funny. I like this version much better.

---

84 *Debatable.*

LIFE WITHOUT MARGARET CHO

―――

By Eric Koester

Originally Published: April 2003

My favorite non-interview story was getting rejected by Margaret Cho's manager and publicist a half-dozen times over four months. They wrote one line replies each time, but I kept pestering them. And when I finally wore down her publicist—who must have gotten tired of me and said he'd set something up—Margaret shot him down because she was preparing for her next tour.

―――

ATTEMPT 1: MARGARET CHO'S PUBLICIST IS NAMED KEN.

Dear Ken –

I got your name from a friend and he recommended I speak with you. I am a writer for a magazine called *Modest Proposal*. I was looking to interview Margaret Cho for an upcoming issue. Do you think you could help?

Kindest Regards,
Eric Koester

RESPONSE 1

Eric,

Thanks, but we are going to have to pass on this one. Good luck with the issue and magazine.

Best,
Ken

ATTEMPT 1.5: THE FOLLOW-UP.

Ken

Thanks for the email, Ken! Can I give you a buzz in a couple months to see if it may work then?

Much appreciated
Eric

RESPONSE 1.5

Eric,

Sure. Why don't you send me a copy of your magazine?

Ken

ATTEMPT 2: MAYBE I'LL TRY TO TALK TO HER MANAGER, KAREN TAUSSIG.

Hello Karen –

I am a writer for a magazine called *Modest Proposal*. I am very interested in the opportunity to interview Margaret for our summer issue. We are doing a feature on Women in Comedy and would love to have Margaret as a feature interview for that topic in this issue. Thanks for all your help.

Kindest Regards,
Eric Koester

RESPONSE 2

No thanks.

Karen Taussig

ATTEMPT 3 (SIX MONTHS LATER): SO MAYBE THAT WAS JUST A BUSY TIME FOR MARGARET...

Karen –

I wrote you in May regarding a potential interview with Ms. Cho for *Modest Proposal Magazine*. I am looking to do a feature interview with Margaret for our focus on Women in Comedy. She has played a major role in the advancement of comedy in the past several years, and I would love to speak to her about that experience.

Eric Koester

RESPONSE 3

Still not interested. Thanks anyway.

Karen Taussig

ATTEMPT 4: LET'S TRY THE PUBLICIST AGAIN.

Dear Ken –

I'm not sure if you remember me, but I contacted you several months back about a possible interview with Margaret Cho. I was curious if you might be able to arrange anything like that for me.

Eric Koester, *Modest Proposal Magazine*

RESPONSE 4

Eric,

What do you guys do? I've never heard of *Modest Proposal*.

Ken

ATTEMPT 5: HE PROBABLY JUST FORGOT...

Dear Ken -

Modest Proposal is a magazine dedicated to featuring innovative comedians and comedy. I'd like to interview Margaret for a feature on Women in Comedy. Can you help? – Eric Koester

RESPONSE 5

Eric,

I vaguely remember getting something from you, but for some reason I can't find the materials anywhere here in the office. I may have sent them onto Margaret and her manager for perusal. Nevertheless, Margaret is not doing press right now. She is testing new material for her next tour, etc.

Maybe when the movie is ready later this year.

Ken

WHAT HAPPENED TO THE LAST ISSUE?

—

By Ron Babcock
Art by Anna Hollingsworth
Originally Published: 2005

There I was putting the finishing touches on Issue 4 at Mill's End, a coffeeshop at (get this) the end of Mill Avenue in Tempe, Arizona. I liked working there because I had a huge crush on the barista named Liz. She had short blonde hair, loved to run, and was relentlessly positive, which at the time I found attractive but would now find absolutely exhausting. I was pretty sure she had a crush on me, too, because she was always giving me iced coffees. *"Who gives free stuff to people they don't like?"* I thought.

I was copy editing the final interview on a Toshiba laptop when Liz offered me this giant sugary latte that was made with skim instead of soy milk. She plunked it right next to the Toshiba, and I remember thinking, *"Maybe that's not a good spot for that?"*

Just then, Ryan walked in to grab the laptop. He was going to put some finishing touches on my finishing touches. Classic Ryan. All of a sudden, Liz turned and hug tackled her co-worker from behind. It felt like watching someone getting mugged but with a hug. Arms flailed next to the latte. You know the story.

Slow motion NOOOO... pfftft. Death.

Later, back at the house, Ryan dried off the laptop and looked at me.

"Should I try turning it on?"

"I don't think that's a good idea," I said.

"I'm going to turn it on."

Pfftffftffftt. If it wasn't dead before, it definitely was now.

When we removed the hard drive, we knew it was bad because it was still sticky with latte. We bought an external hard drive enclosure at Fry's Electronics and ended up recovering most of the magazine, but we spent a week or so redoing what we'd lost.

When Liz saw this piece in the magazine, she got mad because she said it felt like we were blaming her, which we totally were. Who hug-ackles someone from behind at work? I didn't like her as much after that, but we still ended up dating. Ryan's still pissed. It was his laptop.

———————

WHAT ACTUALLY HAPPENED...

...Was a complete accident. Minutes before *Modest Proposal* #4 was going to be declared done, a barista accidentally bumped into her co-worker who then spilled a hot sugary café latte all over our Toshiba laptop. The result was a fried computer, a forty-hour setback, and first-degree burns.

HOW WE INTERPRETED WHAT ACTUALLY HAPPENED...

...Was everything was going really well on Earth, and both God and Satan were bored. They called a truce and decided to play their favorite game, "Who can make two grown men cry in public harder?" Satan won by making a cup of his favorite coffee (cream, sugar and, the *Modest Proposal* laptop). He had help from his demon-coffee urchins whom he personally schooled in the art of a lack of balance and general evil. One of them is pointing to a dotted swirl of smoke, which is what hope resembles when it disappears.

THE HBO ASPEN COMEDY FESTIVAL: A CARTOON DIARY

———

By Mike Hollingsworth
Originally Published 2006

2020 UPDATE

In hindsight, I should have just made this whole comic about my pinkeye story as that is the part of the whole trip that has stuck with me the most fifteen years later.

For accommodations, the Aspen Comedy Festival teamed me up with two other Short Film Directors. I rented one of three rooms in an Aspen condo. One of the other films was *Chad Vader,* a short about Darth Vader managing a grocery store.

Without seeking the approval of me and the other filmmaker *Chad Vader*'s director invited everyone who worked on the short. So suddenly a dozen people are sleeping in the living room and sharing the single bathroom. Well, after one uncomfortable night—for them—a couple of the guys from the *Chad* crew asked if they could sleep with me in my bed.

I should stop here to mention, I paid what was a lot for me to have a private room at this festival—a festival held in one of the most expensive cities in the US. I panicked and told them I would think about it and let them know that afternoon. As I went to festival events I came up with a plan. I told the Chadder Heads that I had noticed that my bed was made up of two single mattresses pushed together to make a queen. So, I thought it made the most sense to simply drag one of those single mattresses out into the living room so they can still be with their friends.

I believe that one or both of those boys later broke into my room and wiped their ass on my pillow.

The *Vader* crew was pretty tickled when they found out I had pinkeye. For the record, the assholes behind that film were Matt Sloan and Aaron Yonda. And in regard to the ER doc who told me that pinkeye was a "disease for dirty little boys," it was Aspen, so she was really, really attractive. Extra humiliating when you fail in front of pretty people.

INTERVIEW WITHS...

—

BY RYAN MCKEE AND RON BABCOCK

2002-2004

INTERVIEW WITH THE GUY IN
THE PLACE WITH THE THING

So, you're that guy?
The one and the same.

In the place?
That's me.

And you had that thing, with the thing?
(He takes a sip of his coffee.)

Yeah, I know. Hard to believe, eh?

INTERVIEW WITH A TRAIN HOBO

Was Jack Kerouac a big influence for you?
Who?

Kerouac? *On the Road* **writer?**
I don't read.

Do most hobos drink moonshine?
I drink what I can get my hands on.

You didn't answer my question. Do *most* **hobos drink moonshine?**
Why? You buying?

(I was not buying.)

Do you prefer the term hobo or bum?
Hobo. A bum is just lazy. A hobo chooses this.

(At this point, he motions to train tracks we're standing on.)

INTERVIEW WITH A GUY WHO ALMOST MADE IT IN LA BUT DIDN'T

You're living with your parents?
Yeah, back in Texas.

Did your momma raise a quitter?
She taught me that you can only get your arm so far up a cow's ass before you know you're in deep shit.

What?
I don't know. I've been drinking. I think it means quit before you're in too deep.

So, what are you doing now, quitter?
I'm thinking of starting up my own... Ah, forget it.

INTERVIEW WITH A GUY WHOSE NAME IS PRONOUNCED "COREY" BUT SPELLED, KAARE

Did you hate your parents growing up?
No, I always liked the attention I got from the unique spelling.

Kids must have called you Carrie a lot?
All those kids now wear NASCAR shirts and work at Big O Tires.

Did you ever wish you were Corey Feldman?
Maybe for a little while after *Meatballs 4* or *Bordello of Blood*.

What about Corey Haim?
Corey Haim, on the other hand, delivered moving performances in such timeless classics as *License to Drive* and *Lost Boys*. We all know the real "Corey" star.

INTERVIEW WITH MY FULL POTENTIAL

WHO I AM: What are you up to?
WHO I AM NOT: More than you.

WHO I AM: Like what?
WHO I AM NOT: Success, popularity, power, fulfillment...

WHO I AM: Okay, I get it. I get it.
WHO I AM NOT: I don't think you do.

WHO I AM: You're right. I just wanted you to stop talking so I can watch TV.

INTERVIEW WITH A MAN ON THE GO

Can I interview you?
I gotta go.

Okay, thanks anyway.
(He gives me a quick wave as he continues walking away at a fast pace.)

INTERVIEW WITH MY YOUNGER BROTHER

Am I first and foremost your hero?
No.

Am I not your hero because Mom and Dad named me a normal name, Ryan, and gave you a fucked-up name, Tyson, and you're jealous?
Yes.

It's not my fault that's your name, you know?
Yes, I know that. I still blame you though.

I wanted a sister, anyway.
(Silence.)

You're supposed to yell, "Well, I didn't ask to be born."
Why?

I'm asking the questions here.

INTERVIEW WITH A BAND NOBODY'S HEARD OF

What's your band's name?
The Antdicks.

Nope, haven't heard of you.
Sorry.

What kind of music do you play?
It's kind of a crossbreed between punk and blues. We like to call it "blunk" or sometimes we call it "plues." It has a tinge of emo, but not really.

How many members are in your band?
There are two, bassist and guitarist. We both sing vocals. However, last weekend the guitarist quit because he didn't like the direction our band was going.

You don't even have a drummer?
We did but he quit 'cause he got caught cheating on a test and wasn't allowed to leave his room. It was a major blow to the band.

Has anyone ever heard of you?
I was in Mexico where this drunk girl started talking on me. I told her I was in a band, The Antdicks, and she told me she had heard of us. She said a buddy of hers on the East Coast had our CD. That was really confusing, 'cause we barely have any songs and they were all on a cassette tape in my buddies car back in Colorado.

It's kind of stupid for me to even interview you, huh, because nobody's ever heard of you.

I guess so, but I brought the cassette tape if you'd like to hear it. No, well you guys are assholes. I'm outta here! The Antdicks RULE!

INTERVIEW WITH A MAN WHO BELIEVES HE'S BEING FOLLOWED

So, do you always take a different route home?

Always. It throws them off.

Them who?

Man, if I only knew, then there'd really be some fireworks.

Don't they know where you live? Why don't they just show up there?

Because, man, that's exactly what they expect you to expect. They don't want you to guess their next move.

Like chess?

Like chess with nuclear weapons, space aliens, the truth behind the Kennedy deaths, and big fucking guns, and fucking hookers.

The Kennedys fucked guns and hookers?

No, man, listen, ahh… never mind, you already know too much. I got to get out of here anyway.

(With that, he put on a pair of dark glasses, a fake mustache, and a tin foil hat. He then got into a '76 Ford Pinto and drove erratically down a dead-end street.)

INTERVIEW WITH THE LETTER U

Why does Q always need you?

I hate it. Q hots all the glory with its cocky spike sticking out. But he's nothing without me. Nothing but a messed-up O. You can tell him I said that.

At least you start words on your own.

Yeah, and what are those words? Unable. Urinary. Unibrow. All words people hate. Q starts words like Quench and Queen. Man, I love that band.

So how U doing?

Oh, that's hysterical. I've never heard that one before. Congratulations, asshole.

INTERVIEW WITH A PUNSTER COMIC

What did you do before this?
I used to be a sharpshooter.

Really?
But then I got fired.

Oh.
I always shot bull's-eyes.

That's cool.
The farmers didn't think so.

Is that supposed to be funny?
No, it's supposed to be punny.

Okay, that's enough.

INTERVIEW WITH GOD

Me: Wow, it's bright in here.
God: Yeah, I get that a lot.

Me: Where's Jesus?
God: Out back, turning water into wine. Want any?

Me: No, I'm cool. Hey, what's your last name?
God: Damnit.

Me: Oh, that makes sense.

INTERVIEW WITH GUY WHO STARTED A FAKE
FRIENDSTER ACCOUNT FOR LENNY BRUCE

**That's pretty funny how you set up a Friendster account for
Lenny Bruce, even though Lenny Bruce is dead.**
Yeah, I know. It still makes me and my friends laugh, and
I've had it up for like six months. Even my non-Friendster
friends get it.

**Where did you ever come up with such an outrageous idea
because, I mean, Lenny Bruce is dead?**
I was surfing Friendster and saw a guy who had a fake George
W. Bush account. I was like, "I can be funnier than that." So,
I took one of my favorite people in history, Lenny Bruce, and
made a fake account for him. And it's funnier than the Bush
account because Lenny Bruce is dead and couldn't possibly
have a Friendster account.

**Yeah, I know. That's what makes your fake Friendster
account so funny.**
I know. My friends and I still laugh at it.

Yeah, you already told me.
Oh yeah, sorry.

**It's cool. How does a man who set up a fake Friendster
account for Lenny Bruce keep it real?**
By slicking my hair and rolling my jeans. And also shooting
down the other fakers on Friendster who have Lenny Bruce
accounts. I'm #1. I have over one hundred friends linked to it!

REVIEWS OF OUR REVIEWS

By Ryan McKee and Ron Babcock
Art by Chad Fogland
2004–2006

We used to review any reviews of *Modest Proposal*. Man, we were so damn snarky back then, I don't know how we didn't get punched more.

FROM *RAZORCAKE MAGAZINE*

A lot of comedy is hit-or-miss. Such is the case with the comedy magazine, *Modest Proposal*: some of the stuff in here is really funny and the rest of it is just kind of "ughhh." I think that if the people who put out this magazine had some kind of quality control it would be a lot better.—Not Josh.

Let me tell you how relieved I was when I found out that it wasn't Josh who wrote this review. Josh and I go way back and even though we don't keep in contact anymore, I still seek his approval on a daily basis. By wearing a "W.W.J.D." (What Would Josh Do) bracelet, I remind myself of that every day. I'm very grateful to the reviewer for specifically telling me that it was Not Josh because Josh is crafty and writes under pseudonyms. I don't know Not Josh, so I read his other reviews in the magazine to find out what he thinks is funny. He liked one zine entitled *Eaves of Ass*, for which he wrote, "I like zines where people just write whatever the hell they want… no telling how drunk this guy was when he wrote this stuff. *Eaves of Ass* is a pretty funny name, too." He's right about one thing… nope never mind, *Eaves of Ass* is not a funny name. —Ryan

FROM *ZINE WORLD*

Modest Proposal Issue 1

Don't be fooled by its drab layout; this cluttered little humor zine offers great interviews with professional comics and comedy writers. David Cross, for instance, chats about the comic fertility of Boston while *Simpsons* writer Brad Abelson details what it was like to land that plush gig at nineteen. Unfortunately, the zine's original humor pieces, such as the "drink recipes" for dorm-room archetypes, made me cringe for the artless undergraduates who wrote them. Still, this first issue is really no worse than its competitors. —Erin Q.

The first three words of this review made The Who's "Won't Get Fooled Again" start playing in my head. Then I kind of zoned out until the part about the "artless undergraduates." I believe this to be an unfair conclusion for Erin Q. to make. If we're so artless, why would The Who have started playing in my head? —Ryan

FROM *ZINE GUIDE*

A few things need refining in *Modest Proposal*, such as the printing, which makes some sections hard to read. But with the content and quality of the first issue being so fantastic it is certain that *Modest Proposal* is on its way to being a truly superior publication. —Alicia Dorr

Alicia deftly walks the line between praising and simultaneously providing a healthy critique, but her responsibility-thick prophetic statement about *Modest Proposal* becoming "a truly superior publication" is ripe with expectations, which makes us nervous. A fairer review would read, "*Modest Proposal* is on its way to being a truly okay publication that may be good, but only if it is not judged against any pre-existing expectations." —Ron

FROM EMAIL

I got your maggie in the mail. I really liked it. It was our "coffee book" on our table for a while. Our friends were interested in it. —Lindsay

I feel so fulfilled because we always aim to be the casual interest of friends' friends. Perhaps one day when we upgrade to a glossy cover, we will graduate to the bathroom or, dare I dream, the bedroom nightstand. No, let's not get carried away. We have to stay focused on being the best at what we are right now. A coaster. A coaster that apparently occupied the coffee table "for a while." —Ron

FROM EMAIL

I fucking love your magazine. It's the kind of magazine that's perfect for those nights at home when you're too stoned to do anything else. Best this [sic] about it is that you don't really have to think about it. Which is a good thing. THANK YOU!" —Jen

_____

Her unique way of wording the language that you and I speak suggests that Jen is lit more than a hippie on fire right now and the greatest compliment she can muster is "best this about it is." Not making people think about things is exactly what we're aiming for, Jen, so you're, um, welcome. I guess. —Ron

FROM EMAIL

Although I haven't thoroughly scanned your magazine yet, it appears to be something right up my alley. —Robby Robb, Afternoon Drive Host X-101.5, St. Petersburg, Florida.

_____

Robby Rob lets out what most reviewers spend their whole lifetime covering up, the fact that they critique things without paying attention to them. The beauty in this review is in its noncommittal affirmation. It might be up this radio host's alley, or it might not. Perhaps it will be up an adjacent road or even an interstate? Let's just hope it's not a dead end… because you always find dead bodies in dead-end roads. (awkward pause) Also, we'll now be known as Ronny Ron and Ryanny Ryan. —Ron

FROM *PHOENIX NEW TIMES*

Modest Proposal Presents is the place to see a rotating cast of young, creative, totally off-the-wall talent doing sketch and stand-up comedy. And did we mention that it's only five bucks? Hey, that's no joke. —the "Best of Phoenix" issue

———————————

The *New Times* is usually a very smart magazine, so I'm not sure how they don't understand the definition of a joke. A joke is something that is funny. If you say something unintentionally funny like, "My grandpa died in bed with a prostitute," and someone laughs, you then have to say, "Hey, that's no joke." But if you just state a general fact, there's no need for it. Can you imagine if the Bill of Rights did that after each amendment? *Eighth Amendment—Prohibition of excessive bail, as well as cruel or unusual punishment. Hey, that's no joke.* —Ryan

FROM *XEROGRAPHY DEBT #14*

For some odd reason my latest obsession has been stand-up comedy. I'm not sure where it started or how it happened, and it'll probably fade away as quickly as it came. Anyhow, this is a funny zine. I liked it, and you should order it unless you have no sense of humor. —Eric Lyde

———————————

We are honored to be declared part of Eric's latest obsession or passing fancy. Who knew we would ever join the ranks of his month-long gym membership? Or that we would be stored on the same shelf as his 35mm camera, which he swore was his best investment ever because he'd always felt he was photographing people's souls when he looked into their eyes? With honor, we accept the invitation that paint brushes, trumpet lessons, a hacky-sack, vegetarian cookbooks, screenwriting courses, and a *Newsweek* subscription have accepted before. —Ron

FROM EMAIL

Last Friday evening I enjoyed some performances at Wet Paint Gallery. The gallery is going in a backward direction by serving alcohol. I was sorry to hear my friend and editor at *Modest Proposal* encouraging people to smoke and drink during the break. I don't think he even smokes himself, so is he trying to impress us that he does or that he condones it? The last singer complained about not being able to smoke inside the gallery because of Tempe's law against it. My partner and I voted for that law. I wouldn't have attended had I been subject to smoke from selfish, self-destructive people like him. Joking doesn't excuse unwarranted insults, either. Done properly, however, one can perform an insult in such a way as to reflect poorly on the insulter, not the insultee. Don Rickles specializes in that kind of insult humour. Performed badly, it can have the opposite effect, but Rickles is a master. —K. Day

---

I disagree that smokers are "selfish, self-destructive people." Whenever I ask them for cigarettes, they give them to me. Maybe you're not asking them the right way. Instead of saying,

"Hey, selfish person, give me some of your self-destruction," you should say, "You are cooler than Don Rickles. Can I bum a smoke?" Our editor is indeed a smoker, and he's not selfish at all. He's constantly giving cigarettes to children at local schools and hospitals. Because of people like him we have today's massive tobacco-settlements. He's just making sure we also have them for tomorrow. —Ron

FROM EMAIL

Dear Ryan,

I saw *Modest Proposal's* "Keepin' It Real" issue in that crepe place on Mill. The guy eating the baby is hot. I brought it down to Australia for my sister and her friends. They thought it was hilarious! And they thought that guy was hot too (I am assuming that was you) just wanted to let you know. —Jacki

P.S. I'm a girl by the way.

Immediately, one has to question the integrity of this writer. We have a binding contract with Waffle House, Inc. stating that it is the only breakfast restaurant with *Modest Proposal* distribution rights. Also in that contract, there is a clause stating that only Waffle Houses located fifty miles or more outside of major metropolitan areas may carry the publication and the copies have to be displayed on the ground, in the dirtiest corner of the men's restroom. That way we reach our target demographic, which are truckers strung-out on

No-Doz and Hank Williams Jr. cassette tapes. So, it is highly unlikely she saw a copy in some uppity crepe place. It is also highly unlikely that Australians would find our highbrow humor hilarious. Have we forgotten so easily that Australia plagued the world with Yahoo Serious, who was really just a crasser version of Carrot Top? Finally, why does the writer feel the need to blatantly state that she is female? Doing so makes me suspect that she is actually a man. That would explain how she got into the men's restroom to procure a magazine. Unless she is using reverse psychology, which is what those heavy-brewed Australians would do. —Ryan

FROM EMAIL

Dear *Mod Props*,

I am writing to let you know that you have a small but devoted European readership. Actually, Kristen Hof is my niece and has sent me a copy of every issue of *MP* to date. Small. But devoted, like I said. Best wishes and put more of Kristen's work in it so she will continue sending me issues.

mit freundlichen Grossen

Paul A. Kachur

Mr. Kachur does not mince words, and that in itself is refreshing. He wants free shit. By us publishing his niece's work, this will allow him to receive free shit via her. Since he lives in Germany, we're going to assume all stereotypes are true: Mr. Kachur must be a very stern, hard-working man with a mustache and is an engineer for Mercedes or BMW or a bratwurst factory. He most likely believes art to be a whimsical thing for children, pot-heads, and homos. Therefore, he belittles his niece, Kristen, for receiving a degree in art. Like an abused child, she still seeks his approval by sending him publications that her work appears in. Not being ones to break a family tradition, we decided to publish more of Kristen's work (pages 30, 35). —Ryan

FROM EMAIL

Ryan,

I was so lucky to be in Flagstaff this weekend to see your performance. I thought it was downright hilarious. I just felt bad for you two because no one else seemed to be laughing very much. My friend even gave me a look when I laughed. I suppose the Northern Arizona University students just do not know funny when they see it. Though, I've always wondered if comedians are sad or disappointed in themselves at all if the audience doesn't seem to like much of their show or if the comedians shrug it off and say that it was just a bad night/a bad crowd. Best regards, Sara

---

I love college students—so cute and naive. Comedians are always sad and disappointed with themselves, no matter what the night or crowd. That is why we *all* drink a lot and do drugs and lose our intimate relationships and will follow in the morbid steps of Lenny Bruce, Jim Belushi, and Bruce Baum (dead career, not body). I think what Sara's really saying here is that she wants to sleep with me. Sara, if you're reading this, don't fight your natural instincts. Meet me out by the dumpster and bring twenty-five dollars. —Ryan

FAIL YOUR WAY TO OKAY

———

By Ron Babcock

June 2020

Ryan and I shouldn't have published this anthology. We instead should be drinking palomas and discussing our upcoming movie on the veranda of our cabin in Big Bear. We shouldn't even have time to consider a project where we have to read our 2003 journal entries for ideas (itself an awful idea). But at every opportunity over the last eighteen years to step toward success, we instead stepped in a pothole full of warm turds.

The real irony is how confident we were about our inevitable march up the mountain of notoriety. We aimed to reach the top by twenty-nine, thirty at the very latest. I'm now forty-one and consider a washer-dryer inside my apartment as one of my greater achievements. And yet, I don't feel regret. I mean, at least not a debilitating amount.

Sure, we haven't hit the top, but we've made it to a nice ledge. Ryan won an Emmy and lives by the beach. I work as an editor on my favorite TV show from when I was a kid and can jump rope like a boxer. I haven't won an Emmy, but I did win an art contest from a seafood restaurant for drawing a picture of a fish. Yes, it was a contest for children, but the point is I won.

To show that you too can fail your way to okay, here are some (but not all) of our biggest blunders.

NEW MEDIA? HARD PASS.

Ryan and I started *Modest Proposal Magazine* in 2002. At the time, many people questioned publishing a physical magazine.

"Print is so expensive. Why don't you start a website?" they said.

Ryan always replied with: "There's just something about holding your work in your hands, you know?" In hindsight, we should've realized there's also something about holding money in your hands.

A WEBSITE? OKAY NERD.

Eric Koester is one of those successful entrepreneur types who makes a button-down shirt look casual. Back in 2002, he was just our buddy Eric whose favorite movie was *Van Wilder*, which Ryan and I hated.

He was campaigning hard that we ditch the magazine and focus on a website (and re-watch *Van Wilder*). When Ryan wouldn't budge, he was adamant that we at least have a website.

Eric had gotten in early on Fark.com, which doesn't mean much now, but at the time was getting millions of hits. Instead of putting content we already had on a website for Fark to push to, we relentlessly made fun of Eric for hanging out on message boards and for liking *Van Wilder*. Now, we just do whatever Eric tells us. He's the one who said we should do an anthology.

VIDEO ON THE INTERNET? YEAH, THAT'S NEVER GONNA HAPPEN.

Fast forward to 2005. A website called YouTube is founded. Ryan and I had been making sketches since 2003 and would show them in packed bars. After a screening, our friend Famous Dave said, "You should put your stuff on this website for videos called YouTube."

I replied, "Most people don't have fast internet. Online video will never catch on, Dave." Dave now owns 10 percent of YouTube. Kidding.

The real reason we didn't use YouTube was I couldn't figure out how to get our videos under 10MB, which was the upload limit at the time. There was a piece of software that could do it, but I was too cheap to get it. It cost seventy dollars.

FOCUS ON ONE THING? BUT WHY WHEN YOU CAN DO EVERYTHING!

Our first paying gig in comedy was opening for Patton Oswalt at the Tempe Improv in 2003. At one point, he asked us, "How long have you guys been doing stand-up?"

"Two years," we said.

"Good. For the first five years, do anything. Literally do anything and everything. Do whatever stupid thing pops into your head. At year five, pick one thing and stick with that."

"Got it."

Ryan and I never did that. In hindsight, you can't be great at stand-up, improv, sketch, acting, filmmaking, and publishing, but you sure can be pretty okay at all of them.

PAID WORK? WE'RE NOT SELL-OUTS!

We moved to Los Angeles in July of 2005. After spending a week setting up our apartment in Los Feliz, we got a call from a guy in NYC who bought the rights to the old humor magazine *Cracked*. He wanted us to do what we were already doing, but just for *Cracked*. He offered us editorial positions in New York City with full-time salaries. So, while trying to make it in stand-up at night, our day job would've been writing comedy. There was only one catch... we had to stop publishing *Modest Proposal*.

Hard pass.

Here was someone who was going to give us money to stop being Sisyphus and we said, "But we love rolling this boulder up a hill!" Instead we threw our hat in with another up-and-coming DIY comedy brand, *The Phat Phree*. Ever hear of them? Exactly.

MOMENTUM? WHOA LET'S SLOW IT DOWN.

It's 2006 and we just finished Issue #6. It is by far the best issue of *Modest Proposal*. The layout, the humor pieces, essays, interviews—it looked like an actual magazine. We had a color cover and even some color pages inside. For the first time, we had a lot of advertisers. Sub Pop Records took the whole back cover! Plus, we finally figured out how to do a full bleed. (That's when the color goes *all* the way to the edge of the page.) We received almost universally positive feedback (except for Greg and you know what, fuck Greg). We finally felt like we knew what we were doing, which is exactly when we stopped.

OKAY, BUT WHAT NEXT?

In 2002, before we designed the first issue, we went to the Circle K behind our house and bought hot dogs and giant sodas. We sat down at Ryan's Toshiba laptop with our junk food haul and fired up Microsoft PageMaker for the first time. It took an hour to just set the page dimensions. When we finally plugged in the right numbers and clicked okay, we watched the page snap to the correct size.

Ryan and I high-fived each other and went, "Yeah!" We did it. We finally figured out how to format... a blank page.

We looked at each other and said, "So what should we put on the cover?"

We had written an entire magazine and didn't once think about what would go on the cover. Our ability to focus on only what was in front of our faces was just breathtaking. We never stopped to ask ourselves, "Okay, but what next?"

IT'S COOL. WE TURNED OUT ALL RIGHT

Instead of a website, we published a magazine with a finite number of copies. Instead of posting videos online, we focused on DVDs, another tangible object that can only go so far. Instead of making better web videos, we spent all our calories on live shows that only fifty to a hundred people would see. And then we would scrap that material and start over. We never thought, "Hey is all this time and effort learning magazine design, finding advertisers, burning DVDs, rehearsing sketches, etc. the best use of our time and energy?"

I don't highlight these missteps so you feel sorry for us. Believe me, my inner voice is saying *"Awww poor straight white male comedian, did only some of and not every single dream of yours come true?"* I mention them because it's easy to focus on your missteps when it feels like everyone else is running so much faster than you. But then one day you look around and realize everyone has regrets. The successful ones just don't let missed opportunities bog them down.

If I'm really being honest, I have very little to complain about, and that's always been a problem. Happy-go-lucky is an awful character trait for a comedian. A comedy manager once put their hand on mine in the middle of lunch and said, "Ron, it's okay to want more." It took me a moment to realize she wasn't talking about ordering dessert.

OKAY, BUT WHAT NEXT... NOW?

Can I be honest and tell you what a complete mind fuck it has been working on this anthology? I feel like we've been riding the coulda-woulda-shoulda carousel for months now, which makes sense when you're reading your 2003 journal entries (just awful). No one looks at their past and thinks, "Welp that went perfect, no notes!"

But for two guys who supposedly blew it, we sure have done a lot: a magazine, festivals, tours, commercials, scripts, series, consistent industry work, DVDs, an album, and now a book. We didn't just spend our twenties and thirties drunk and high. I mean, we did, but at least we traveled the country performing while doing it. *Modest Proposal* is some of the happiest times we've had doing comedy, which is the whole reason we started in the first place. We'll keep creating because it feels good.

So, that's what's next. Ryan will keep writing things that I thankfully won't have to lie about when I say they're good. And I'll still do stand-up because I love it and why stop doing something you love? Maybe we'll even finally take Patton's advice and focus.

We've come to the realization that it's not about how high you go but just the fact that you climb in the first place. Even if we don't climb any higher, we'll have failed our way up to a pretty good view. We hope you enjoyed it as much as we did.

CONTRIBUTOR BIOS

We wrote these bios as we would have in 2003, when we published the first issue of *Modest Proposal*, and then added our current bios. It's not intended to make a grandiose statement about how far we've come. It's mostly an opportunity to make fun of our younger selves. Just a quick heads up: you won't find contributions from every person listed below in the book. However, every person here contributed to the original magazine in one way or another.

RYAN MCKEE

2003

Ryan McKee worked two fire seasons with the Payson Hotshots and then used the money to found *Modest Proposal*. He's written for *State Press Magazine*, golf punk magazine *Schwing!* and Arizona's finest porno mag *Playtime*. In addition, he's been rejected over a dozen times from *McSweeney's*. Currently he's working on his first novel, *The Hole We Dug in Frank's Front Yard*, and can almost land a kickflip.

2020

Ryan McKee worked at *The Late Late Show with James Corden* for five years, wrote the Emmy-winning short form series, *James Corden's Next James Corden*, and is a producer for the CBS show *Game On!* He is also the editorial director at Sports Gambling Podcast Network and hosts *NBA Odds Pod*. Based on Facebook messages from people in his hometown, this is more than anyone expected him to accomplish. Ryan and his wife Annie adopted two dogs since they cannot conceive their own. He never finished his novel, never landed a kickflip, and never had anything published by *McSweeney's*.

RON BABCOCK

2003

Ron Babcock (desperately wants to be) a filmmaker. In his senior year in college, he made an hour-long documentary about a demolished hotel in Scranton, Pennsylvania. It made a lot of old people cry, at least a dozen. For his final three credits to graduate, he made *Three Credits to Freedom*, a sketch comedy show about not wanting to make the show. In his free time, he juggles devil sticks and is coincidentally a virgin. He recently moved to Phoenix to pursue stand-up comedy, which his parents are still coming to terms with.

2020

Ron Babcock has been on TV. Not enough to be super famous, but enough to make kids from high school impressed. He's appeared on *Adam DeVine's House Party* on Comedy Central, *Last Comic Standing* and other canceled shows. He has written and produced digital series for Tasted, Mashable, MTV, AOL and many other defunct platforms. He's edited on HBO's *Life and Times of Tim* (canceled), Adult Swim's *Mr. Pickles* (canceled) and Disney's *Muppet Babies* (probably soon to be canceled). All Things Comedy ranked his debut comedy album *THIS GUY.* as a "Top 5 Album of 2017." He no longer juggles devil sticks and is coincidentally not a virgin.

ERIC KOESTER

2003

Eric Koester is an accountant. He secretly longs to do something more "creative" with his life, so he jumped at the chance to help out with an up-and-coming comedy magazine. If this magazine doesn't work out, he'll probably go to law school.

2020

Eric Koester has started and run numerous technology startups, is a venture capital investor and a professor of entrepreneurship and innovation at Georgetown University. He's the founder of the Creator Institute, where he has coached more than five hundred authors to create and publish their first books. As you might have guessed, he *did* go to law school but after a few twists, turns and soul-searching moments in the corporate legal world he finally broke free, found his creative muse and fell in love with the energy of the startup world. He lives in Washington, DC and is married to Allison with three daughters Quinn (five), Parker (three) and Aven (one).

ANDREA GOLLOHER

2003

Andrea is a research assistant on a study of drug dependence (*wasn't quite sure what to do with herself after she graduated so she stuck around St. Louis*). She's contemplating what to do next. (*Everyone she knows is having a better time on either coast. Plus, St. Louis is super cold.*) She recently learned about a disorder called autism (*there was a time when people didn't know what autism was*) and has decided to start working with kids with autism to see what that's all about. (*She also needs the money. RAs don't make much.*)

2020

After completing her MA and teachers credential in early childhood special education at Vanderbilt in Nashville, Tennessee, she moved to California (*where it's much warmer than St. Louis and much less humid than Nashville*). After teaching for a bit, she went back to school again (*again*) for her doctorate in special education at UC Berkeley. She's now an Assistant Professor in the Department of Special Education at San Jose State University. (*It pays a little better than an RA position.*) When she's not working, she enjoys spending time with her husband and two daughters.

BRANDON HUIGENS

2003

Brandon Huigens is a new, super ambitious cartoonist, writer, and singer with big aspirations... and he really wants to be like Ron and Ryan, who told him to stop trying to be "lovably angry," great advice he does not understand.

2020

Brandon Huigens is a broke, single, finally sober father trying to continue making cute art for the sake of showing his daughter to never quit. Brandon has published over sixty comics, produced over fifty songs, and contributed to dozens of zines and publications. He runs a successful yearly forty-eight-hour film festival in downtown Phoenix called Dinerwood and considers his time working with *Modest Proposal* to be one of his favorite achievements in life.

BRODIE FOSTER HUBBARD

2003

Brodie Foster Hubbard is a musician and writer from The Valley of the Sun who loves punk rock, comedy, zines and comics, pro 'rasslin', and LIFE! He is excited to finish his screenwriting studies and English Literature degree, maybe an MFA in Creative Writing next? But for sure, a move to Hollywood to find the future that awaits! Movies, television, publishing, concerts... there is so much to explore! Thanks, Ron and Ryan!

2020

Editor's Note: Request for an updated bio was sent to an address in Los Angeles, the last known location for this contributor. Two years later, a young girl with a dirty face and dressed in fatigues arrived at our office, riding a pale white horse and unveiling a package postmarked "HIGLEY, ARIZONA." It contained a microcassette, and the following is a transcript of the audio contained:

"What are these names you speak? I haven't heard them in years... there is only Hub now. Yes, I do miss *Shakeytown* sometimes. It was the greatest place on Earth. But those songs, those jokes, those pamphlets... they're buried in a forgotten world, under bloody soil, paved over in skull and bone. Where we live, you cannot find on a map, it cannot be annexed, it cannot be gerrymandered. We remain, even now hidden in shadows, fighting back through subversive art and media. HubUnofficial.com is a light in the darkness. Tell them... the hydrological cycle is a hint at the true meaning of life. Tell them... we are all connected. Tell them... live without fear but heed the warnings before you. See you in Valhalla. Oh wait... which one asked? The funny one, or...?"

CAROL PINTA

2003

Carol Pinta recently graduated college and apparently has her whole life ahead of her. She needs some coffee first. She was a successful publicist working across fourteen movie and TV studios but realized early that she prefers lying and faking enthusiasm for things only in her personal life. She reads a lot, writes for a TV show that doesn't pay her, and recently moved back to her hometown of Pittsburgh, Pennsylvania.

2020

Carol Pinta lives in New York City and works all over the world. She builds software and does other shady things involving computers. No one is more surprised than she is that she grew up and got paid for the non-funny ideas in her brain. These days she finds her stage on conference calls and consults on music and writing projects because thankfully, her friends still encourage her to follow their passions. She is currently working on her first novel. Allegedly.

CHAD FOGLAND

2003

Chad has only been living in LA for about two and half years and boy howdy does he love it! I bet he will never never NEVER get married and move away. With his Art Degree in his back pocket and his fondness for fake mustaches in his duffle bag, Chad prances about the Los Angeles Comedy Underground like the idiot he was always meant to be. Who knows? Maybe he'll be an Andy Kaufman Award Finalist in 2007, and no matter what, he'll find a way to work that in every bio about himself.

2020

Chad has been living in LA for seventeen and half years, and he's been engaged for one year. It looks like he might just move away because he doesn't have a million dollars for a house. With his tattered old Art Degree in his back pocket and his even greater affinity for fake mustaches in his now three duffle bags, Chad prances, more modestly and with greater self-awareness these days, dipping his toe in the Los Angeles Comedy Underground as often as he can, now that he likes taking naps. Don't get me wrong, he still loves comedy and will never quit, but I bet he'll live in Wilmington, North Carolina, by 2020 and do comedy there. In fact, I'm willing to put twenty bucks on it. That and my reputation as a 2007 Andy Kaufman Award Finalist!

CHRIS KEENER

2003

Chris Keener is a preditor (producer/editor), actor, and all-around good dude. He graduated from Temple University and has been working in all aspects of the film business, hoping to catch a break. His whirlwind world-travel on the Semester at Sea program triggered a fiery wanderlust that is unlikely to be extinguished in the near future. He lives in a cool old artsy warehouse in North Philadelphia where the *pièce de résistance* is a couch suspended from the ceiling by ropes.

2020

Chris Keener/Goldenbear has spent a very healthy number of years creating, directing, and producing content for outfits like National Geographic, Discovery Channel, PBS, NYT, Dow Jones, ESPN, and the Travel Channel. He has been founder and principal of two production companies: Goldenbear and Goodfight Media. He recently directed the five-part series *We Speak Dance* for Netflix and helmed the Webby-Award winning docuseries *Conflict* for Netflix and the *Atlantic*. He also teaches a mind-blowing wellness method called Goldenair breathwork.

CHRYSTYNA GOLLOHER

2003

Chrystyna Golloher was born in Northern California and grew up in Tempe, Arizona. Chrystyna graduated from Arizona State University with a BA in Elementary Education, a major specifically chosen after watching a very inspiring episode of *Oprah*. Upon graduation, and a quick stint in South Bend, Indiana, she accepted a teaching job and just started her second year teaching sixth grade. People often ask her if she enjoys teaching, and she always exclaims, "Oh, my god! I love it!" when secretly she just kind of likes it. Chrystyna is currently working for the weekends and feels fortunate she can spend her free time hosting *Modest Proposal*'s stand-up open mic nights and acting in *Modest Proposal* videos and sketch shows.

2020

Chrystyna Golloher and her boyfriend, David, moved to Portland, Oregon six years ago. They want everyone to know they are not economic refugees from California but just a couple of people who really like the Pacific Northwest. How could they have known that literally everyone was moving there too? After four years of teaching sixth grade and eight years advising elementary and secondary education students, Chrystyna decided she had had enough of that and spruced up the ol' résumé. She currently works for a startup called Househappy in their two-person accounting department. She has discovered that multiple-hat-wearing, constant change, and a busy schedule are quite fitting to her personality. Chrystyna is still working for the weekends and feels fortunate to live in such a beautiful state and a city, despite its flaws, that offers lots to do, eat, and drink. Chrystyna and David do not have, nor do they want, any human children but are raising three cats, and after the adoption of the third, have accepted the fact they are indeed, cat people.

JEN WOOD

2003

Jen Wood is a full-time newspaper reporter and a part-time waitress at a wine bar. She interned at *Jane* magazine, where she once got to address a package to Charlize Theron and recently won two state press awards for an article about a bathroom attendant. Jen is not sure where any of this is going, so will soon quit both jobs and move back to New York City to live out of a suitcase in a studio apartment where she shares a futon with her best friend and lives off a single slice of pizza every day.

2020

Jen Wood has styled windows for Nordstrom, created art displays for Anthropologie and moonlighted as a wedding planner. So, the sincerity in her father's voice is palpable when he says, "I'm still surprised you have a nine-to-five job." Jen has been working at an electric and gas utility for the past ten years where she leads an Experience Design team and lives in Minneapolis with her husband Chris and their two dogs. She really likes where this has gone.

JACKI O.

2003

Jacki O. is an artist and zine maker in Phoenix, Arizona. She loves to make beer, ride bikes, and explore the desert. She hates bios!

2020

Jacki O. is a multi-media artist working in upcycled digital and analogue mediums and is co-founder of *PoolBoy Magazine* (www.poolboyfm.com), a feminist adult media company about hot dick. She still hates bios!

JOEY SULLIVAN

2003

Second Lieutenant Joey Sullivan.

2020

Lieutenant Colonel Joey Sullivan. Married with two daughters and three cats. The cats are not his. They are his wife's and his mother's, who recently passed away. Karma is real. Joey is paying for all his past mistakes.

JOHN ESPINOZA

2003

John Espinoza is a native of California attending graduate school at Arizona State University in Tempe, Arizona. He took advantage of writing for *Modest Proposal* to explore other writing modes such as satire and farce.

2020

Since writing for *Modest Proposal*, John Espinoza has published one book and has taught writing and literature at two universities in California. He currently works as a writing consultant.

KENA RAY

2003

Kena just graduated from ASU with a degree in English Literature and writes a weekly column, "Tough Titty," for *College Times* newspaper, waxing unpoetic about the meaning of quarter-life discoveries and adventures. Ron and Ryan call her the "Furor of Fashion" because she forces hipster makeovers upon her friends. She is hungry, looking under every rock for a snack and even inside cubicles for a real job. She is throwing a Quinceañera with a piñata for her twenty-sixth birthday, which she doesn't yet realize is cultural appropriation.

2020

Kena lives in a cool old condo in Tempe with her emotional support beard owner Fred, her sweet teenage stepdaughter Madeleine, and bariatric-geriatric dog Tank. She found herself on her HOA board as the "Furor of Flyers," which mostly involves getting screamed at by antichrist-reincarnate neighbors. She found a cubical career as an Instructional Designer at ASU, creating and editing educational materials, where she staunchly defies office decorum with her constant laughter and stretch pants wardrobe. She also teaches power vinyasa yoga classes, which is her midlife outlet for making meaning out of this strange world. She threw herself three separate, culturally inoffensive birthday parties for her fortieth.

KEVIN POLOWY

2003

Holy shit this magazine came out in 2003? I don't think he had even gone through puberty yet. Let's see, Kevin Polowy lives in New York City—Brooklyn, specifically, which hasn't gotten overrun by fucking hipsters yet. It's still gritty and cool even if he's afraid of all the bars within walking distance. At this point he's probably an editorial assistant at Moviefone.com, also writing about hip-hop for other ill-fated magazines like *URB*, and slowly cracking into NYC's DJ scene. He'll never move to Los Angeles.

2020

Kevin Polowy lives in Los Angeles, and he fucking loves it. He's now a senior correspondent/ host for Yahoo Entertainment. He still DJs a little bit, but mostly he's working on various side projects as a writer, director, and producer—like the recently released comedy *Standing Up, Falling Down* starring Billy Crystal and Ben Schwartz. He still dreams of the day he'll get to write for a real comedy magazine.

KRISTEN HOF

2003

Kristen just graduated from the University of Arizona with a Bachelor of Fine Arts degree the year before and works in the receiving office at La-Z-Boy in Tucson full time—benefits and everything! She lives in a two-bedroom apartment alone with one room as her art studio, which feels very luxurious, and painted an accent wall, which feels very grown up. She is on the hunt for that perfect career, where she can be creative and love what she does, and only be "charmingly" broke, like *real* artists are until they die and get super famous. She also had some pet fish, but that ended badly.

2020

Kristen has worked in home custom art production, sales, design, assisting the elderly in downsizing, finance, and now, human resources. *(Insert John Oliver clip about why not to get an art or art history degree. He nailed it so painfully.)* She still commissions some art for friends and family, though. And, it turns out, turning something you love into a job has the potential to make it unlovable, and being broke is *not* charming. She moved in with her film student boyfriend, got a dog, got married, traveled, tried to have kids, (thankfully) failed, ran obstacle course races, and lost touch with independent music (not necessarily in that order). So, ya know, she got old, but gives very few shits about what people think of her now, and actually likes HR. It's perfect for people who kind of hate humanity but enjoy people on a case-by-case basis.

MAT SNAPP

2003

Mat Snapp joins the rag-tag crew from *Modest Proposal* as he pursues his dream of having his own freelance writing company. He assumes freelance writing will afford him all the time and financial freedom he needs to finish off his collection of short fiction and his first full-length novel.

2020

Mat Snapp has found, as many English Literature majors with focuses in Creative Writing, wild success in a field completely unrelated to English, Literature, or Creative Writing. He currently oversees the beverage programs for a nationally recognized restaurant company, makes references during cocktail classes to Edmund Burke, and corrects people's spelling and grammar—much to their chagrin.

MAX BURGER

2003

Max Burger grew up in Tempe, Arizona, and graduated from Arizona State with a business degree. After some time at a "real job" in Silicon Valley, Max decided that cubicles weren't his thing and moved back to Arizona. He just got his real estate license like everyone else in Arizona. He has also started doing stand-up comedy as some sort of deranged therapy to deal with him being broke, unemployed, and back living with his parents. Rather than sell tons of houses, he hopes to sell just one extremely expensive home for the massive commission and call it a day.

2020

Max Burger lives in Phoenix and works for a local utility company. After long consideration, he realized that cubicles actually *were* his thing and works a nine-to-five office gig. He enjoys playing golf and dreams of making the senior tour in a dozen years after suddenly getting really good. He also likes playing guitar and has played in a few cover bands over the years—his solo album is currently a twenty-year project and will rock your socks off if it ever drops. He is married to his wife, Melissa, of thirteen years and they have two boys.

MELISSA CUNDIEFF

2003

Melissa works at Hooters and buys every meal from the Circle K on the corner of Maple and University in Tempe, Arizona. She can't wait until she's old enough to buy Vendange wine from the Circle K, and she is 1.5 years away from being a college dropout. Melissa likes to write and listen to Silver Jews.

2020

Melissa graduated from college via online efforts in 2010 and received an MFA in creative writing from Vanderbilt in 2012. Her poetry collection *Darling Nova* was selected by Alberto Rios and published by Autumn House Press in 2018. She currently teaches at the University of Minnesota and hangs out with her two kids in Saint Paul.

MIKE BAOULE

2003

Los Angeles-based stand-up comic living at home with his mom. Also thought-contributor to *Modest Proposal.*

2020

Ex-comic. Failed life participant.

MIKE HOLLINGSWORTH

2003

Mike's been doing comedy for seven years now and he's not sure it's working out. <u>He thinks</u> he's really, really, really funny, but the crowds don't always agree. *guuurgleguurgle.* Sorry, that was his stomach. He's so hungry all the time. He would love a juicy steak. He must figure out a way to buy food to put in his stomach. He can kinda draw. Maybe he should try to put his jokes in cartoons he makes. Maybe that could be his ticket...

2020

Mike Hollingsworth has the distinction of being the first animator hired at Netflix back in 2013 when the now-dominant streamer rolled out its fourth original show, *BoJack Horseman.* After six seasons of steering the ship as the Supervising Director and Co-Executive Producer of *BoJack*, one season of *Tuca & Bertie*, and many awards, Mike is now an Executive Producer at Netflix's new in-house animation studio. *guuurgleguurgle!* Why is he still so hungry? He's achieved so much. Oh! What's all this liquid? What's happening? Did his water break? He can see a head! It's—It's a baby! She's beautiful! He wasn't a hungry comedy failure! He was just pregnant with a baby for a nearly two-decade-long gestation! And what's that? She has steaks! One juicy factory-sealed steak under each arm. He's the luckiest man-mother in the world! Thank you, Netflix!

NIC WEGENGER

2003

Nic Wegener graduated from Arizona State University two years ago, where he performed with Farce Side Comedy Hour and Barren Mind improv. Upon graduation, he moved to LA where he has worked at a company that sells commercials to TV stations and at a well-known spa as the guy that's supposed to keep people from pleasing each other in the men's locker area. He can be seen around town in odd open mics and poorly planned sketch shows.

2020

Nic Wegener graduated from Arizona State University where he performed with Farce Side Comedy Hour and Barren Mind improv. Upon graduation he moved to LA where he worked at a well-known spa as the guy that's supposed to keep people from pleasing each other in the men's locker area. Then he did a bunch of other stuff. After that, he joined the seminal Los Angeles sketch group The Midnight Show and became a writer for the TV show *American Dad*.

TARA CARPENTER

2003

Tara grew up in Guilford, Connecticut, as a comedy-loving oddball with dreams of living somewhere warm and different. After graduating from the University of Connecticut, she moved to Arizona, which fit the warm and different criteria, and was immediately disoriented. Tara held a variety of jobs while searching for the right fit, finally landing a gig in the exciting field of local government. She met Ron and Ryan through the Phoenix comedy scene and was fortunate to be able to contribute to their charming comedy movement as a managing editor for an issue of *Modest Proposal*.

2020

Tara is still a disoriented oddball—now with dreams of living somewhere not so warm. She solves literary mysteries and plays an excessive amount of *Animal Crossing* in her free time. Let it be known that all her book reviews get an extra star when the killer is a woman. Between 2003 and now, Tara earned a master's degree in Library and Information Science, worked in various libraries, and currently oversees adult education at a local garden. She is known as an indie wrestling enthusiast that sometimes cosplays as Orange Cassidy.

TERESA AGUILERA

2003

Teresa Aguilera is a graphic designer and sometimes-journalist trying to find meaningful work in the burst-bubble rubble of San Francisco. She's written and designed for *State Press Magazine* and produced a few small design exhibitions but is currently employed as a visual merchandiser/store associate at Old Navy's fabulous flagship store.

2020

Teresa Aguilera lives in San Francisco where, after a decade of being the only lonely designer at approximately a million startups, she finally sold out to her original corporate overlords and works with a whole team of user experience designers at Gap, Inc. (which does still include the fabulous Old Navy). She was also a member of the art and design studio Rebar, through which her design work appeared in shows in New York City, Amsterdam, Athens, and at the Venice Biennale Architettura. Teresa and her husband Ben have a daughter named Zelda and three chickens.

CONTRIBUTORS WHO HELPED WITH THE ORIGINAL MAGAZINES BUT WEREN'T ABLE TO GET US A BIO FOR ONE REASON OR ANOTHER:

Adam Rust, Amy Seimetz, Anna Hollingsworth, Annie Worth, Bill Ross, Bonnie MacFarlane, Bryan Hollingsworth, Brian Stolfa, Brittany Avignan, Charlyne Yi, Chris Dunham, Chris

Fairbanks, Christopher Hamilton, Dan Piatkowski, Dave Maass, Drew Sullivan, Eddie Shoebang, Emily Stone, Erin Borcherding, Flex Flavin, Giuliano Giuliani, Graham Annable, Genevieve Lamb, Greg Burosh, Jack Sullivan, James Begley, Jen Kirkman, Jim Mahfood, Joe Gentile, Joe Klocek, John Delacruz, Kirk Buckout, Kiyoshi Nakazawa, Korky Day, Landon Lyon, Lev, Lindsay Post, Lora Bodmer, Luster Kaboom, Lynn Shawcroft, Mary Mack, Mel Cowan, Melissa Bradsher, Michael Capozzala, Michael Rayner, Mike Montaya, Mike Lee, Mikey Cramer, Miki Ann Maddox, Mishka Shubaly, Neil Campbell, Paul Goebel, Paul Williamson, Rhonda Aburomi, Rich Nemonk, Ryan Lossing, Scott C., Sean Anders, Skeet Link, Sterling Bartlett, Todd Hibbeler, Todd Valdini, Trevor Seigler, Troy Conrad, Tyson McKee, and Yasmin Tabi.

THANK-YOUS

———

My wife Annie Worth never wavered in her enthusiasm for this book. That's incredibly impressive since I second-guessed it twenty times a day for two years, and then every minute of every day during three months of shelter-in-place when I did most of the work. She was stuck in a small house with this whiny, brooding writer during a pandemic and worldwide social unrest, yet she always remained supportive and patient. She did so much writing and rewriting and punch-up and editing for this book and never asked for credit. Without her, I'd be hiding in the fetal position under my bed.

My partners Ron Babcock and Eric Koester, as well as their significant others Jamie Reed and Allison Jones Koester. Over twenty years of friendship and collaboration and somehow, we still don't hate each other. Our partnership will no doubt last another twenty months or so… still an impressive run.

Everyone at New Degree Press, especially my marketing and revisions editor Pea Richelle White, copy editors Amanda Brown and Gina Champagne, layout designer Zoran Maksimović, cover designers Josip Perić and Gjorgji Pejkovsk, as well as Brian Bies, Leila Summers and Grzegorz Laszczyk.

My family, especially my parents who taught me the importance of tenacity, even if everyone is making fun of me for the thing I'm doing, and who've always supported me, even though many of my decisions made them nervous.

Dave Eggers.

Everyone who contributed to *Modest Proposal*, our live shows, and this book, especially: Chrystyna Golloher, who gets the MVP award in those early years; Melissa Cundieff, who read many early versions and gave such great notes; and Mike Hollingsworth, who provided so many amazing comics, cover designs, and illustrations and recruited his even-more-talented wife Anna Hollingsworth and brother Bryan Hollingsworth to do the same; and Jack Sullivan, who patiently taught two idiots (Ron and me) how to design a magazine.

All the comedians and bands who performed at our shows, especially our original crew: The Great 1, Jared Blake, Todd Hibbeler, Genevieve Lamb, Dan Goff, Kirk Buckhout, Tara Munson, Chris Bennett, Josh Skalniak, Josh McDermitt, Jaqi Furback, Steve Maxwell, Manny Yanez, Kass McPherson, Matt Martin, Ronnie D, Erik Miller, John Buber, Cristin Davis, Fatigo, Brodie Foster Hubbard, Male Pattern Radness, Paul Wade, Steve Faulkner, Famous Dave, Jose Gonzalez and Galapagos, Sean Latham, Mark Fry, Dévyan DuMon, The Christers, and all the kids from Barren Mind and Farce Side.

Dawn Admire-Sanders for sharing Scott with us.

Chris and Jim McClennon from Trash City Entertainment for doing so much for Phoenix comedy.

Our early supporters and advertisers: Noreen Strehlow, Leslie Barton & Kimber Lanning from The Modified Arts, JRC and Steph Carrico from The Trunk Space, Dan Schlissel from Standup! Records, Jack Vaughn from Comedy Central Records, Henry H. Owings from Chunklet, Drew Sullivan from Ash Ave Comics, Arizona Roller Derby, and Dan Mer from Tempe Improv.

Kenny and Miguel from Rio Salado Brewing Company.

Gina and Gabe Brooks for allowing us to photograph their baby, Dylan, on a plate.

Rich Yanez for teaching me most of what I know about writing.

Anyone who let us crash and gave us food, especially Theresa Rigoli, Paige Oneshoe Wilson, Kena Ray, Jacki O., Katherine Mosher, Gregg Thibodeau, and most of Ron's family.

———————

History is written by the winners… and by people who raise enough money to publish a book via a crowdsource campaign funded predominantly by friends, family, and his mother's friends (because she's wonderful at group texts).

A-LIST TALENT

Joey Sullivan, Kristin Morse

EXECUTIVE PRODUCERS

Allan Lyon, Cathryn Tusick, Chris & Jim McLennan, Dean & Dana Erickson, Jennifer Fowke, Lyndsey & Donovan Sullivan, Maria Menconi, Mike & Anna Hollingsworth, Rob Engalla, Teri & Mike McKee

LINE PRODUCERS

Adam Hatch, Cameron Omoto, Carole & Dennis Omoto, Chris Moeser, Chrystyna Golloher, David Guerrero, Jamie Reed, Karen Randall, Madison & Matthew Borunda, Melissa Cundieff, Nick Bernstein, Paul Wade, Ty Clancey, Tyson & Kirstin McKee

PRODUCERS

Charles Tsai, Duane Whitcraft, Erica Owens, Garrett Omoto, Hillary Tusick, Jan Parsons, Jess & Marty Beckerman, JJ Tusick, Joseph & Karen Tusick, Julie Hanssen Harris, Justin Harvey, Kara Isaac, Kevin & Pixie Polowy, Kristen Hof, Michael Busch, Michele Kerulis, Mike Baoule, Nicole Ellis, Nic Wegener, Oren Kessler, Rob Reich, Sam Nowak, Michael & Tanya McKee, Tim & Doreen Tusick, Tina Jackson, Westyn Hinchey

ASSOCIATE PRODUCERS

Adam Abramson, Alex Mazzurco, Andrea Bishop, Andrew Meader, Andy Erikson, Barbara Babcock, Barbara Underwood, Brandon Goldstein, Brian Sharp, Cara Garfield, Casey Krehbiel, Chris Albright, Chrissy Mahlmeister, David Pischke, Diane Jackson, Ed Baker, Edward Salazar, Emily Sullivan, Ethan Fixell, Fischer Family, Grant Lyon, Jacki O., Jason Elliott, Jenifer DeLemont, John Espinoza, John Sumners, Karen & Russell Morse, Kathe & John Ketchem, Katherine & Matt Daniels, Kyle Patterson, Lawrence C. Tusick, Leana McDougal, Lexa Payne, Linda & Jim Idoine, Lisa Beth Johnson, Maddox, Madeline Roth, Matt Tusick, Michael & Aarti Williams, Mishka Shubaly, Morgan Evans, Neil Gladstone, Patricia Hochwarth Sheehan, Raj Desai, Rhonda Newman, Roger Carnow, Sandy & Ray Tusick, Sara Simpson, Scott Boxenbaum, Sean Green, Sean Kantrowitz, Shannon Smith, Shawn Harris, Tara Carpenter, Taylor Newman, Teresa Aguilera, Thomas Salitsky, Troy Conrad, Wende & Forrest Waggoner

Made in the USA
Middletown, DE
11 December 2020